the cinema of STEVEN SODERBERGH

DIRECTORS' CUTS

Other select titles in the Directors' Cuts series:

the cinema of TERRY GILLIAM : *it's a mad world*
edited by JEFF BIRKENSTEIN, ANNA FROULA & KAREN RANDELL

the cinema of TAKESHI KITANO : *flowering blood*
SEAN REDMOND

the cinema of THE DARDENNE BROTHERS : *responsible realism*
PHILIP MOSLEY

the cinema of MICHAEL HANEKE : *europe utopia*
edited by BEN McCANN & DAVID SORFA

the cinema of SALLY POTTER : *a politics of love*
SOPHIE MAYER

the cinema of JOHN SAYLES : *a lone star*
MARK BOULD

the cinema of DAVID CRONENBERG : *from baron of blood to cultural hero*
ERNEST MATHIJS

the cinema of JAN SVANKMAJER : *dark alchemy*
edited by PETER HAMES

the cinema of NEIL JORDAN : *dark carnival*
CAROLE ZUCKER

the cinema of LARS VON TRIER : *authenticity and artifice*
CAROLINE BAINBRIDGE

the cinema of WERNER HERZOG : *aesthetic ecstasy and truth*
BRAD PRAGER

the cinema of TERRENCE MALICK : *poetic visions of america (second edition)*
edited by HANNAH PATTERSON

the cinema of ANG LEE : *the other side of the screen*
WHITNEY CROTHERS DILLEY

the cinema of STEVEN SPIELBERG : *empire of light*
NIGEL MORRIS

the cinema of TODD HAYNES : *all that heaven allows*
edited by JAMES MORRISON

the cinema of ROMAN POLANSKI : *dark spaces of the world*
edited by JOHN ORR & ELZBIETA OSTROWSKA

the cinema of JOHN CARPENTER : *the technique of terror*
edited by IAN CONRICH & DAVID WOODS

the cinema of MIKE LEIGH : *a sense of the real*
GARRY WATSON

the cinema of NANNI MORETTI : *dreams and diaries*
EWA MAZIERSKA & LAURA RASCAROLI

the cinema of DAVID LYNCH : *american dreams, nightmare visions*
edited by ERICA SHEEN & ANNETTE DAVISON

the cinema of KRZYSZTOF KIESLOWSKI : *variations on destiny and chance*
MAREK HALTOF

the cinema of GEORGE A. ROMERO : *knight of the living dead*
TONY WILLIAMS

the cinema of KATHRYN BIGELOW : *hollywood transgressor*
edited by DEBORAH JERMYN & SEAN REDMOND

the cinema of WIM WENDERS *the celluloid highway*
ALEXANDER GRAF

the cinema of KEN LOACH : *art in the service of the people*
JACOB LEIGH

the cinema of
STEVEN SODERBERGH

indie sex, corporate lies, and digital videotape

Andrew deWaard & R. Colin Tait

WALLFLOWER PRESS LONDON & NEW YORK

A Wallflower Press Book
Published by
Columbia University Press
Publishers Since 1893
New York • Chichester, West Sussex
cup.columbia.edu

A complete CIP record is available from the Library of Congress

ISBN 978-0-231-16550-1 (cloth : alk. paper)
ISBN 978-0-231-16551-8 (pbk. : alk. paper)
ISBN 978-0-231-85039-1 (e-book)

Series design by Rob Bowden Design

Cover image of Steven Soderbergh courtesy of the Kobal Collection

Columbia University Press books are printed on permanent
and durable acid-free paper.
This book is printed on paper with recycled content.
Printed in the United States of America

c 10 9 8 7 6 5 4 3 2 1
p 10 9 8 7 6 5 4 3 2 1

CONTENTS

ACKNOWLEDGEMENTS

Every book is the product of much support and feedback, especially in the case of a couple of eager graduate students who figured 'Why not? Let's write a book.' Our tenure at the University of British Columbia was a wonderfully collaborative time in both of our lives, despite the tiny office we shared, and we first and foremost wish to thank the three brilliant amigos who guided us through our Masters degrees and the early stages of this book: Brian McIlroy, Lisa Coulthard, and Ernest Mathijs. A more enlightening, understanding, and downright fun trio of mentors is difficult to imagine, and this book would not exist without their help. Ernest deserves a special mention for generously recommending us to a great publisher. We would also like to give a hearty shout-out to our man Brent Strang, and a heart-felt thank you to Colleen Montgomery, to whom we are eternally indebted for reading through our first draft with a fine-toothed comb.

Colin would like to thank Tom Schatz, who truly went above and beyond in his support for this project, as well as Mary Kearney, Janet Staiger, and Caroline Frick at the University of Texas at Austin; Charlie Keil, Corinn Columpar, Peter Fitting, and Manuela Gieri at the University of Toronto; and Chris Kanurkas, Michelle Urquhart and Michelle Mama for helping to reignite the flame of inspiration when there didn't seem to be any gas left in the tank. Andrew would like to thank Keir Keightley, Amanda Grzyb, Brian Wall, and Michael Zryd at the University of Western Ontario, for opening his eyes during his undergraduate education and inspiring him to continue with graduate studies. The number of good friends we would like to thank is too long to list, but a few of those who contributed to this book in ways they may not have even known include Matt Payne, Anne Helen Petersen, William Moner, as well as many others at UT to whom Colin sends his Canadian love, while Andrew says *merci* to Laura DeVries, Alicia Bond, Ian Dahlman, Brian Fauteux, and Matthias Stork.

We would also like to thank the students of 'FIST 338: Film Authorship and Steven Soderbergh,' who willingly submitted themselves as guinea pigs to this material as it was being formed, and whose feedback was often incisive and always honest. We are also very grateful to the Social Sciences and Humanities Research Council of Canada for providing funding throughout our graduate careers. For our contributions to *The Philosophy of Steven Soderbergh*, we are very grateful for the excellent editing and advice from Steven Sanders and Barton Palmer. And finally, we are indebted to Yoram Allon and Jodie Taylor at Wallflower Press for their incisive feedback and suggestions, and for pushing us to develop our ideas further.

Colin would like to thank his father for introducing him to his love of movies, his mother for nurturing it, and his sister for over-indulging him with the VCR. Special and heartfelt thanks go to Cathy and Barry Gay. Biggest thanks of all go to his partner in crime Sarah Gay, who is always inspiring him to be a better man, husband, and father, and without whose patience, love, and support none of this would have been possible. Andrew would like to thank his mom for the countless grilled cheese sandwiches she brought him while he wasted his childhood in a basement watching movies, and the rest of his family for supporting his academic aspirations. And to Terra, his love for whom spans from YXU to YVR to LAX.

A note on previously published and presented work
This book was the product of many years of work, and some of these thoughts and essays were published and presented in earlier forms over the past several years in a variety of formats. We are thankful for the feedback and editorial support we received along the way, which vastly improved all of these thoughts and pieces. We presented 'sex, lies and digital videotape: Steven Soderbergh as Digital Auteur,' and 'The Global Social Problem Film,' at the Film Studies Association of Canada Conference in 2007. An earlier assessment of the 'sellebrity auteur,' applied to Spike Lee's directorial persona, appeared as 'Joints and Jams: Spike Lee as Sellebrity Auteur,' in *Fight the Power: The Spike Lee Reader* (eds. Janice D. Hamlet and Robin R. Means Coleman) in 2008. An early version of Chapter 8 appeared as "You Shook Sinatra's Hand, You Should Know Better': Competing Modes of Capital in *Ocean's 11*,' and an early version of Chapter 6 appeared as 'The Blend of History: Intertextuality, Broken Mirrors, and *The Good German*,' both in *The Philosophy of Steven Soderbergh* (eds. R. Barton Palmer and Steven Sanders) in 2010.

To Terra, Sarah and Stella

PREFACE

by *Thomas Schatz*

Among the most important and elusive filmmakers in contemporary Hollywood, Steven Soderbergh both demands and defies scrutiny. Since *sex, lies, and videotape* in 1989, one of the most impressive debuts in movie history, Soderbergh has carved out a career that puts him in a class by himself among active auteurs. And yet he has avoided even routine coverage by journalists, let alone the kind of celebrity treatment that most other Hollywood filmmakers more readily cultivate. Nor has Soderbergh's remarkable body of work been subjected to close analysis by critics or scholars, who seem either unwilling or simply unable to deal with the filmmaker's varied and voluminous output.

That reluctance is understandable, given both the range and pace of Soderbergh's work. In terms of sheer productivity, his performance has been astounding. Soderbergh has directed two dozen films since 1989, a record matched only by Woody Allen (who also has directed 24 over the same period), and well ahead of the other top American directors – Clint Eastwood with 19, Steven Spielberg with 17, Spike Lee with 16, Martin Scorsese with 14, the Coens with 13, Tim Burton with 12, and so on. Soderbergh has also produced over twenty films, which further distinguishes him from his contemporaries. The only other top Hollywood director with serious producing credits, other than on his or her own films, is Spielberg, who through Amblin and DreamWorks has taken producer (or, more usually, executive producer) credit on some three dozen films. Most of these are nominal credits with little if any active involvement on Spielberg's part, however, whereas Soderbergh's role has been not only active but invaluable in most cases. Indeed, he has backed and contributed to a number of risky, innovative films that may not have been made without his participation – films like Richard Linklater's *A Scanner Darkly* (2006), Todd Haynes' *I'm Not There* (2007), and Tony Gilroy's *Michael Clayton* (2007).

The risk and innovation in these films is indicative of Soderbergh's own work, which without question is more eclectic and daring than that of any other contemporary American director. In terms of budget level, production conditions, subject matter, narrative form, and film style, Soderbergh's films run the gamut, from no-budget digital experiments and low-budget independent art films to mid-range star vehicles and big-budget studio blockbusters. He has enjoyed his share of critical and commercial success in these wide-ranging efforts, although he has had his share of failures and misfires as well. The misfires were most painful and pronounced early on, and in fact Soderbergh's mere survival in the early to mid-1990s was a feat in itself. *sex, lies, and videotape* was a true phenomenon, putting not just Soderbergh on the industry map but Miramax and Sundance as well, and going on to win the top prize at Cannes and jump-start the American indie film movement. While that movement caught fire, though, Soderbergh suffered through a string of commercial and critical flops – *Kafka* (1991), *King of the Hill* (1993), *The Underneath* (1995), *Gray's Anatomy* (1996), and *Schizopolis* (1996). He had joked in his 1989 acceptance speech for the Palme D'Or at Cannes that "it will be all downhill from here," and for nearly a decade that turned out to be precisely the case. One measure of that downhill slide came after the Academy Awards in early 1997, at the Miramax party celebrating the Oscar sweep by *The English Patient* (1996). Writer-director Anthony Minghella invited Soderbergh to the Miramax bash, and upon arrival he was denied entrance to the special VIP section, where he spied Minghella through a glass partition as a big-screen TV played trailers of Miramax's signature hits, including *sex, lies, and videotape*.

After the failure of *Schizopolis* Soderbergh took a studio assignment, *Out of Sight* for Universal, and it was this 1998 release which sparked a career revival that went into overdrive in 2000 with back-to-back critical and commercial hits, *Erin Brockovich* and *Traffic* – two more mid-range studio films, both of which garnered multiple Oscar nominations (including Best Picture and Best Director), restored Soderbergh's credibility with American critics, and grossed over $200 million at the box office. *Out of Sight* also marked a career breakthrough for George Clooney, who teamed with Soderbergh to launch Section Eight, an independent company whose first production, *Ocean's Eleven* (2001), took both of their careers to the proverbial next level while cementing their partnership. That slick, all-star heist film grossed nearly half a billion dollars worldwide for Warner Bros., securing the new company's relationship with the studio and Soderbergh's standing among Hollywood's filmmaking elite. In the wake of that flurry of hits, Soderbergh has been able to make the films he wants to make on his own terms, and he's been able to get other films made as well. In 2002 alone, his signature was on an astounding seven films – five as producer, including *Far From Heaven* (Todd Haynes), *Insomnia* (Christopher Nolan), and Clooney's directorial debut, *Confessions of a Dangerous Mind*, along with two risky and vastly different projects of his own, *Full Frontal* and *Solaris*.

Soderbergh followed those dicey projects with *Ocean's Twelve* in 2004 and, after another pair of ambitious, offbeat films, *Bubble* (2005) and *The Good German* (2006), with *Ocean's Thirteen* in 2007. Both *Ocean's* installments were global hits with all-star casts (including Clooney, Brad Pitt, and Matt Damon) that ensured the financing, creative control, and artistic license on Soderbergh's other projects – a price the film-maker has been altogether willing to pay, particularly since all involved in the *Ocean's* franchise seem to be enjoying themselves. The blockbuster *Ocean's* films and his asso-ciation with Clooney have been crucial to Soderbergh's success, obviously enough, and both are indicative of far more than his commercial instincts. Glimpsed in *sex, lies, and videotape* but not coalescing until *Out of Sight*, *The Limey* (1999), and *Traffic*, Soder-bergh has become an "actor's director" *par excellence*. He consistently gets terrific – in many cases career-best – performances out of his cast, and he is a director with whom top talent, from character actors and independent stalwarts to marquee stars, are eager to work. And like Woody Allen and the late Robert Altman, Soderbergh is also a masterful ensemble director – an artist who is at his best when handling multi-strand narratives with multiple principal characters.

Soderbergh also shares with Allen and two other veterans of the Hollywood renais-sance, Scorsese and Eastwood, an artistic fervour and an obsessive work ethic – traits that are altogether rare in contemporary Hollywood. Despite repeated announcements over the past several years that he will take a break from filmmaking and refocus his creative energies on painting, Soderbergh continues to produce and direct films at a furious pace. He remains as productive, as eclectic, and as ambitious as ever, seemingly oblivious to the industry conditions and constraints that force his contemporaries to go two to three years (or longer) between films.

As Soderbergh approaches fifty and threatens to retire (or refocus), one wonders what the coming years might hold in store, and what to make of his remarkable career. Andrew deWaard and R. Colin Tait initiated *The Cinema of Steven Soderbergh* when the filmmaker first threatened to retire, which seemed an opportune time to under-take this project. That was at least four films ago, and Soderbergh has as many in the works. Thus the authors may well be providing a mid-career assessment, although that scarcely diminishes the significance of this book, which stands as the first comprehen-sive, in-depth examination of Soderbergh's films and filmmaking. This is no mean feat, given the range and diversity of his work and his working methods. The authors note that Soderbergh has described himself as a "chameleon" due to his capacity to adapt to an array of projects and production situations – one key reason, no doubt, that critics and film scholars have shied away from Soderbergh as the subject of serious study and have been reticent to rank him among today's canonised auteurs.

deWaard and Tait display no such qualms, readily acknowledging Soderbergh's multi-faceted filmmaking career, celebrating its rich diversity while identifying the key characteristics and signature effects of his work. Indeed, the authors approach Soder-bergh as a radical text case for contemporary auteur analysis – a multivalent filmmaker who continually moves through varied modes of production and market sectors, from Hollywood to Indiewood to the fringes of the independent realm. They celebrate this mobility as a key marker of Soderbergh's singular style, while tracing the permutations of that style in each of these varied filmmaking venues. The authors celebrate, too, the risks Soderbergh has repeatedly taken in terms of both film technology and film technique – his pioneering forays into digital cinema, for instance, and his compulsive experiments with narrative continuity. They also trace the development of key motifs in Soderbergh's films, most notably the recurrent narrative-thematic tropes of detection and disease. While virtually all movies – or all good ones, anyway – are suspense films and many of Soderbergh's films are outright detective films, deWaard and Tait show how the process of detection in a Soderbergh film, for the viewer as well as the principal characters, is operating on a far more intricate and sophisticated level than in most films. They also trace his steadily deepening fascination with corruption and contamination, whether on an individual, a communal, or a more broadly social (even global) scale. The "contagion" in his recent hit is both a medical and a social condition, and the narrative itself is an instance in which a frequent thematic undercurrent in Soderbergh's films bursts through to the surface with alarming, visceral force.

Assessing Soderbergh's eclectic career also requires deWaard and Tait to chart the development of the American film industry at large, as their subject veers from the mainstream to the margins, from global blockbusters to specialty films, from very traditional filmmaking projects to cutting-edge digital experiments. Soderbergh's work as a multi-hyphenate producer-director-cinematographer (and occasional writer, editor, composer, *et al.*) also requires them to rethink film authorship, which is a signal strength of this study. And as they examine Soderbergh as auteur, as brand-name empressario, and as "corporate revolutionary," they demonstrate how very complex the issue of authorship has become in contemporary cinema – particularly for a film-maker who refuses to stay put. Indeed, the figure that emerges in *The Cinema of Steven Soderbergh* is an agent of constant change and relentless independence. Soderbergh may have pioneered the indie movement and learned to operate within the vastly complex machinery of conglomerate Hollywood, but he has remained a consummately free agent within an increasingly deadening, convention-bound industry. And while other top filmmakers locate their comfort zones and market niches and signature styles, Soderbergh just keeps pushing himself, his audience, and the expressive range of cinema itself.

INTRODUCTION

Because the house always wins. Play long enough, you never change the stakes, the house takes you. Unless, when that perfect hand comes along, you bet big, then you take the house.

Danny Ocean, Ocean's Eleven

Gambling, like cinema, is a game of chance – and endurance. The art of the long con is the ability to plan with purpose, to be patient, and when the opportunity presents itself: to pounce. Uncertainty and unpredictability unite the gambler and the film-maker, each profession more known for its spectacles than its careers. Romanticised enterprises both, the true story of gambling and cinema is one of minor acts, repeated over and over and over – in other words, labour. Prolonged labour does not lend itself to narrative though; it prefers sensational moments of exaggerated importance and overwrought imagery. The true story of gambling and filmmaking – equal parts banality and bombast – is rarely glimpsed. Instead, we have the Cincinnati Kid, as depicted by Steve McQueen in the 1965 film of the same name, a precocious young poker player who goes all in on that one all-important deal, the prototypical gambler. And we have the Sundance Kids, as formulated by James Mottram in the 2006 book also of the same name, to describe the new generation of American filmmakers who arose in the 1990s out of the Sundance Film Festival, starting with Steven Soderbergh. A trivial tale of 'mavericks taking back Hollywood,' this book – along with other titles like *Rebels on the Backlot*, *Cinema of Outsiders*, and *Down and Dirty Pictures* – mythologises the American independent film movement and obscures the true nature of filmmaking at this time. The real story, as it is wont to be, is far more complex. In particular, Steven Soderbergh – with nearly thirty films as director and dozens more as producer – is by far the most prolific filmmaker of his time, and as such, irreducible to any singular, romanticising narrative.

Despite his well-publicised and oft-mythologised debut at Sundance (then called the US Film Festival) and Cannes in 1989, Soderbergh has directed, produced, written, edited, photographed, and starred in such a diverse array of projects in his continuously evolving twenty-plus year career that he has not been pinned down by any concrete brand name. Quentin Tarantino has his violent pop-culture mash-up, David Fincher his gritty, gloomy palette, Spike Lee his political provocations, Wes Anderson his precious nostalgia, Sofia Coppola her tragic tales of youthful desperation, the Coen Brothers their darkly comic absurdity[1] – all finely-crafted artistic personas that are easily marketed and easily championed in this brand-heavy, publicity-centric era. What about Steven Soderbergh? We are hard-pressed to capture his oeuvre with a comparable encapsulation. Though he is a distinct aberration in the field of contemporary American Hollywood directors – and is responsible for more films than the combined total of his aforementioned kin – compared to his peers, there is precious little scholarly attention devoted to this important director. What accounts for this omission?

Our initial response to this question is simple: he is too inconsistent. The range of his filmmaking practice varies widely. Formally, generically, stylistically, and aesthetically, Soderbergh refuses to work within any one paradigm; in fact, he prides himself on his ability to continually experiment with new forms and styles. The scale of his films deviates considerably as well, from the humble, independent roots of *sex, lies, and videotape* (1989) – and its 'spiritual sequel' *Full Frontal* (2002), which retained its minor scale but added A-list celebrities working 'for scale' – to the immense budgets of *Ocean's Eleven* (2001), *Ocean's Twelve* (2004), and *Ocean's Thirteen* (2007). Even his digital experiments cover a wide range: minor, *Bubble* (2005); epic, *Che* (2008); and special-effects intensive, *Solaris* (2002). Finally, the success of his films, whether measured critically or commercially, fluctuates like a wild heartbeat. Considering these three factors in tandem, it should become apparent that Soderbergh is inherently unclassifiable. As critic Ty Burr elegantly summarises, his multiple 'personae can be ticked off like stations on a commuter line: neophyte genius, sophomore slumper, tasteful artiste, B-film train-wreck, committed avant-gardist, crime-film genre master, Godard's heir, king of Hollywood blockbusters, Oscar-winning directorial godhead, smug insider, and… romantic visionary.'[2]

Steven Soderbergh's story is one of constant r/evolution. His career could be conceived of as a long series of cinematic interjections from a diverse range of angles: historical, political, industrial, digital, ideological, economic, aesthetic, and textual. Having quickly moved from indie darling (*sex, lies, and videotape*) to industry pariah with a string of unsuccessful films, from *Kafka* (1991) to *Schizopolis* (1996), Soderbergh clawed his way back into relevance by learning nearly every major above-the-line creative role in filmmaking and then establishing a tenuous relationship with Hollywood, eventually resulting in the tremendously profitable *Ocean's* trilogy. Alongside this mainstream work, Soderbergh continues to carve out a niche for himself by funding his own low-key, esoteric fare.

Emblematic of many of the significant shifts within cinema in the last two decades, Soderbergh adopts and emulates the various forms emerging in the cinematic *zeitgeist*: a polished period piece, *King of the Hill* (1993); a brooding neo-noir, *The Underneath*

(1995); a Tarantino-esque crime film, *Out of Sight* (1998); a disjunctive non-linear narrative, *The Limey* (1999); an American Dogme-inspired film, *Full Frontal*; a science-fiction spectacle yet love-letter to his arthouse influences, *Solaris*; a meta-fictional reality television series, *Unscripted* (2005); a brazen pastiche, *The Good German* (2006), and a zany corporate satire, *The Informant!* (2009). Documentary has been a continual concern for Soderbergh: *Gray's Anatomy* (1996) stylises one of Spalding Gray's incomparable monologues, while *And Everything is Going Fine* (2010), released a few years following Gray's death, crafts a fitting tribute to the unique artist, presenting a mosaic of clips from throughout his life. The effect is the construction of a thoughtful narrative allowing the monologist to present his own eulogy in his own words. These are in addition to his ongoing and frequent experiments with digital filmmaking and High Definition technologies, most notably *K-Street* (2003), *Bubble*, *Che*, and *The Girlfriend Experience* (2009). His most recent features – *Contagion* (2011), *Haywire* (2012), *Magic Mike* (2012), *Side Effects* (2013), and *Behind the Candelabra* (2013) – continue this recent digital preoccupation, applied to a variety of distinct genres.

Soderbergh is an interesting object of study if only for the fact that he is the only contemporary mainstream filmmaker who affords himself the creative and financial freedoms to take such huge risks. Nominated for both *Traffic* (2000) and *Erin Brockovich* (2000), Soderbergh is only the second filmmaker in history to compete against himself and win (and lose) for the Best Director category at the Academy Awards. This significant achievement, in addition to multiple awards for his actors, was the decade-long fulfillment of the promise made with his debut, *sex, lies, and videotape*, which won the Audience Award at Sundance, the Palme D'Or at Cannes, the Independent Spirit Award for Best Director, and the Academy Award for Best Screenplay. Awards and prestige are only half the story, though, as what enamours Soderbergh to the studios – in contrast to the Michael Bays and James Camerons of the industry, or the bloated budgets of the 1970s' 'movie brat' generation – is his consistent ability to be on time and on budget.

Both a celebrated artisan and a savvy businessman, Soderbergh cashed in some chips amidst his successful run of films from *Out of Sight* to *Traffic* and established his own production company, Section Eight Productions, with his new partner in crime, George Clooney. From 2001 to 2009, Section Eight not only provided Soderbergh and Clooney more control over their own productions – as long as they continued to deliver massive global box office with the *Ocean's* trilogy – it also allowed them to facilitate production deals for challenging Hollywood fare from some like-minded directors: *Far From Heaven* (Todd Haynes, 2002), *Insomnia* (Christopher Nolan, 2002), *Syriana* (Stephen Gaghan, 2005), *A Scanner Darkly* (Richard Linklater, 2006), and *Michael Clayton* (Tony Gilroy, 2007), amongst others. In addition, Clooney directed his first films through Section Eight: *Confessions of a Dangerous Mind* (2002) and *Good Night, and Good Luck* (2005). Soderbergh's documentary fixation exists in his producing role as well, including *Who is Bernard Tapie?* (Marina Zenovich, 2001), *Tribute* (Chris Currie and Rich Fox, 2001), *Playground* (Libby Spears, 2009), *Roman Polanski: Wanted and Desired* (Marina Zenovich, 2010), and *His Way* (Douglas McGrath, 2011). In this regard, a comprehensive analysis of

Soderbergh would need to include more films than his already large body of directorial work.

To return to our question of why Soderbergh has been underexplored by contemporary film scholarship, then, we posit a second answer, in addition to the fact that he is too inconsistent: he is too complex. Thirty films, even more productions, a dizzying array of forms, styles, and themes – we are faced with the dilemma of how to approach such a complex figure. In the early days of this book's planning, we developed a series of different outlines and potential critical frameworks as we evaluated how best to construct a methodology to analyse the director's work. Reviewing these proposed structures should provide further insight into just how complex Soderbergh is as an object of study, as well as a suitable overview of the many factors at play in the director's career.

How Do You Solve a Problem Like Steven Soderbergh?: Methodology and its Discontents

> I want John Huston's career. I want a lot of movies over a long period of time. And then we'll go back, if we want to – I don't want to, but somebody else can – and sort it all out.
>
> Steven Soderbergh[3]

> [Soderbergh] is another director of obvious significance, though of exactly what kind I remain uncertain. I cannot seem to get a firm grasp on his films.
>
> Robin Wood[4]

One avenue of exploration to attempt 'a firm grasp' on Soderbergh's body of work would be a film-based, chronological assessment that uses in-depth textual analysis of each individual film, the standard methodology for most director-focused studies. Soderbergh has far too many films for this type of approach though; the result would be a limited survey and each chapter's analysis would suffer without the opportunity to establish larger patterns between films. A selective focus on Soderbergh's key films would be another strategy, one that reads larger issues into certain films:

1. *sex, lies, and videotape* (1989): preoccupation with film and video apparatus, contribution to American independent film
2. *Schizopolis* (1996): experimental urge, mastery of key creative roles
3. *Traffic* (2000): political resonance, networked narratives
4. *Ocean's Eleven* (2001): blockbuster impulse, high-concept celebrity
5. *Bubble* (2005): digital and industrial impact
6. *The Informant!* (2009): global vs. local
7. *Contagion* (2011): synthesis of all these concerns

However, this approach would minimise the importance of his other films – including our personal favourites, *Out of Sight* and *The Limey* – and take away from our belief that, for Soderbergh, the whole is greater than the sum of its many, many parts. Instead, a system of stages in the director's career was established:

1. Early success and experimentation: *sex, lies, and videotape* to *Schizopolis* (1989–1996)
2. Indiewood renewal: *Out of Sight*, *The Limey*, *Erin Brockovich*, and *Traffic* (1998–2000)
3. Section Eight Productions (2001–07)
4. Blockbuster: *Ocean's Eleven* to *Ocean's Thirteen*
5. Esoteric: *Full Frontal* to *The Good German*
6. Digital: *Che* to current (2008–12)

These stages seemed forced and arbitrary for such a wide-ranging body of work, however, and many of the director's films cross these boundaries and do not fit so neatly into such categories. Setting aside a chronological organisation, formal patterns present themselves as a useful point of departure, as they play such a prominent role in the director's oeuvre. As one of the few contemporary filmmakers who often performs multiple key creative roles on his films, Soderbergh's 'alter-egos' and pseudonyms provide a convenient categorisation:

1. Peter Andrews (his father's first and middle name): Director of Photography
2. Mary Ann Bernard (his mother's maiden name): Editor
3. Sam Lowry (the hapless hero of Terry Gilliam's *Brazil* [1985]): Screenwriter
4. Section Eight (military term for discharge due to mental instability): Producer[5]

Formal structures would provide a suitable jumping off point; a specific focus on editing, for example, could lead into a fruitful analysis of the director's preoccupation with memory and consciousness. But again, a formal schematic is too limiting, even if it is broadened to include the digital, industrial, and performative ways in which Soderbergh is experimental. Genre is another potential organising principle, but this would prove as unwieldy a list as the films themselves: noir, crime, comedy, political, period, melodrama, biopic, social problem, documentary, docudrama, psychological, and thriller, not to mention the various combinations and hybrids, of which most of his films are to some degree.

Conceptual and thematic organisation proved to be the only way to comprehensively cover all the issues we wished to include, but this presents its own problems. Typically, following the money is a useful enterprise, and the ways in which Soderbergh's films are financed and/or distributed is a valid categorical tool:

1. Blockbuster: Warner Brothers, Universal Studios, and 20th Century Fox – *Ocean's* trilogy, *Out of Sight*, *Erin Brockovich*, *Solaris*
2. Indiewood: 'mini-majors' like Miramax, Warner Independent, and USA – *sex, lies, and videotape*, *Kafka*, *King of the Hill*, *The Underneath*
3. Independent: Artisan, Jersey Films, IFC, Northern Arts, Relativity Media, Nick Wechsler Productions – *The Limey*, *Gray's Anatomy*, *Haywire*, *Magic Mike*
4. Socially-conscious: Participant Media – *The Informant!*, *Good Night, and Good Luck*, *Syriana*, *Contagion*

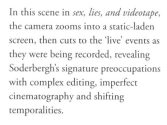

In this scene in *sex, lies, and videotape*, the camera zooms into a static-laden screen, then cuts to the 'live' events as they were being recorded, revealing Soderbergh's signature preoccupations with complex editing, imperfect cinematography and shifting temporalities.

5. Television: HBO and Showtime – *Fallen Angels* (1993–95), *K-Street*, *Unscripted*
6. Digital: Magnolia Pictures, 2929 Entertainment, and HDNet – *Bubble*, *The Girlfriend Experience*

Again this appeared too prescriptive, but also inaccurate, as many of his productions involve companies from across the spectrum; for instance, *Erin Brockovich* was produced through Jersey Films but distributed by Universal Studios and Columbia Pictures. Many of Soderbergh's films blur the lines between these divisions of production, and many exhibit elements of one within another. *Solaris*, though large in budget, is humble in its arthouse aspirations; *sex, lies, and videotape*, though small in scale, went on to gross twenty times as much as its budget. The economic realities of contemporary Hollywood are far too complex for such a reductive categorisation.

Confronted with these many tensions, we developed a series of binaries with which to grapple the many dualistic forces within Soderbergh's work:

1. Independent vs. Mainstream
2. Experimental vs. Traditional

3. Form vs. Function
4. Art vs. Commerce
5. Reality vs. Artifice
6. Insider vs. Outsider

This schematic appeared the closest to what we hoped to accomplish, as it would allow us to explore the many formal and thematic concerns within a larger framework, and mix a variety of critical approaches along the way.

Concurrent to the planning and writing of this book, we were honoured to be included in an edited collection entitled *The Philosophy of Steven Soderbergh*, the first substantial book to deal with the director from a scholarly perspective. Its solution to the Soderbergh complexity dilemma is the formation of wide-ranging thematic clusters:

1. Knowledge, Truth, Sexuality
2. Genre, Temporality, Intertextuality
3. Self-Reflexivity, Self-Centeredness, Autobiography
4. Politics, Morals, Methodology
5. Simulacra, Space, *Solaris*

Due to the nature of a collected work such as this – sixteen individual authors working independently on individual films – each essay exists as an island, with bridges formed after the fact by the editors' introductions and categorisation. All of these essays are highly refined, insightful analyses (which we will refer to throughout the rest of this book), and we cannot recommend the book enough. However, a series of individual arguments and analyses paints a fragmented mosaic of the director. As appropriate as a mosaic structure is in this case, with a director as fragmented as Soderbergh, only a dedicated, comprehensive study can hope to connect the multitude of dots that Soderbergh's prolific career has established. Rather than a series of islands, then, we hope to construct an ecosystem out of these many concerns, fostering a space of diverse interaction. Instead of choosing one of the proposed structures, we opted to put them all in contact with each other, in an effort to produce a holistic picture of the director.

The idea of an intertwined, multifarious methodology seemed appropriate for a director whose work is so multifarious itself. At the risk of descending into *too* convoluted an analysis, potentially confusing the reader, we have structured the book in a very regimented manner, as a series of nested dialectics. The book is divided into three parts, each of which contains three chapters, each of which orients around three main points in dialectic tension. The relation between chapters and parts is also dialectical, so the groupings of chapters speak to each other (e.g. the tension between chapters one and two produces chapter three), as do the overall parts (Part Three is the result of Parts One and Two). With this structure, we are provided with the freedom to establish larger patterns among the films and issues, yet are contained within a distinct trajectory. Juxtaposing this wide array of factors and characteristics together in an attempt to fully capture the many contradictory elements in his career, we realised the third and final answer to our question of why Soderbergh has been largely ignored by contemporary film scholarship. In addition to being too inconsistent and too complex, he is too paradoxical. There is no solving a problem like Soderbergh, only revelling in the problem's many contradictory impulses. A method embracing this paradox is necessary.

Dialectics, as a method of reasoned argument in search of truth using the conflict of opposing forces, dates back to at least Ancient Greece, and is generalised as a process that produces a synthesised viewpoint: (hypo)thesis plus antithesis equals synthesis. As one of the basic foundations of philosophy, the dialectic method is deceptively simple yet immanently complex. For Slavoj Žižek, the dialectic is an explicit *acknowledgement of contradiction*. 'Far from being a story of its progressive overcoming,' Žižek claims as his thesis in *The Sublime Object of Ideology* (1989), 'dialectics is for Hegel a systematic notation of the failure of all such attempts – "absolute knowledge" denotes a subjective position which finally accepts "contradiction" as an internal condition of every identity.'[6] It is our contention that Soderbergh's body of work represents an acute opportunity to investigate such a contradictory cinematic condition through the dialectical method.[7] In short, Soderbergh's oeuvre is *paradox in praxis*.

Part One – 'Author, Brand, Guerrilla' – is comprised of three different analyses of authorship that explore the different ways in which Soderbergh creates film. Chapter one is a traditional auteur analysis, looking at the conflicting characteristics of Soderbergh's cinematography, narrative, editing, and performance. The overall result of this multi-faceted style produces what we call a 'dialectical signature.' Chapter two considers extratextual factors of Soderbergh's filmmaking practice, outlining the issues of finance and fame that must be negotiated by the 'sellebrity auteur.' Soderbergh and Clooney's production company, Section Eight, provides a suitable example of this economic position in filmmaking. In chapter three, we look at the legacy of Third Cinema and find elements of 'guerrilla,' 'imperfect,' and 'minor' filmmaking within Soderbergh's vast body of work.

Part Two analyses the role of the detective in Soderbergh's body of work, exploring three particular varieties of detective characters and formal strategies that concern 'History, Memory, Text'. Chapter four investigates the 'schizophrenic detective' in *The Limey*, and its accompanying themes of nostalgia, memory, and influence. *Solaris* and its 'psychoanalytic detective' are the focus of inquiry in chapter five, where issues of temporal, psychological, and societal trauma are rendered bare onscreen. Chapter six is concerned with history, and explores the 'intertextual detective' that mediates the past through cinema in *The Good German*, a film that embodies the many interrelated factors at work in Soderbergh's oeuvre.

Part Three – 'Crime, Capital, Globalisation' – contains three genre-based arguments and is concerned with the form and socio-economic-political meaning of Soderbergh's crime films. In chapter seven, the classification 'New Crime Wave' is given to the broad resurgence of Hollywood crime films during the 1990s, and Soderbergh's unique 'anti-crime' iteration within it. A close reading of *Out of Sight* illustrates the alternative values system that Soderbergh proffers with his criminal characters. Contextualised by the heist film genre, chapter eight reinterprets the *Ocean's* trilogy as an allegory of capital which produces a utopian undercurrent to its blockbuster caper. Chapter nine isolates a unique cycle of films utilising networked narratives, docudrama, and themes of social justice that we term the 'global social problem film.' We outline this sub-genre's characteristics and iconography in *Traffic* (the first film in the cycle), *Syriana*, *The Informant!*, and *Contagion*.

In addition to this regimented trajectory, structured by nested three-part dialectics, the subtitle of the book acts as an overarching thematic. 'When I finished the script, I did not know what I was going to call it,' Soderbergh recalls about his debut film. 'I asked myself how someone like Graham, direct and honest, would describe the film. And I thought about these three words, which by the way seem to summarize all the themes of the film, which are also the themes of modern America: the selling of sex, the practice of telling lies, and the invasion by the video.'[8] Twenty years later, we can imagine Graham updating this triad for twenty-first-century America: indie sex, corporate lies, and digital videotape.

By 'indie sex,' we refer to the way 'independence' and 'indie' have by and large become mere markers of distinction, and valuable marketing properties within contemporary American culture, the film industry in particular. Sex sells, and so does independence. 'Indie sex' can also refer to Soderbergh's debut, which combined both elements, and to two of his most brilliantly crafted sequences: the non-linear sex scenes featuring his muse (George Clooney), with Jennifer Lopez in *Out of Sight* and Natascha McElhone in *Solaris*; we will analyse both scenes in depth. 'Corporate lies' is fairly self-explanatory, but Soderbergh works to expose them and promote social justice in a variety of ways: with a linear melodrama and an endearing performance by Julia Roberts in *Erin Brockovich*, through a complex, globe-spanning networked narrative in *Syriana*, using digital cameras and real politicians in the faux-documentary *K-Street*, profiling the controversial enigma that is *Che*, utilising satire and enjoyable retro absurdity in *The Informant!*, and simulating a global pandemic with a networked narrative in *Contagion*. Finally, we have 'digital videotape,' which has come a long way since the 'primitive' video used in Soderbergh's debut. An early-adopter, Soderbergh has used the latest digital cameras throughout his career, from mini-DV on *Full Frontal* to the 'ultra high definition' RED One camera on *Che*, *The Informant!*, and *Contagion*. The apparatus of cinema and video is a recurring diegetic motif within his body of work, emblematic of the way mediation occupies a central role within American society.

Because Soderbergh is too inconsistent, too complex, and too paradoxical, critical analysis of his work requires a wide-ranging investigation into underlying assumptions of concepts as diverse as authorship, independent cinema, genre, capital, globalisation, trauma, and history. We move in and out of these concepts, returning to them throughout the book from different perspectives. We also approach the films in the same way, which might get repetitive at times, as we briefly recap certain scenes or ideas in an effort for chapters to be able to stand on their own. In order to avoid lengthy plot descriptions and jump right into the films at any time, we have appended an in-depth filmography to the end of the book and would suggest all but the most serious Soderbergh-philes begin there, if only to briefly browse through the dozens of films that he has directed and produced. We have also set up a website at www.cinema ofstevensoderbergh.com that contains an extended filmography along with clips and full-colour images to accompany the scene analyses we will enact over the course of the book. It is a large corpus that we take as our subject matter, and we will not be offering any biographical trajectory or plot summaries as we go. There is little time to explain the rules of the game; we're going 'all in' on an analytic heist.

With such a diverse, multivalent object of study, *The Cinema of Steven Soderbergh* aims to provide not just a critical overview and interpretation of Soderbergh's career, but a 'criminal' investigation into many of the central concerns that colour both Soderbergh's oeuvre and the contemporary cinematic culture at large. Just as Soderbergh bets big when that perfect hand comes along, exploiting his creative and industrial connections for each new project, we intend to use Soderbergh to perform our own theoretical 'heist.' We are encouraged by Theodor Adorno to commit such an act: 'Dialectics as a philosophical mode of proceeding is the attempt to untie the knot of paradoxicality by the oldest means of enlightenment: the ruse.'[9] For us, Soderbergh is not just a prolific author and purveyor of the long con; he is a fertile site in which to witness and examine the circulation of some of the key cultural, social, aesthetic, and technological ideas of the last two decades. He is not merely the quintessential auteur *of* our time, but the quintessential auteur *for* our time, and all its noisy, incomplete, digital fragmentation.

Notes

1   Spike Jonze his satirical eccentricity, P.T. Anderson his disciplined formalism, David Lynch his nightmarish symbolism, Christopher Nolan his darkened subjectivity – we could go on, but the point is well established: most contemporary American directors stick to what they know. Admittedly, they do this very well, but rarely do they venture beyond their wheelhouse, at least in comparison to Soderbergh.

2   Ty Burr, '*Solaris* Remake is a Space Odyssey into the Human Heart,' *Boston Globe*, November 27, 2002, D1.

3   Anthony Kaufman, *Steven Soderbergh: Interviews*, (Jackson: University Press of Mississippi, 2002), 106.

4   Robin Wood, *Hollywood from Vietnam to Reagan – and Beyond* (New York, NY: Columbia University Press, 2003), xxxviii–xl.

5   It should be noted that Soderbergh has also acted as producer and executive producer on many other films outside of the Section Eight enterprise.

6   Slavoj Žižek. *The Sublime Object of Ideology* (New York: Verso 1989), 6.

7   We acknowledge that the application of the dialectical method to a filmmaker's *oeuvre* is not in itself unique or necessarily new; for an example, see James Monaco's application of this method to François Truffaut's work in *The New Wave: Truffaut, Godard, Chabrol, Rohmer, Rivette* (New York: Oxford University Press, 1976), 47. Rather than the systematic methodology that we apply, Monaco's comments refer mostly to a possible 'pleasure' for Truffaut in having his films received in dialectical opposition.

8   Kaufman, *Steven Soderbergh: Interviews*, 20.

9   Theodor W. Adorno. *Negative Dialectics* (New York: Seabury Press, 1973), 141.

PART ONE

AUTHOR, BRAND, GUERRILLA

CHAPTER ONE

The Dialectical Signature: Soderbergh as Classical Auteur

I don't consider myself an artist or a visionary… There are the Fellinis, the Altmans – even someone like Gus Van Sant – who push the film language, who bend and twist the medium to suit their vision. You look at their movies and you can't imagine anyone else making them. I'm not that kind of filmmaker. I'm a chameleon.

Steven Soderbergh, 1993 [1]

Since its development more than half a century ago, auteur theory – the conceit that a film director's personal creative vision is the predominate force in shaping the artistry of a film – has remained a contentious, heavily fragmented discourse.[2] As with most other arts, film theory's relationship with authorship has morphed and evolved through various iterations, due in large part to historical context and competing ideologies. Nevertheless, a common, if shaky, approach to cinematic authorship has coalesced in film criticism, and its formulation and application to Steven Soderbergh will be the focus of the current chapter. Subsequently, we will update auteur theory for the age of New Hollywood,[3] Indiewood,[4] and Conglomerate Hollywood,[5] adding to it the dimensions of celebrity and fame to formulate the 'sellebrity auteur.' We will then follow that chapter with a decidedly non-traditional application of 'Third Cinema,' considering Soderbergh as a 'guerrilla auteur,' whose repossession of the means of production represents a significant advancement in the art form. But first, we will situate the director within the discourse of 'classical' auteur theory, identifying the prevailing patterns of Soderbergh's work within this traditional view of authorship. As Soderbergh refuses to play by the rules, we will quickly see how our subject matter exceeds the increasingly limited boundaries of auteur theory, not to mention the classical paradigm. That being said, a brief rehearsal of auteur theory seems necessary, if only to analyse how well, paradoxically, the frame does in fact suit the director.

In the mid-1950s, film critics at the influential French journal *Cahiers du cinéma* set out to elevate the status of its most beloved film directors by championing the creative vision of luminaries like Alfred Hitchcock, Jean Renoir, and Howard Hawks. As a consequence of this central objective, these critics sought to diminish the role held by the screenwriter, who at that time was perceived to be the film's true author. Led by François Truffaut, Jean-Luc Godard, and Eric Rohmer, the *Cahiers* group also sought to demonstrate how the true individual artist rose above the industrial formation of the Hollywood system to clearly relate their unique visions, particularly within set genres. Three predominant criteria of auteurism took hold, which could elevate a filmmaker to the status of auteur: a distinctive visual style, achieved through technical mastery; a continued, intentional set of thematic concerns and patterns; and finally, a struggle with the industrial process of cinema's production, embodying the unavoidable tension between art and commerce. In short, a personal creative vision defined the auteur.

When the theory travelled to the Anglophone world in the 1960s, it was popularised by American and British critics, most notably Andrew Sarris and Peter Wollen. Sarris's influential essay, 'Notes on the Auteur Theory' (1962), was the first iteration of this critical trend, followed by *The American Cinema: Directors and Directions 1929– 1968* (1968). Sarris synthesised many of the French ideas and privileged the American context over all others. Sarris elaborated on Alexandre Astruc's notion of the *caméra-stylo* (camera-pen), the instrument through which the director expresses their distinctive creative vision or 'signature.' As a result, Sarris created a hierarchical system, still in operation today, that isolates a 'pantheon' of directors, ranked in order of importance. Despite critical, scholarly, and industrial attempts to dislodge the director as the centre of all filmmaking, the canonising of important figures remains firmly in place today, just as it does in literature, despite similar attempts. Admittedly, this very book participates in the reductive capacity of canonisation, elevating Soderbergh to the status of 'important artist.' At the same time, however, we can use the opportunity to measure the flaws in classical auteur theory by what it excludes and why many productive filmmakers stand outside of the critical canon. As Soderbergh has been equally privileged by and dislodged from a larger canon throughout his career, it is worth mapping the moments and aspects by which he has been anointed as a *bona fide* auteur, as well as exploring those where he has not.[6]

What is often forgotten in the auteur debate is that the theory itself has been divided since its inception, and oriented in opposite directions between French and Anglophone perspectives. As Maitland McDonagh reminds us, the French critics venerated the director who worked within the system, and whose signature emerged despite the interference from the studio. The 'new generation' of auteurs, prompted by Sarris, privileged 'film as art' and a 'medium for personal expression' without regard to the industry that produced them.[7] The irony of dealing with a figure like Soderbergh is that he neither emerges as the romantic auteur, nor the 'studio hack.' His status remains uncertain, despite the reality that he is actually closer to both analytic models than many other contemporary directors. This is also why he doesn't quite fit. Soderbergh thus offers an opportunity to view his career-long trajectory amidst other trends and a larger model that does not exclusively view him as a practitioner whose works express, as Sarris would have it, the 'élan of his soul.'[8] Rather, Soderbergh is a complex figure whose intersections with many collaborators, contexts, and technologies require that we reach beyond Sarris-inspired criticism to find a new structure that accounts for the many tensions and paradoxes that the contemporary Hollywood industry provides us.

Auteurism fell out of favour when its flaws and limitations were articulated, and a multitude of alternative discourses in film theory gained prominence in its place, but there has been a reconsideration of cinematic authorship in recent years. Dudley Andrew poignantly welcomes back auteurism: 'Breathe easily. *Epuration* has ended. After a dozen years of clandestine whispering we are permitted to mention, even to discuss, the auteur again.'[9] 'Auteurs are far from dead,' in Timothy Corrigan's view. 'In fact, they may be more alive than at any other point in film history … within the commerce of contemporary culture, auteurism has become, as both a production and interpretive position, something quite different from what it may have been in the 1950s or 1960s.'[10] Hollywood is a constantly changing and evolving industry; there is no reason why considerations of authorship in Hollywood should not evolve correspondingly. By understanding its theoretical limitations and shifting industry conditions, we may reformulate the concept of the 'auteur' according to these new contexts.

The primary modification of auteurism has been in terms of the reliance on Romantic and individualist notions of the author. Prompted by such grand literary revelations as Roland Barthes' 'The Death of the Author'[11] in 1968 and Michel Foucault's 'What is an Author?'[12] in 1969, auteur theory has been overhauled in terms of its breadth and scope. Rather than perceiving an auteur film as some sublime expression of individual genius, it is now regarded as a discursive *site* for the interaction of biography, institutional context, social climate, and historical moment. In this rendering, auteurism is meant to 'emphasize the ways a director's work can be both personal *and* mediated by extrapersonal elements such as genre, technology, [and] studios.'[13] What began as an attempt by the French critics of *Cahiers du cinéma* to elevate the director to the status of an artist has since evolved into a complex theory containing various interrelated theories and positions.

Nevertheless, auteur theory continues to be a useful categorical tool for the film critic, if only for the simple reason that a distinctive authorial signature is still readily perceived in directors to this day. Authors remain an important site for critical analysis. While we have already noted the difficulties in pinning down Soderbergh to any distinct brand on account of his prolific output and his formal, thematic, and stylistic promiscuity, broad strokes of his signature are visible to varying degrees throughout his body of work. When dealing with a canon approaching thirty feature films, as well as dozens of others that have borne his name as producer, patterns are sure to reveal themselves. At first glance, cinematography would be an easily identifiable trademark: Soderbergh's films often exhibit a colour-coded visual pattern, matching stories, characters, or settings with carefully chosen, symbolic colour palettes. On closer inspection, one might isolate editing as his tool of choice; flashbacks, temporal shifting, and non-linear editing pervade the bulk of his work. Thematically, arguments could be made for technological alienation, conflicted subjectivity, or institutional absurdity. Alternatively, armed with some meta-filmic knowledge, Soderbergh's inventive use of his actors and stars or his deft navigation of the financial aspect of Hollywood production might well be his defining feature. Upon completion of an in-depth study of the man's entire oeuvre, however, one comes to realise that Soderbergh is not so much painting with many cinematic brushes, but *orchestrating* his films with a mastery of nearly all the major roles of film production. And not just the creative ones.

In an effort to move beyond the Romantic notion of authorial genius, we might reverse the importance given to raw talent versus 'mere' skill. No doubt Soderbergh did appear a considerable talent when his debut film – *sex, lies, and videotape* – seemingly came out of nowhere to win the Audience Award at Sundance, the Palme D'Or at Cannes, the Independent Spirit Award for Best Director, and the Academy Award for Best Screenplay. More impressive than this precocious feat, however, is what he did next. Prophetically claiming that 'it's all downhill from here' in his acceptance speech at Cannes, Soderbergh – determined to hone his craft – followed his debut success with two minor, middling experiments (*Kafka, The Underneath*), one critically acclaimed film (*King of the Hill*, one of the best reviewed films of 1993), and one of the most abysmal failures in contemporary American cinema history. Though *Schizopolis* was seen by few and enjoyed by even fewer, Soderbergh took the opportunity to experiment and develop his skill in all aspects of film creation. As director, writer, cinematographer, editor, composer, and even actor, in these multiple roles, Soderbergh assimilated all the necessary skills needed on a film set.

With this newly-minted holistic approach, Soderbergh returned to Hollywood with the one-two crime-genre punch of *Out of Sight* and *The Limey*, showcasing his new signature to much acclaim. This would be followed by *Erin Brockovich* and *Traffic* the next year, each landing him a Best Director nomination at the Academy Awards (the first dual nomination in more than sixty years). There is no defining element or characteristic that unites all of these films – nor any of the increasingly experimental works to follow – so much as there is a Soderberghian ethos or spirit that pervades his entire body of work. And work it most certainly is; Soderbergh has fulfilled his desire to rival the career of John Huston, constantly working and prolifically releasing films: almost thirty as director and another thirty or so as producer. Aggressive with his visuals and storytelling, political and antagonistic with his thematics, loose and deceptive with his performances, and ceaselessly experimental, the Soderberghian signature is not a brush stroke, but a full-on filmmaking factory.

Though a holistic approach to filmmaking defines Soderbergh's signature, four major categories can be isolated as his most radical: cinematography, editing/narrative, performance, and production. Each of these categories can be subdivided to highlight not only their opposition to conventional Hollywood modes, but to exhibit the dynamic internal tensions within each designation. Not content with a single visual style, editing structure, or performance expectation, Soderbergh constantly experiments with different styles oscillating along a spectrum, their disjuncture forming a *signature-as-dialectic*. His style itself is working through the formal and aesthetic possibilities of the medium. This formal fluctuation is inherently bound to Soderbergh's choice of material; he bounces from esoteric arthouse project, to digital experiment, to high concept blockbuster, to genre staple, to period piece, to special-effects laden project, and back again. With such a diverse range of subject matter, it is appropriate that the accompanying form and style should oscillate as well. Tracking this dialectical dynamism requires a wider view towards patterns that exhibit themselves only across many films.

Considering the wide scope of Soderbergh's work, we might designate one end of the spectrum as 'classical', referring to his more traditional impulses, and the other 'chaotic', representing his experimental qualities. By 'classical', we mean the painterly compositions, glossy three-point lighting, and smooth camera movements of his cinematography and *mise-en-scène*; the linear continuity and 'invisibility' of his editing; the traditional heroes and genres of his narratives; the Method-influenced 'realism' of his performances; and the big studio budgets of his productions. By 'chaotic', we refer to the stunted framings, lack of lighting, and erratic camera movement of his cinematography; the jarring, non-linearity of his editing; the anti-heroes and abstract narratives; the Brechtian distanciation and fabricated nature of his performances; and the independent and alternative modes of financing and distributing his productions. His mainstream films lean more toward the 'classical', while his experimental films, particularly those filmed digitally, drift more toward 'chaotic'. However, there are elements of both in every one of his films, and it is the oscillation between and paradoxical synthesis of these two modes that defines the Soderberghian signature.

Table 1: Soderberghian signature elements

	Classical/Thesis	Chaotic/Anti-thesis	Paradox/Synthesis
Cinematography	• painterly compositions • 3-point glossy lighting • smooth tracking	• stunted framing, digital, ugly • no lighting • erratic handheld movement	• collage • filmed mosaic • triptych
Editing/ Narrative	• continuity • invisible • hero • genre	• non-linear • jarring • anti-hero • abstract	• modular, network • reflexive • noble thief • genre hybridity
Performance	• Stanislavski / naturalism / realism / Method • amateur, or star as 'real person' / historical figure • style: open framings, long takes, method, monologue, depth	• Brecht / artifice • star, star as themselves • style: quick, post-modern, ironic, wit, banter, off-the-cuff, surface	• hyperbolic • hybrid ensembles • 'dirtied' stars
Production	• studio • high-concept	• independent • limited budget	• Indiewood • mini-major • Section Eight

Soderberghian cinematography can be charted along a lengthy axis, often mixing styles within the same film, sometimes even within a single scene. On one end, we have the painterly Soderbergh, whose keen eye is set to capture careful compositions, in large part achieved with an expert knowledge of cameras, lenses, filters, gels, and other cinematic equipment. Whereas a director working with a director of photography might envision the objective of their scene, then consult their DOP on how to best achieve this formally, because Soderbergh acts as his own director of photography – starting with *Schizopolis*, then everything from *Traffic* on – his scenes are designed in direct accordance with how they will be shot. It is this hands-on formalism that leads to films so intrinsically linked to their precise visual style.

For example, the complexity of *Traffic*'s networked narrative is aided by its geographically matched colour palettes: the East Coast scenes are shot in bright daylight to produce icy blue, monochromatic tones; the Mexican scenes are overexposed and use 'tobacco' filters for grainy, bleached-out sepia tones; and the San Diego scenes use the risky tech-

The complexity of *Traffic*'s networked narrative is aided by its geographically matched colour palettes: overexposed 'tobacco' coloured film for Mexico, icy blues for the East Coast, and flashed negatives for sunny San Diego.

nique of 'flashing' the negative for a halo effect to complement the vibrant hues. An alternative use of colouring, quite literally, is in *Kafka*, which is presented mostly as a black-and-white, *film noir*-inspired world, but colourises on occasion, in order to represent a heightened perception of reality. Another fitting example of this precise cinematography is *The Good German*, which takes on the technical challenge of producing a film under the technological constraints of Classical Hollywood. Using only fixed focal-length lenses, boom mics, rear projection, incandescent lighting, and other technology from the 1940s, Soderbergh creates a film that hinges on its very method of production and visual style, such is the man's commitment to 'form = function.'

On the other end of his cinematographic spectrum, in opposition to this orderly, painterly impulse, Soderbergh exhibits a flawed, chaotic method that is characterised by speed and movement. Highly kinetic and bearing the influence of both *cinéma verité* and the French New Wave, as well as the 1970s' American cinema, this purposefully imperfect style is embodied in handheld camera work, canted framings, unmotivated zooms, and erratic motion. This raw impulse is more readily discernable when he works with a digital camera, whereby mobility and experimentation are afforded both technologically and financially: *Bubble*, *Che*, and *The Girlfriend Experience* mark his most prominently unhinged camera work – apart from *Schizopolis*, of course. However, traces of this erratic cinematography can be found in even the broadest of his films. Each entry in the *Ocean's* trilogy contains one or more aberrant scenes of unexpected delirium that stand in stark contrast to its otherwise slick, big-budget aesthetic. The brief, nostalgic recounting of previous failed attempts at robbing a Las Vegas casino in *Ocean's Eleven* and the high-speed climax of *Ocean's Twelve* are played for light-hearted whimsy in these contexts, but are easily linked to Soderbergh's other more distraught renderings of this raw style of camera work.

Incorporating disparate types of film and video – such as Hi-8, 16mm film stock, and various incarnations of digital video – is another method of adding incongruity in his style of cinematography. Ever since *sex, lies, and videotape*, with its juxtaposition of film and diegetic VHS videotape, right through to his recent usage of the RED One digital camera and 5k digital video – which has five times higher resolution than current 'high definition' Blu-Ray discs – Soderbergh has been experimenting not only with what the camera is capable of capturing, but with the camera and medium itself. A self-described 'gear-head,' accounting for his expert knowledge of filmmaking equipment, Soderbergh's fetishisation of the audio-visual apparatus continually finds its way into his films. Sepia-tinged scenes from *Poor Cow* (Ken Loach, 1967), an old Terence Stamp film, are cleverly used as flashbacks in *The Limey*, while security tape footage is the key to the heist in *Ocean's Eleven*, tricking both the villain and viewer alike. *Full Frontal*, the 'spiritual sequel' to *sex, lies, and videotape*, produced a little over a decade after his debut, represents the culmination of all three of these cinematographic impulses: a highly polished, elegantly filmed story – staged on the set of a Hollywood production – is contrasted with a 'raw,' behind-the-scenes story shot on grainy digital video. The film-within-a-film structure is revealed to be yet another filmic contrivance, and the full extent of Soderbergh's cinematography is on display.

It is on the visual plane that we can make a case that Soderbergh is attempting to produce a new and accurate vision of what the late 20th/early 21st century looks like, as well as how it is to be recorded. The filmmaker's experiments with the texture of film is only part of this process, as is his innovation in the realm of digital cinema. Just as 16mm camera technology informed the movement from Italian documentary film to what we call Italian neorealism, Soderbergh is an early adopter in every sense of the word when considering his cinematographic practices. In this same fashion, he pushes older technologies beyond their limits, by flaring camera lenses, flashing and burning film stocks, and tinting digital images with sickening blue and red hues. Though filmmakers such as David Fincher and Peter Jackson are often attributed as the key pioneers in Hollywood's embrace of digital innovation, Soderbergh was, in fact, experimenting with these technologies years before the wholesale digital conversion.

As with any attempt to specifically demarcate technological and aesthetic innovations, the logic of before and after prevail. Following Roland Barthes' 'The Death of the Author,' we might say that Soderbergh's 'author-function' embodies the specific logic of 'a *before* and an *after*.'[14] When speaking about cinematography, we tend to point to specific films in which the directors of photography accomplished something different, shifting the paradigm of vision. This is certainly true of Gregg Toland's innovative work in *Citizen Kane* (Orson Welles, 1941), Gordon Willis's sombre tones in *The Godfather* (Francis Ford Coppola, 1972), and Christopher Doyle's painterly motion in *Chungking Express* (Wong Kar Wai, 1994). For Steven Dillon, Soderbergh's cinematographic experimentation in the 1990s establish him as the artist 'who has most deliberately sought to retool the visual potentiality of [contemporary] American film,' and it is Soderbergh who led the way in a decade that 'saw more rapid shifts in color design than ever before.'[15]

Traversing Soderbergh's experiments in cinematic artifice, Dillon pinpoints *The Underneath* as a pivotal film in the evolution of digital visual texture. True to its title, the film is a work of denaturalisation and desubstantialisation, achieved primarily through a foreboding and haunting system of colour. A noir remake that purposefully carries none of the baggage of its cliched style – 'No wet streets, no smoke, no hats, no long shadows'[16] – *The Underneath* uses colour, framing, and tonality to capture the anxiety and alienation that noir achieved with chiaroscuro. Instead of a heavy-handed voice-over, the film cuts back and forth across its timeline unannounced, in effect denaturalising both time and space. Dillon proclaims the film 'a more significant contribution to the visual development of American film than Stone's *Natural Born Killers*,'[17] and oddly enough, despite the film's own cerebral pace, the influence of *The Underneath* is seen most directly on MTV: '[n]early all of Spike Lee's films after *Clockers* [1995], for example, manipulate film through a method taken straight from Soderbergh. Now every MTV video looks like *Clockers*, but the impulse in the 1990s to color, to tint, and to denaturalize came above all from Soderbergh.'[18]

Once again, the logic of 'before and after' prevails in Dillon's thinking, as he asserts that Soderbergh, and *The Underneath* in particular, should be seen as a historical marker. In an era when presumably everything has already been said, Soderbergh's work as a cinematographer still produces images that have yet to be seen. Aided by advancements in technology, Soderbergh produces unique, painterly visions of the world.[19] Accordingly, we can tie him more directly to a legacy of visual, film, and video artists like Stan Brakhage, Hollis Frampton, Michael Snow, Maya Deren, Chantal Akerman, Bill Viola, Matthew Barney, and Stan Douglas. In other words, perhaps it is more appropriate to judge some of Soderbergh's 'failed' films as belonging to a failure of imagination on the part of his middlebrow critics to see them as part of another legacy, more accurately befitting a 'high art' culture.[20] As visual art is most often the field that evokes comparisons to high culture, it is worth exploring whether Soderbergh's work on the visual plane should be judged outside the traditional evaluative apparatus Hollywood films receive.

On *The Underneath*, Soderbergh and his crew used Ektachrome film stock, overexposed it, and developed it as a negative, a process that favoured the distinctive, anxious green hue that pervades the film. According to Kodak, this technique had never been tried before,[21] and Soderbergh would continue this chemical experimentation on films like *The Limey*, where he 'flashed' the film stock before using it, producing the eerie, flared glow that accompanies the flashbacks. Does this kind of physical cinematographic experimentation deserve to be placed alongside Stan Brakhage's etching and painting on film, rather than be characterised as 'yet another Hollywood remake'? Tellingly, the credit Soderbergh hoped to take for *Traffic*, before clashing with the Directors' Guild of America, would have read 'Directed and Photographed by Steven Soderbergh'; by insisting on calling his work photography, and including it as his main title, he privileges this role as equal to the task of directing.

Somewhat hesitantly, Dillon claims that Soderbergh's lack of any clear style or theme means 'that the adjective "Soderberghian" will never be as meaningful as "Lynchian", "Scorsesian", or "Kubrickian."'[22] Dillon seemingly contradicts his own earlier insight, when he responds to the claim that 'critics and Soderbergh himself always emphasize how different Soderbergh's films are, one from another,' yet 'all of Soderbergh's films work through the absent presence of cinema.'[23] This self-reflexive mediation of cinematic fantasy – Dillon's own thesis that many contemporary American films enact 'the Solaris Effect' – is but one of the possible thematic signatures we might ascribe to the meaning of 'Soderberghian.' In referencing a French critic, Dillon provides us with an even more suitable metaphor: 'la machine Soderbergh.' Like a machine, many interlocking components are needed. Only when this impressive cinematographic vision is connected to a complex editing and narrative structure does this machine start to hum, and can we then begin to get a sense of the multivalent Soderberghian signature.

Ripping it Apart: Soderberghian Editing and Narrative Structure

Parallel to the cinematographic range that runs between orderly composition and erratic movement, Soderberghian editing and narrative structure spans a similar spectrum between classical and chaotic. On the traditional end, there is a distinctly Classical Hollywood mode of storytelling based on the interplay of range and depth of narration, the hero's quest to overcome adversity, and the structures of a traditional genre. On the classical side, there is an ironic and dialectical relationship between what is seen onscreen and what is heard through dialogue, urging the viewer to question the events as they occur. On the other end of this editing and narrative spectrum, we have a schizophrenic, non-linear editing style that destabilises time and space, complemented by a tendency to shade the protagonists as flawed heroes who cannot achieve closure in their narrative struggles. Soderbergh's films conform to an era of increased postmodern fragmentation to the point that they undermine traditional rules of storytelling and reflect the contemporary subject's struggle to make sense of their fractured, media-saturated environment.

To varying degrees throughout his oeuvre, Soderbergh's cutting destroys linear temporalities, disrupts space, and ultimately destabilises the viewer's expectation as to where and when the film is taking place. Accordingly, the storytelling pushes at the boundaries of narrative convention with frequent flashbacks, flashforwards, and repeated events. Soderbergh also varies and restricts story narration to such an extreme that part of the experience of watching one of his films is deciphering the mystery of the film's form. The 'how' is added to the 'where' and the 'when', while the 'why' is concealed behind a flurry of formal fluctuation. Thus, in *The Limey* it is ultimately revealed that Wilson (Terence Stamp) is flying away from the US, rather than arriving, forcing the spectator to reorganise the story, and realise the non-linear progression of the story is actually a result of the character's unreliable memory. This effect also occurs in *The Girlfriend Experience* as a final montage reorganises the order of events, in a manner that somehow surpasses the narrative device of *in medias res*. As Chelsea (Sasha Grey) makes her way to the restaurant to be interviewed by a journalist, we discover that this event occurs at the very end of the movie, as opposed to the beginning as the narrative has fooled us into believing.

Though we maintain that Soderbergh's signature is the result of a mastery of multiple creative roles, it should be noted that editing and narrative structure in particular are very closely intertwined, hence their consideration here as a single creative element. For Soderbergh, editing is part of the writing process, even from the most preliminary stages of production. In his rejected screenplay for *Moneyball* (Bennet Miller, 2011), Soderbergh states directly on the script: 'an important portion of this film will be written in the editing room… This isn't a cop-out,' but 'entirely by design.'[24] A preoccupation of his from the beginning, considering the innovative splicing of home video in *sex, lies, and videotape*, again it is *The Underneath* in which Soderbergh first asserts his stylistic potential: 'Our physical bodies go through life in a chronological, linear way from birth to death, while in the mind it's different,' Soderbergh explains. 'Every time something happens to us, we think about a similar experience in the past and we imagine the consequences in the future. There is a constant back and forth. Our minds are totally non-linear.'[25] In addition to the deep visual texture mentioned previously, *The Underneath* emphasises this denaturalised time and space with an elaborate editing structure that mimics the protagonist's recollection and regret. *The Limey* was also designed in order to allow the editing to shape the film and emphasise the fractured nature of the mind: 'That was always the my intention. To go and shoot a bunch of stuff and then go in and just rip it apart.'[26] The result is a unique drift through

Wilson's mind, where conversations float above different scenes, flashbacks meander, and impossible memories of his daughter are seen through evocative flares.[27]

The relationship between Soderbergh's editing and his soundtracks is yet another illustration of the director's oscillation between classic and chaotic. His most frequent musical collaborator is Cliff Martinez, who composed the scores for Soderbergh's first six films, as well as *The Limey*, *Traffic*, *Solaris*, and *Contagion*. The slow, moody scores of Martinez are evocative and contemplative, a far cry from the breezy, jovial scores of DJ/ composer David Holmes, who worked on *Out of Sight*, the *Ocean's* trilogy, *The Girlfriend Experience*, and *Haywire*. Holmes' scores set a quick, enjoyable pace and tone that keeps pace with the editing, whereas Martinez's music is much more sombre and cerebral, befitting of a classic Hollywood score. More recently, Soderbergh has expanded these musical collaborations to include the moody acoustic stylings of Guided by Voices leader Robert Pollard (*Bubble*), the peppy retro stylings of composer Marvin Hamlisch (*The Informant!*), and the acoustic Latin guitar of Spanish composer Alberto Iglesias (*Che*). In each case, Soderbergh uses the soundtrack as a consistent frame upon which he can overlay his complex editing, while at the same time establishing an evocative mood.

Soderbergh uses sound bridges and jumbled dialogue from several differing temporalities to suggest a unity of space and time, as seen in the hyper-stylised love scene between Karen Sisco (Jennifer Lopez) and Jack Foley (George Clooney) in *Out of Sight*.

Soderbergh also extensively uses sound bridges and jumbled dialogue from several differing temporalities to suggest a unity of space and time, despite its staggered nature or its being taken from altogether different time frames. A notable example of this technique takes place in the hyper-stylised love scene between Karen Sisco (Jennifer Lopez) and Jack Foley (George Clooney) in *Out of Sight*, wherein a conversation over drinks is provocatively intercut with images of both characters as they undress; *Solaris* features a similarly brazen love scene between Kris Kelvin (Clooney) and his wife Rheya (Natascha McElhone), also provocatively intercut between the past and the present, dream and reality. The most extreme example, however, takes place in *The Limey*, where the plot's staggered chronology is as much a mystery to the viewer as the film's story. Each of these examples find their origins in *Schizopolis*, where Soderbergh overlays a dense array of staggered chronologies on top of each other, complicating the viewer's understanding of where and when the narrative is actually taking place.[28]

Beyond such general, overarching characteristics of his editing and narrative structure, we can isolate unique plot formations according to formalist critic Charles Ramírez-Berg's 'A Taxonomy of Alternative Plots in Recent Films: Classifying the "Tarantino Effect."'[29] This useful, comprehensive schematic surveys contemporary films that utilise unorthodox and experimental narration and categorises them according to twelve different structures. After exploring the historical antecedents, Ramírez-Berg claims that Quentin Tarantino is responsible for popularising this latest trend of alternative film narration, or what other scholars have called network narratives (David Bordwell[30]), modular narratives (Allan Cameron[31]) and puzzle films (Warren Buckland[32]). One cannot dismiss the popularity and cultural impact of Tarantino in the 1990s, particularly the long shadow cast by *Reservoir Dogs* (1992) and *Pulp Fiction* (1994), but for his purposes, Ramírez-Berg would have been better off choosing Soderbergh as his exemplar, as his films can be seen to exhibit *every single one* of the twelve structures, many more than once (see Table 2), while Tarantino only fits three. *Schizopolis* is a notable oversight, as it exhibits some of the rarer formations (Multiple Personality, Daisy Chain, Repeated Action, Repeated Event), as well as the more common (Jumbled, Subjective, Existential) in a single, hybridised (and appropriately titled) example, providing a textbook case study for the trend of experimental narrative structure in the 1990s and beyond. Just as Dillon proclaims that MTV started to look a lot like Spike Lee films, but the source of this innovative visual texture is actually Soderbergh, we would contend that though the influence of Tarantino is felt far and wide in film and television, the actual source of much of the narrative experimentation at the time is in fact Soderbergh. In other words, a more accurate subtitle would have been 'The Soderbergh Clause to the Tarantino Effect.'

Performing Reality: Soderberghian Performance

Soderbergh's direction of actors is another important aspect of his filmmaking process, which has inspired loyalty from a repertory of Hollywood talent, and has coaxed unexpected performances out of non-professional actors. As with the previous characteristics, Soderbergh's direction of actors oscillates between two major impulses. The first of these is

Table 2: Charles Ramírez-Berg's Taxonomy of Alternative Plot Formations, with Soderbergh's Films as Examples.

Plots Based on the Number of Protagonists
1. The Polyphonic or Ensemble Plot – multiple protagonists, single location *Full Frontal*
2. The Parallel Plot – multiple protagonists in different times and/or spaces *Traffic, Syriana, Contagion*
3. The Multiple Personality (Branched) Plot *Schizopolis*
4. The Daisy Chain Plot – no central protagonist, one character leads to the next *Schizopolis*, elements of *The Good German*
Plots Based on the Re-ordering of Time; Non-linear Plots
5. The Backwards Plot *The Last Time I Saw Michael Gregg*, elements of *The Limey* and *The Girlfriend Experience*
6. The Repeated Action Plot – one character repeats action *Schizopolis*, elements of *Out of Sight* and *The Limey*
7. The Repeated Event Plot – one action seen from multiple characters' perspectives *Schizopolis*, elements of *Out of Sight* and *The Limey*
8. The Hub and Spoke Plot – multiple characters' story lines intersect decisively at one time and place *Full Frontal*
9. The Jumbled Plot – scrambled sequence of events motivated artistically, by filmmaker's prerogative *Out of Sight, The Limey, The Underneath, Schizopolis, Solaris, The Girlfriend Experience, Che*, elements of the *Ocean's* trilogy
Plots that Deviate from Classical Rules of Subjectivity, Causality, and Self-Referential Narration
10. The Subjective Plot – a character's internal (or 'filtered') perspective *The Limey, Solaris, King of the Hill, Schizopolis*
11. The Existential Plot – minimal goal, causality, and exposition *Schizopolis, Solaris*
12. The Metanarrative Plot – narration about the problem of movie narration *sex, lies, and videotape, Schizopolis, Full Frontal*

rooted in 'naturalism' and 'realism,' which in Soderbergh's usage are conceptsthat certainly necessitate scare quotes to indicate relativity. From Stanislavski, to the Method school of acting, to considerations of historical accuracy, this performance style embodies the classical end of the spectrum. The opposite impulse employs reflexivity and artifice, rooted in Brechtian distanciation, where performances engage with star persona, either by embracing and playing with its contours, or by radically acting against type. Again, the paradoxical synthesis of these impulses leads to hybrids in which performances are pushed in tense, hyperbolic directions, leading to alienation, reflection, and ironic indulgence.

Soderbergh's loose style lends itself to acting of either stripe, as his open framings allow for direct, complex performances, which anchor his stylistic excesses. Because he is also the Director of Photography, Soderergh is often behind the camera within a few feet of the action, maintaining an intimate relationship with his actors, whispering directions to avoid interrupting the flow of the shoot. This technique has obviously won him a great deal of loyalty from his recurring collaborators, from A-list stars (George Clooney, Julia Roberts, Brad Pitt, Matt Damon, Michael Douglas, Catherine Zeta-Jones), to a growing repertory of noted character actors (Luis Guzmán, Don Cheadle, Catherine Keener, and Eddie Jemison). In addition, Soderbergh has experimented with unique performances from non-professional actors, such as KFC manager Debbie Doberener (*Bubble*), Bill Clinton advisor and Democratic pundit James Carville (*K-Street*), adult film star Sasha Grey (*The Girlfriend Experience*), and mixed-martial arts star Gina Carano (*Haywire*).

On the realist and naturalist end of the spectrum, Soderberghian performance can be traced through three categories: 'typage,'[33] Stanislavskian realism leading into 'the Method,' and an emphasis on historical accuracy. The first of these categories draws from the film traditions of early Soviet silent cinema and Italian neorealism, where non-professional actors who look like the parts they play are asked to portray characters who have similar lives to their own. A long history of this effort to capture 'realistic' performances through non-professional actors and location shooting exists in cinema, from *Battleship Potemkin* (Sergei Eisenstein, 1925), to Vittorio De Sica's *Bicycle Thieves* (1948) and *Umberto D.* (1952), to more recent examples, like Pedro Costa's *Colossal Youth* (2006). Soderbergh has embraced this style in *K-Street, Bubble, The Girlfriend Experience,* and *Haywire*, which echo the works of Eisenstein and De Sica by relying on verisimilitude to provide the basis for realistic performance.

This 'authentic' trend within Soderbergh's films is first visible in James Carville's role in *K-Street*, in which he portrays a meta-fictional political analyst in Washington, D.C. named James Carville. *Bubble* continues the geographic/non-professional actor connection with its West Virginia factory workers, including Debbie Doberener, who Soderbergh found in a KFC drive-through and cast as the lead. Filmed at the height of the financial crisis in New York City, Chelsea, the high-end escort in *The Girlfriend Experience*, is played by notorious adult film star Sasha Grey, lending the film some scintillating cache to its tale of bodily exchange. Finally, *Haywire* hinges on the athletic performance of Mallory, the hard-as-nails spy played by mixed-martial arts champion Gina Carano. For her part, Carano is mostly called upon to perform physical tasks throughout the film, such as running, fighting, sleuthing, and executing acrobatic manoeuvres, as the camera stays locked on her performing these tasks. Because these characters exist in environments and contexts that resemble those of the actors' 'everyday' lives, their performances strike us as gritty and 'real'; however, our knowledge of the film *as* film potentially pushes the performances towards being considered contrived. Of course, perceiving of the actor's 'real' life being portrayed as 'reel' life is

Soderbergh experiments with performance by working with non-professional actors, such as KFC manager Debbie Doberener (*Bubble*) and mixed-martial arts star Gina Carano (*Haywire*), while also subverting and 'dirtying' star images, such as Gwyneth Paltrow in *Contagion* and Matt Damon in *The Informant!*

part of the interpretative tension, and the viewer's perception of the film would vary according to their degree of extratextual knowledge.

This devotion to realism in performance derives from a much longer tradition in the theatre, emerging from Russia in the late nineteenth and early twentieth centuries. The teachings of actor-turned-director Konstantin Stanislavski are central to this technique, as he sought to find dramatic truth in performance through psychological realism and emotional authenticity. [34] The core of this practice would travel stateside mid-century and be interpreted by American teachers such as Lee Strasberg and Stella Adler, directors like Elia Kazan and Arthur Penn, and depicted onscreen by Marlon Brando and Robert De Niro, among others.[35] The common thread between all these teachers, directors, and actors is that realism and 'truth' lie at the heart of authentic performances.

Soderbergh's own work in theatre may be partially responsible for his use of this approach, in addition to his admiration of figures like Mike Nichols, whose cinematic style translates theatricality to the screen. *Who's Afraid of Virginia Woolf* (1966), *The Graduate* (1967), and *Carnal Knowledge* (1971) all employ this method, allowing their actors to roam and pace, as well as providing longer dialogue scenes, complete with long takes, slow camera movements, and long pauses for acting, which could involve specific rhythms of speech, applying regional dialect, or physically interpreting a character's mannerisms that are apart from the actor's own. When Soderbergh directed Jonathan Reynolds' play *Geniuses* at Louisiana State University's Swine Palace theatre in 1996, he received directing advice from Nichols over the phone.[36] Years later, following her work with him on *The Good German*, Academy Award-winning actress and Sydney Theatre Company artistic director Cate Blanchett invited Soderbergh to write and direct a play for the company's 2009 season, entitled *Tot Mom*, based on the coverage of the Casey Anthony murder trial. In addition to this rigorous theatrical production, in typical prolific Soderbergh fashion he recruited the cast to film an improvised comedy during production and in between rehearsals. Entitled *The Last Time I Saw Michael Gregg*, this meta-narrative concerns a company mounting a theatrical production, focusing on a husband and wife team who lead the troupe, not unlike Cate Blanchett and her husband Andrew Upton.

As Soderbergh has been involved in theatre and deeply influenced by directors who emerged from the stage, it is worth exploring how theatricality works in Soderbergh's films. *sex, lies, and videotape* provides a suitable example of this theatricality on film, as his actors are given the full range of expressive dialogue, dramatic monologues, and pensive pauses. In these instances, Soderbergh lets the camera roll, providing wide open shots, framings, and space for his actors to interpret the scene, creating the impression that events are occurring spontaneously, despite the fact that the film was fully scripted in advance. A heightened theatricality is also predominant in *Full Frontal*, as characters engage in lengthy reflections and soul-searching through long takes and voice-overs. A subplot also involves a small live-theatre production called 'The Sound and the Führer,' allowing Nicky Katt to indulge in the absurdity of Hitler on stage; though Soderbergh is not known for his comic sensibility, a surreal, understated absurdity, rendered theatrically, pokes through here, as well as in *Schizopolis, The Limey*, the *Ocean's* trilogy, and *The Informant!*

In terms of Stanislavskian realism, many of Soderbergh's films allow his actors free rein to revel in character detail, nuance, and motivation. Details like regional accents are common, such as Terence Stamp's adoption of a lower-class cockney accent in *The Limey*, or Benicio Del Toro, whose Academy Award-winning immersion into the character of Javier Rodriguez in *Traffic* necessitated that he speak a Mexican dialect of Spanish, despite his native Puerto Rican heritage. Ensconcing themselves in the 'grammar of acting,' many of Soderbergh's characters are driven by an existential motivation, such as Clooney's bemused, brooding Chris Kelvin in *Solaris*, Stamp's regretful, nostalgic Wilson in *The Limey*, and del Toro's calm, meditative Che.

Che brings us to the final category at the realistic and classical end of the Soderbergh performance spectrum: historical accuracy. In channeling Che, a long-gestating role and project Del Toro had been preparing for years before production, the actor interprets and internalises the real-life figure by incorporating the patterns, tics, personality traits, and details of Ernesto 'Che' Guevara's life. A great deal of research is required to portray such a controversial political figure, resulting in a synthesis of the many documents read, interviews conducted, and footage screened. This research-oriented approach is indebted to Stella Adler's American variant of 'the method' in which details studied include everything from a character's social class and historical context to their clothing, mannerisms, and physicality. The context of *Che*'s production also aided in this detail-oriented method, as the film was shot in Spain, Puerto Rico, and Mexico with the assistance of local crews, and in an extremely non-commercial decision, the original Spanish language was retained; when del Toro met Venezuelan President Hugo Chávez after a screening of the film, he could confidently tell Chávez that *Che* was 'a totally Latin American movie.'[37]

In addition to this dedication to performance and contextual accuracy, del Toro owes his Best Actor Award from the Cannes Festival to the unconventional structure of the film. Unlike the typical Hollywood biographical film, *Che* is comprised of two campaigns and divided into two parts – the successful revolution in Cuba, followed by the failure in Bolivia – viewed through a stripped-down depiction of events lacking the perceived gravitas of Hollywood's sentimentalism. Such a frank rendering of the man thus relies heavily on del Toro's subdued incarnation. Other Soderbergh films to engage in historical biography include Julia Roberts' Academy Award-winning turn as Erin Brockovich, a clever, melodramatic usage of her star image in the role of a scrappy heroine, and Matt Damon's portrayal of Mark Whitacre, whose weight gain and absurd appearance emphasise the character's bipolar instability, and stands in contrast to the massive institutional corruption at hand.

Turning back to the full spectrum of Soderberghian performance, if Stanislavski represents one pole, then the opposite pole would be Bertolt Brecht and his 'epic theatre.'[38] Using a modernist approach to the theatre, Brecht's techniques assured that his audience was fully aware they were watching a play and his actors were instructed to play their characters reflexively. Brecht's shows attempted to dispel the bourgeois notions of the theatre as well as the ideological structures that held it up. Through reflexivity, and irony on the part of both the spectator and the actor, Brecht sought to engage the spectator in a critical, rather than emotional or escapist fashion. Considering the naturalistic tendencies of Soderberghian performance we have outlined, one might question how Brecht applies to the director's work, but the key tenets of the acting technique should leave little doubt: fragmentation, contradiction, and interruption. Moreover, Brecht later came to prefer the term 'dialectical theatre,' so its inclusion here accounts for Soderbergh's intentions and serves our own analysis.

In cinema, and its corresponding star market, the relationship between an audience's extratextual knowledge and expectation of an actor and the onscreen fulfillment or subversion of that knowledge and expectation is a key site for interpreting performance. Though Soderbergh may seem an odd choice in comparison to more famous practitioners of Brechtian technique (Jean-Luc Godard, for one, who utilised techniques such as breaking the fourth wall, excessive filters, and narrative interruptions[39]), the overdetermined nature of many of Soderbergh's films, particularly those featuring A-list stars, warrants our inclusion of Brecht in the director's toolkit.

Soderbergh's use of reflexivity is most apparent in the *Ocean's* trilogy, which features some of Hollywood's biggest stars: George Clooney, Brad Pitt, and Matt Damon star in all three; Julia Roberts in two; Catherine Zeta-Jones, Bruce Willis, and Al Pacino in one each. In an era where box office is seen to be largely determined by celebrity, many directors hope to snag just one of these bankable movie stars; the *Ocean's* trilogy remains a unique franchise for the sheer quantity of star power. Saturated with such high-calibre celebrity, it is no wonder Soderbergh takes the opportunity to ruminate on the star phenomenon. This begins by casting the stars as thinly-veiled versions of their own star persona: Clooney's classic charisma, Pitt's handsome rebel, Damon's earnest modesty, and Roberts' generous heart and smile, these personas are embodied in their characters to such an extent that the viewer feels they are watching glamorous versions of the celebrities themselves, rather than their respective characters. When Clooney and Pitt finish each other's sentences, or Damon is charmingly awkward, the pleasure in watching these interactions is derived from witnessing megastars George Clooney and Brad Pitt clowning around as stereotypes of characters, not from the experience of watching Danny Ocean and Rusty Ryan as believable characters located in the diegesis of the film.

This reflexive engagement with the audience, which we would call the distancing effect or distanciation under Brecht's rubric, is further pronounced in an early scene in *Ocean's Eleven* in which the celebrity-characters of the film world interact with celebrity-actors from the 'real' world. Rusty (Brad Pitt) is seen teaching poker to a group of 'teen idols' who were all starring in popular teen-oriented television shows at the time: Holly Marie Combs of *Charmed*, Topher Grace of *That 70's Show*, Joshua Jackson of *Dawson's Creek*, Barry Watson of *7th Heaven*, and Shane West of *Once and Again*. A quick-cut from Rusty at the bar to Danny (George Clooney) at the poker table, and we can barely hear Danny asking, 'Isn't it a big move from TV to movies?' Topher Grace responds, 'Not for me, dude,' having just made the move to film the previous year in Soderbergh's *Traffic*. The joke relies on the viewer's extratextual knowledge of Clooney's much more publicised transition from *ER* to film. This crack in the façade of celebrity is driven home when the whole gang leaves the bar and screaming fans hound Topher Grace for an autograph, while Clooney and Pitt waltz by unaffected.[40]

Ocean's Twelve pushes this self-awareness to breaking point with its infamous 'Julia Roberts playing Julia Roberts' scene. With half of the crew in jail, Tess (Roberts) is called on to play a role in the heist, pretending to be none other than Julia Roberts. What results is basically one giant in-joke, with Julia Roberts' star image being the linchpin of the gag. First, we get Linus (Matt Damon) coaching Tess in how to act like Julia Roberts: 'She needs a southern accent... You're from Smyrna, Georgia... You're playing an actress, they're insecure!' Many references are made to her previous films: *Four Weddings and a Funeral* (Mike Newell, 1994) is mistaken for *Notting Hill* (Roger Michell, 1999), a similar film also written by Richard Curtis in which Roberts also played a version of herself; Tess is later incarcerated with prostitutes, alluding to her breakthrough role in *Pretty Woman* (Garry Marshall, 1990); and the 'real' Bruce Willis plays himself, a real-life friend of the real-life Julia Roberts, who co-starred with Roberts in the fake movie within a movie in *The Player* (Robert Altman, 1992). The appearance of Bruce Willis also creates the opportunity to riff on the cultural impact of his film *The Sixth Sense* (M. Night Shyamalan, 1999), as well as make a jab at his lack of Academy Award appeal. 'You know, that little statue on the mantle starts smirking at you after a while, you know what I'm saying?' Linus asks, to which Willis replies, 'Not really, Glen, no' (Damon and Roberts are both Academy Award winners, Willis has never been nominated). The viewer is left with one final fissure in the credits. Jokingly referring to Hollywood's highest-paid female star as an ingénue, the credit 'And introducing Julia Roberts as Tess' in *Ocean's Eleven* is followed by the intertextual reversal in *Ocean's Twelve*: 'And introducing Tess as Julia Roberts.'

This explicit level of reflexivity is just scratching the surface, as subtle homages and in-jokes proliferate in the series. Character names Virgil and Turk are an homage to *The Godfather*; the concluding scene in front of the Bellagio fountains in *Ocean's Eleven* is an homage to *The Right Stuff* (Philip Kaufman, 1983). Terry Benedict (Andy Garcia) is heard denying a request to 'Mr. Levin,' recommending he instead watch the boxing match on TV, because 'surely he must have HBO.' Gerald Levin is chairman of Time-Warner, the parent company to both HBO and Warner Brothers, the film's distributor. Reprising his cameo role from the first film, Topher Grace claims he 'totally phoned in that Dennis Quaid movie,' referring to *In Good Company* (Paul Weitz, 2004), the preview of which was seen before *Ocean's Twelve* in many theatres. The franchise ends on a final reflexive note, in which Pitt's character tells Clooney that for next time, 'try to keep off the weight in between,' referring to the actor's weight gain for *Syriana*. As a retort, Clooney tells Pitt to 'settle down' and 'have a couple of kids,' referring to his much-publicised relationship and family with Angelina Jolie.

We could continue this referential catalogue, but suffice to say, the tenuous connection between the 'reel' world and the 'real' world is continuously put on display – to varying degrees depending on one's inter/extratextual knowledge – within the world of *Ocean's*. By explicitly pointing to film *as* film and stars *as* stars, Soderbergh is in turn able to use his celebrity-filled high-concept blockbuster to comment on celebrity-filled high-concept blockbusters. In addition to playing *with* star image, Soderbergh also plays *against* star image, and this is where we see the paradoxical synthesis of the two poles of Soderberghian performance. The most direct synthesis of both Stanislavskian and Brechtian impulses is in Soderbergh's use of what we might call 'dirtied stars,' in which a performer will dull the shine of their star persona by adopting a gritty, naturalistic character, often by transforming their bodies through weight gain and other alterations, or by playing a radical departure from their usual roles. Julia Roberts' Academy Award-winning performance in *Erin Brockovich* is emblematic, as the actress plays a scrappy, down-on-her-luck, lower-class character, yet one who uses her beauty as a weapon in the diegetic story. A clever use of her star persona, Roberts is able to be both 'real' yet seductively charming; she is portrayed with both selfless tenacity and charismatic sentimentality. The paradox here is that the naturalism is ultimately achieved only through sheer artifice.

Similarly, George Clooney's first acclaimed movie role, beginning his transition from television heartthrob to 'serious' film star, came with the working-class, kind-hearted ex-convict and criminal Jack Foley in *Out of Sight*. Another charming, criminal role in *Ocean's Eleven* would cement this rugged, mysterious, 'Classical Hollywood'-type persona, before exploring more dramatic, existential roles for Soderbergh in *Solaris*, *Syriana*, and *The Good German*. Matt Damon's turn in *The Informant!* belongs in the 'dirty star' category as well, his appearance and performance a far cry from his marquee idol star persona seen in the *Bourne* trilogy. In this case, Damon's appearance – weight gain, hair piece, and unsightly moustache – is played for comic absurdity, as opposed to Clooney's weight gain and world-weary demeanour in *Syriana* that indicates 'heavy drama.' Fittingly, both films involve stories of widespread, global corporate malfeasance, and the institutional weight of these topics is literally embodied in each performance. But the most explicit example of the 'dirty star' is Gwyneth Paltrow's role in *Contagion*, in which she not only dies early in the film, transmitting the deadly virus, but suffers the indignity of having her face peeled from her skull during an autopsy. Her pale, sickly visage was used extensively in the marketing campaign, signalling that this film would enact all manner of unsightly trauma upon its A-list ensemble cast. Kate Winslet would also be unceremoniously dispensed with by the pandemic.

The Limey features a dual example of this performative synthesis, with Soderbergh exploiting the countercultural image and 1960s' legacy of Terence Stamp and Peter Fonda. In a sort of 'washed-up star' or 'past-their-prime star' variant, *The Limey* features two characters/actors who both peaked in the 1960s; Stamp as a career criminal who did time for robbing a Pink Floyd concert, and Fonda as a promoter in the music industry. We are first introduced to Fonda's Valentine in a montage set to 'King Midas in Reverse' by the Hollies, and later, we see him driving up the Californian coast with Steppenwolf on the soundtrack, surely evoking Fonda's iconic Captain America from *Easy Rider* (Dennis Hopper, 1969). For Stamp's Wilson, his background is established in flashbacks which are actually taken from a film from 1967, Ken Loach's *Poor Cow*. On one hand, the performances portray a naturalist quality – these characters 'really are from the 1960s,' with the mannerisms to prove it – but on the other hand, we are distanced from them for the very same reason; the actors each bring too much cultural baggage to be believable as anyone but themselves. A similar paradox is achieved with Michael Douglas and Catherine Zeta-Jones as morally conflicted characters on opposite sides of the law in *Traffic*, and Tobey Maguire destroying his heroic *Spider-Man* (Sam Raimi, 2002) persona in *The Good German* as Tully, the soldier turned con-man, whose physical violence, excessive swearing, and sexual vices stand in stark contrast to both Maguire's good-natured star persona and the Hay's Code-era cinema the film is imitating.

Finally, no discussion of Soderberghian performance would be complete without at least a cursory mention of Soderbergh's own appearances within his films and others. He has a series of self-deprecating auteur cameos: in *Ocean's Eleven*, credited as the 'incompetent safecracker'; in *Full Frontal*, as the film-within-a-film's director, whose face is edited out with a black censor block; and *Contagion*, as Paltrow's adulterous love interest, heard only briefly at the beginning of the film as a voice over the telephone. Animated through rotoscoping, Soderbergh's visage pops up in Richard Linklater's *Waking Life* (2001), recounting a story about Louis Malle and Billy Wilder: Malle has just made a film (*Black Moon* [1975]) costing two and a half million dollars, and tells

Wilder it's about a dream within a dream, to which Wilder responds: 'Well you just lost two and a half million dollars.' Soderbergh has also performed the role of critic and cultural authority on the DVD commentaries of films he was heavily influenced by: *The Third Man* (Carol Reed, 1949), *Clean, Shaven* (Lodge Kerrigan, 1993), *Point Blank* (John Boorman, 1967), *The Graduate*, and *Who's Afraid of Virginia Woolf?*

Last but not least, in *Schizopolis* Soderbergh plays the main character, Fletcher Munson, and his *doppelgänger*, Dr. Jeffrey Korchek.[41] We will have more to say about this esoteric little experiment in later chapters, but for now, it's worth mentioning that Soderbergh spends a great deal of time alone on camera, performing in front of it. *Schizopolis*'s mirror scene, literally and figuratively a moment of reflection, has the director standing in a bathroom making faces at himself. One of these faces would grace the front cover, and nine others the back cover of *Getting Away With It: Or: The Further Adventures of the Luckiest Bastard You Ever Saw*, a book containing Soderbergh's interviews with his hero and mentor, Richard Lester, as well as a collection of Soderbergh's diary entries providing insight into the period between *Schizopolis* and *Out of Sight*. A fitting cover image, the many different faces (and personas and titles and roles) of Soderbergh is something that, by now, should be more than apparent in the man's expansive oeuvre.

Cinema of Economy: A Steven Soderbergh Production

For all the experimentation and variability of the Soderberghian signature in cinematography, editing, narrative, and performance, these are common tools in an auteur's arsenal. Production, and its direct involvement in the business side of the film industry, however, is not a role we often associate with the romantic view of the auteur genius. Yet this is where Soderbergh's most confounding challenge to the auteur system lies. As demonstrated by the previous categorical assessment, Soderbergh is a resolute auteur, not only a master of the technical apparatus of filmmaking, but someone who pushes the boundaries of the medium itself. The rest of the book will investigate the thematic, social, and cultural implications of his impressive body of work. But what do we make of Soderbergh's industrial role?

Once again, we can plot a spectrum to illustrate the extent to which the economic and industrial nature of Soderbergh's productions vary. On the 'classical' end, big Hollywood productions, funded and distributed by one of the big studios; on the 'chaotic' end, smaller independent productions, experimental distribution strategies, and his own production company, Section Eight. In the middle, Soderbergh is emblematic (and considered one of the founders) of the most explicit, literal case of paradoxical synthesis we have seen yet: the formation of so-called 'mini-major' production companies within the industry, and the short-lived fantasy of 'Indiewood.' We will investigate this axis of production in the next chapter, when we complicate auteur theory by also considering how fame and celebrity enter into the business side of being a film director in the new 'New Hollywood.'

In conclusion, we can return to the epigraph that began this chapter, and consider Soderbergh's own evaluation of his craft. After four films, he describes himself as a chameleon rather than an artist or visionary; instead of imposing his own style, he finds the right style for the right material. Thirty films later, we can certainly see the vast variability in how he applies his wide range of style to a wide range of material, but is this not artistry? Is it the lack of a singular, concrete artistic vision? Perhaps we have just never had someone like Soderbergh in Hollywood before. He compares himself to John Huston and Howard Hawks, but these men never pushed and struggled at the boundaries of the medium quite like Steven Soderbergh. And though his personal characterisation of himself as a chameleon is accurate, there is a thread that binds the many facets of his form and style together: experimentation. In the next chapter, we will look at another extremely experimental position for an auteur: wearing a suit.

Notes

1   Anthony Kaufman, *Steven Soderbergh: Interviews*, 69.
2   For an extensive history, see John Caughie, *Theories of Authorship*, 2001; Virginia Wright Wexman, *Film and Authorship*, 2003; David A. Gerstner and Janet Staiger, *Authorship and Film*, 2003; and Barry Keith Grant, *Auteurs and Authorship: A Film Anthology*, 2007.
3   See Thomas Schatz, 'The New Hollywood,' 1993.
4   See Geoff King, *Indiewood U.S.A: Where Hollywood Meets Independent Cinema*, 2009.
5   See Thomas Schatz, 'The Studio System in Conglomerate Hollywood,' 2008.
6   For a typical example of this trend, see Robin Wood, *Hollywood from Vietnam to Reagan – And Beyond*, 2003. On the one hand, there is a recognition that Soderbergh is not a typical director, while on the other this exceptional status occludes him from easy identification because of some confusion as to what to do with him. Wood explains that he is 'aware of the absence of Steven Soderbergh' in his book despite his 'obvious significance,' though he is 'uncertain' of what his significance is, admitting that he 'cannot seem to get a firm grasp on his films.' This recognition of Soderbergh as simultaneously belonging to, but excluded from a canon is typical, as is the assumption that scholarly inquiry has caught up with the need to address the director and his films. For Wood, this omission comes down to the filmmaker's emotional impenetrability, the idea that he does not 'know' the director after watching his films. The lack of the personal, so it seems, is part of the larger problem. Moreover, there is a tendency to view this lack of a coherent personality as a bad thing, as if the issue of biography were more important to the issue of artistry and authorship than the effect of watching a movie.
7   Maitland McDonagh, 'The Exploitation Generation, or: How Marginal Movies Came in from the Cold,' in *The Last Great American Picture Show: Traditions, Transitions and Triumphs in 1970s Cinema*, eds. Alexander Horwath, Noel King, and Thomas Elsaesser (Amsterdam: Amsterdam University Press, 2003), 111.
8   Andrew Sarris, 'Notes on the Auteur Theory in 1962', in *Auteurs and Authorship: A Film Reader*, ed. Barry K. Grant (Malden, MA: Blackwell, 2008), 43.

9   Dudley Andrew, 'The Unauthorized Auteur Today,' in *Film and Theory: An Anthology*, eds. Robert Stam and Toby Miller (Malden, MA: Blackwell, 2000), 20.

10   Timothy Corrigan, 'Auteurs and the New Hollywood,' *The New American Cinema* (Durham: Duke University Press, 1998), 60.

11   Roland Barthes, 'The Death of the Author,' in *Image. Music, Text*, trans. Stephen Heath (New York: Hill and Wang, 1977), 142–148.

12   Michel Foucault, 'What is an Author?,' in *Textual Strategies: Perspectives in Post-Structuralist Criticism*, ed. Josué V. Harari (Ithaca: Cornell University Press, 1979), 141–60.

13   Robert Stam, *The Author: Introduction*, in *Film and Theory: An Anthology*, eds. Robert Stam and Toby Miller (Malden, MA: Blackwell, 2000), 6.

14   Barthes, 'The Death of the Author,' 145.

15   Steven Dillon, *The Solaris Effect: Art & Artifice in Contemporary American Film* (Austin, TX: The University of Texas Press, 2006), 22.

16   Soderbergh quoted in Kaufman, *Steven Soderbergh: Interviews*, 83.

17   Dillon, *The Solaris Effect*, 29.

18   Ibid., 22.

19   It is fitting, then, that Soderbergh has suggested he might take up painting in his 'sabbatical' from filmmaking.

20   See Pam Cook, 'The Point of Self-Expression in Avant-Garde Film,' in *Theories of Authorship: A Reader*, ed. John Caughie (London: Routledge, 2000), 272. 'Traditionally the relationship of the avant-garde film-maker to her or his work has been artisanal, i.e. the film-maker, like a craft worker, is in control of all aspects of the process of production and distribution/exhibition, retaining rights of ownership over her or his film. The artisanal mode of production has several levels: it implies a particular mode of production which is small-scale and therefore, in a capitalist economy, lies outside the dominant system.'

21   Kaufman, *Steven Soderbergh: Interviews*, 73–4.

22   Dillon, *The Solaris Effect*, 26.

23   Ibid., 17.

24   Steven Soderbergh, *Moneyball*, Revised Version of Script, June 22, 2009, 1.

25   Quoted in Kaufman, *Steven Soderbergh: Interviews*, 75.

26   Ibid., xv.

27   For a more comprehensive analysis of the relationship between these two particular films see R. Barton Palmer, 'Alain Resnais Meets Film Noir in *The Underneath* and *The Limey*,' in *The Philosophy of Steven Soderbergh*, eds. R. Barton Palmer, and Steven Sanders (Lexington, KY: University Press of Kentucky, 2011), 69–90.

28   See Drew Morton, '*Schizopolis* as Philosophical Autobiography,' in *The Philosophy of Steven Soderbergh*, eds. R. Barton Palmer, and Steven Sanders (Lexington, KY: University Press of Kentucky, 2011), 173–193. Morton's assessment of the film offers the following corrective, stating that '*Schizopolis* stands as an odd film out, a misunderstood film in a complex and far-reaching filmography due to its emphasis on surrealist comedy and stylistic flourishes'. In an interview with the director that ends the essay, Soderbergh states that he 'was working with fractured

narrative, playing with color schemes, mixing shooting styles' while 'test-driving things' he would 'later fuse with better material'. Ibid., 190.

29 Charles Ramírez-Berg, 'A Taxonomy of Alternative Plots in Recent Films: Classifying the "Tarantino Effect,"' *Film Criticism* 31, no. 1–2 (Fall 2006): 5–61.

30 David Bordwell, *The Way Hollywood Tells It: Story and Style in Modern Movies* (Berkeley, CA: University of California Press, 2006), 99–103.

31 Allan Cameron, *Modular Narratives in Contemporary Cinema* (Basingstoke: Palgrave Macmillan, 2008).

32 Warren Buckland, *Puzzle Films: Complex Storytelling in Contemporary Cinema*. (Chichester: Wiley-Blackwell, 2009).

33 *Film Theory*, eds. Sergei Eisenstein, and Jay Leyda (New York: Harcourt Brace, 1949), 8–9.

34 Though Stanislavski's technique changed over time, his main, influential works remain, Konstantin Stanislavsky, *Building a Character* (New York: Routledge/ Theater Arts Books, 1989) and Konstantin Stanislavsky, *An Actor Prepares* (New York: Theatre Arts Books, 1948).

35 See Foster Hirsch, *A Method to Their Madness: The History of the Actors Studio* (New York: W. W. Norton, 1984) for a comprehensive history. It is also useful to distinguish between Stella Adler's attention to detail and Lee Strasberg's emotional detail, as seen in Stella Adler, *The Technique of Acting* (Toronto: Bantam Books, 1988) and Lee Strasberg and Evangeline Morphos, *A Dream of Passion: The Development of the Method* (Boston: Little, Brown, 1987).

36 Steven Soderbergh, *Getting Away With It, Or: The Further Adventures of the Luckiest Bastard You Ever Saw* (London: Faber and Faber, 1999), 167.

37 Quoted in Xan Brooks, 'Revolution in the air as Benicio Del Toro Meets Hugo Chávez,' *The Guardian*, March 5, 2008, accessed March 6, 2009.

38 For an in-depth analysis of Brecht's technique, the gold standard (in our view) remains Martin Esslin's description, as found in Martin Esslin, *Bertolt Brecht* (New York: Columbia University Press, 1969).

39 Peter Wollen discusses Godard's adoption of Brechtian technique in film in 'Godard and Counter-Cinema: *V'ent d' Est,'* in *Narrative, Apparatus, Ideology: A Film Theory Reader*, ed. Philip Rosen (New York: Columbia University Press, 1986), 120–130.

40 The tradition of actors playing themselves is a long one, ranging from a similar poker game in *Sunset Boulevard* (Billy Wilder, 1950) where, famously, Buster Keaton and other notables play themselves in a poker game at Norma Desmond's (Gloria Swanson, playing a thinly-veiled version of herself) house and where Cecil B. De Mille delivers the final, famous line in the film, when Desmond is 'ready for her close up.' The tradition continued in the 1970s where Elliott Gould and Julie Christie made appearances in Robert Altman's *Nashville* (1975) and the aforementioned *The Player*, where cameo appearances by Jack Lemmon, Malcolm McDowell, and Willis and Roberts brings this tendency to its natural ebb.

41 In a deleted scene, Soderbergh plays a third character who inexplicably wears an afro-wig.

CHAPTER TWO

Impresario of Indiewood: Soderbergh as Sellebrity Auteur

It's an idea that's as old as cinema, almost. The idea behind it [F-64, an aborted plan for a production company to be formed by Soderbergh, Spike Jonze, Alexander Payne, and David Fincher], which is very similar to what we're doing in Section Eight, is getting a group of artists together who aren't driven by money, to try and gain greater control over their work, from the content to how it's sold. But it's complicated.

– Steven Soderbergh[1]

Perhaps a slight cognitive slip on Soderbergh's part, it is indicative of the economic dimension in which Hollywood directors now find themselves that Soderbergh would consider the director's concern of 'how it's sold' to be an idea 'that's as old as cinema'; for most of Hollywood film history, directors have been ceded little control in determining how their movies were sold, marketed, or distributed. Particularly in the 'golden age' of Classical Hollywood Cinema, studio executives were notorious for marketing films on their sensationalistic rather than artistic merits, and even editing films for commercial reasons; recently, adjusting films for maximum appeal according to the fickle demands of test screening audiences has become *de rigueur*. For Soderbergh to so instinctively consider the promotional end of the film industry to be an integral part of controlling his own product just goes to show how much has changed in the tensions between art and commerce. Contemporary cinematic authorship is promoted and highlighted to an unheralded degree, and yet the traditional notions of auteurism no longer seem to account for how the industry works. Conventional conceptions of film authorship fail to grasp the nuances and complexities of this new model that Soderbergh espouses, thus necessitating new formulations for auteurism, both for critics and the auteurs themselves. As Soderbergh muses, 'it's complicated.'

We propose the term *sellebrity auteur* as a paradoxical concept that signals the complexities and contradictions of contemporary commercial cinematic authorship.[2]

Soderbergh has exploited the celebrity of his A-list co-conspirators – such as Matt Damon, George Clooney, and Brad Pitt – in order to sustain his prolific cinematic output over several decades.

It highlights, on the one hand, the cultural-economic factors involved in a film's creation, the industrial context in which marketing and promotion have taken centre stage, and the struggle between art and commerce that this process involves; on the other, it acknowledges the need for an analysis of the auteur-as-celebrity, looking at the auteur's brand identity and celebrity cachet as they are exploited both by the auteur in order to get a film made, and by the studio in its marketing system. In short, the sellebrity auteur injects a consideration of commerce, promotion, and celebrity into conventional theories of authorship.

Steven Soderbergh will prove an exemplary case study for the sellebrity auteur, as he occupies a unique position within Hollywood with regards to both economics and celebrity. Catapulted into the spotlight and studio executives' embrace when his debut film grossed more than twenty times its budget, Soderbergh has since failed to recoup his budget on many films, yet he has also earned Warner Brothers more than a *billion* dollars for the *Ocean's* franchise. He has produced more than thirty films outside his own directorial features, and Section Eight, his production company formed with George Clooney, focused on distributing challenging films to the multiplex and shielding them from studio interference.[3] Furthermore, this concern for economics manifests itself within Soderbergh's films (*Erin Brockovich*, *Traffic*, his many films in the crime genre and so on), as does the role of celebrity (*Ocean's* trilogy, *Full Frontal*). Soderbergh's own increased economic power has been due in large part to his skill in branding the Soderbergh name; the result has been the transformation of his name into a valuable, reliable commodity. From his ability to channel the *zeitgeist* and choose topical, volatile subject material, to his various production and distribution enterprises, Soderbergh has exploited his celebrity, as well as that of his A-list co-conspirators, in order to sustain his prolific cinematic output over several decades.

The Economics of Auteurism: Blockbusters, Indiewood, Conglomerate Hollywood

Before delving into Soderbergh's sellebrity status, a consideration of the contemporary auteur's economic context requires a brief foray into the economic situation of Hollywood itself. As true now as when he wrote it nearly twenty years ago, 'blockbuster hits,' Thomas Schatz admits, rather reluctantly, 'are, for better or worse, what the new Hollywood is all about, and thus are the necessary starting point for an analysis of contemporary cinema.'[4] Following the enormous successes of George Lucas and Steven Spielberg in the 1970s and 1980s (*Jaws*, the *Star Wars* franchise, the *Indiana Jones* franchise and so on), the high-concept blockbuster film became Hollywood's staple product.[5] [6] With every major studio subsumed by a huge transnational corporation and mercilessly focused on the bottom line, movies were thought of as mere products more than ever; reliable profits and growth were sought through formulaic plot lines, intense market research, a reliance on sequels and remakes, bankable movie stars, and inoffensive topics.

In the 1990s, as blockbuster films were increasingly produced with a global audience in mind, a middle tier developed within the industry as a result of the rise of niche marketing and the increased economic importance of film festival and award show success, exemplified by Sundance and Miramax, respectively.[7] In 1989, it was Soderbergh's *sex, lies, and videotape*, debuting at Sundance then marketed and distributed by Miramax, that, according to Alisa Perren, 'ushered in the era of the "indie blockbuster" – films that, on a smaller scale, replicate the exploitation marketing and box-office performance of the major studio high-concept event pictures.'[8] Costing much less to produce, independent films were found, on rare occasions when marketed and distributed correctly, to have better profit-to-cost ratios than the most carefully planned blockbuster; *sex, lies, and videotape* set the standard for this approach, with Miramax finding even greater success with Tarantino's *Pulp Fiction*. Hollywood's distribution structure began to follow a tripartite model:[9] majors, independents, and the newly formed 'major-independents,' speciality companies such as Miramax which focused on 'quality' movies that aspire to the status of 'art.' In response to a range of newly discovered/developed intermediate markets, every major studio (Paramount, Columbia, Fox, Universal, Disney, and Warner Bros.) fostered a stable of subsidiaries (Miramax, Focus Features, Fox Searchlight, New Line, etc.) that were to operate with a high degree of autonomy.

Thomas Schatz, who first documented the rise of blockbusters and 'New Hollywood,' followed this seminal economic analysis with its logical successor: 'Conglomerate Hollywood.' Tracing the corporate mergers and (de)regulatory overhauls that led to such a moment, Schatz claims that '[i]n a five-year span from 1990 to 1995, the New Hollywood rapidly transformed into Conglomerate Hollywood, as a new breed of media giants took command of the US film and television industries and became the dominant powers in the rapidly expanding global entertainment industry.'[10] Every studio was beholden to its parent company (News Corp. owns Fox, Viacom owns Paramount, Sony owns Columbia, etc.) and along with the 'indie film' divisions, television and cable networks, and other media holdings, studios became 'players in a game they no longer control.'[11] Schatz notes the paradox in the rise of the independent film movement occurring simultaneous to the conglomerate era, with media giants eventually subsuming the most successful independents like Miramax and New Line, while also forming their own indie divisions, such as Focus Features and Fox Searchlight.

Exploring this murky middle tier is Geoff King, with an impressive methodology that combines industrial context, textual analysis, and audience reception in *Indiewood, USA: Where Hollywood Meets Independent Cinema*. '[A] part of the American film spectrum in which distinctions between Hollywood and the independent sector appeared to have become blurred',[12] King characterises Indiewood 'not as a "thing in itself" but… its relative position in a wider field.'[13] Shading his analysis with a Pierre Bourdieu-inflected consideration of distinction and niche marketing, King explores both film and distribution company case studies, before settling on Soderbergh as 'an individual whose work illustrates as well as any the ability of some filmmakers not just to move between Hollywood and the independent sector, but to produce hybrid features that occupy the ground between the two.'[14] A particularly effective reading of *Traffic* shows how even in the pre-production stages, the film was being pulled in two directions: on one hand, a studio-sized budget and negotiations with Michael Douglas and Harrison Ford; on the other, a controversial topic, an unconventional multi-arc story, and a unique visual style. The final product itself formally embodies this tension, with a complex narrative structure, erratic camera work, and unconventional sound design balanced with the Hollywood tendency to focus on the actions of individuals rather than collective action, and in its multi-perspective approach and avoidance of any radical political interpretation. While the tension in production and execution seemed to serve *Traffic* well, considering its commercial and critical success, the two forces pulling at *Solaris* (challenging art film and science-fiction crowd pleaser) seem to have prevented it from finding an audience.

Now that the corporate 'package' system has slowly replaced the studio system following its collapse in the late 1960s – with the hazy notion of 'independence' hovering ever since – many film projects are put together on a one-off basis by varying groups of key creative personnel. In this system, the Hollywood director often operates as a kind of 'free agent.'[15] In order to attain funding and distribution, the director – sometimes aligning with a producer or attached star, forming the 'package' – pitches a film to a major or major-independent studio, or is recruited for a specific project already being planned. As a free agent, the director must navigate this complex terrain of art and commerce, independent and corporate sensibilities, arthouse and mass marketing, minis and majors. Soderbergh is a fitting example of this varied negotiation, having worked through his own production company (Section Eight), with independents (Magnolia Pictures, Artisan Entertainment, Jersey Films, Lightstorm Entertainment, IFC Films, Relativity Media, Nick Wechsler Productions), with mini-majors (Miramax, USA Films), and with major studios (Warner Bros., Fox, Universal), to produce smaller films (*sex, lies, and videotape*, *Kafka*, *The Good German*), middle tier 'Indiewood' fare (*Erin Brockovich*, *Traffic*, *The Informant!*, *Contagion*), big-budget blockbusters (*Ocean's* trilogy, *Solaris*), digital experiments (*Full Frontal*, *Bubble*, *The Girlfriend Experience*, *Haywire*), and television (*K-Street*, *Unscripted*). It is necessary to keep this shifting playing field in mind as we consider Soderbergh and the sellebrity auteur, as attending to a range of economic concerns is increasingly one of the primary responsibilities of the contemporary auteur.

The previous chapter's discussion of classical auteur theory explored the key artistic elements that might 'elevate' a filmmaker to the status of auteur: a distinctive set of thematic concerns and a personal visual style – the director's 'signature.' While much debate surrounds these two formal features that are taken to indicate individual authorship, the other, potentially more provocative side of auteur theory, is the consideration of the auteur's relationship to the industrial structure of film production. Both commercial and collaborative, the creative autonomy of the auteur will inevitably be under constraint in the filmmaking environment; thus, the tensions between the artist and the industry have been central to auteur theory. Fifty years after the inception of the auteur theory, in an industry now dominated by sensational summer spectacles, big box-office business, corporate conglomeration, and massive marketing manoeuvres, what are we to make of the auteur today?

Much of the recent critical analysis surrounding contemporary auteur theory makes use of the term *blockbuster auteur*, a designation we find lacking because of its reduction of the director to their generic product.[16] Instead, the more evocative term *sellebrity auteur* can incorporate the brand identity and celebrity cachet that is now so integral to today's auteur, while foregrounding the centrality of economic imperatives without limiting the discussion to Hollywood blockbusters. As we explore other critical forays into the intersection between auteurism and commerce, we will witness an evolution in both the actual practices of the contemporary auteur, as well as the theoretical conception of the auteur, eventually arriving at the sellebrity auteur's unique synthesis of fame and economics that Steven Soderbergh personifies.

Taking as its starting point the recent trend towards focusing on the box-office success of a film as the dominant measure of its value, Jon Lewis analyses the careers of George Lucas and Steven Spielberg in order to come to terms with contemporary auteurism. Over the last thirty years, no two filmmakers have reached a wider international audience nor been considered more emblematic as 'American movie-men.' According to Lewis, Lucas and Spielberg exemplify the trend that auteurs now 'gain notoriety less for a signature style than for a signature product.'[17] If a director's claim to auteur status were to be determined solely by the degree to which he or she has control over a project, then Lucas and Spielberg would be auteurs of the highest order. One method by which they have achieved control of their product, one which marks a shift in auteurism writ large, is through an aggressive business strategy.

Warren Buckland continues this line of thought, arguing that auteur status in contemporary Hollywood is no longer achieved simply by mastery of the filmmaking process; the director must control external factors such as production, financing, and distribution as well. Lucas and Spielberg are, of course, exemplars of this process, each director having constructed a veritable empire out of their commercial enterprises. Lucas's special effects facility, Industrial Light and Magic, has become a central component in the Hollywood economy by establishing itself as the world's premier special effects company. The Lucas empire also includes his production company, Lucasfilm; his sound divisions, Skywalker Sound and the THX Group; his video-gaming company, LucasArts Entertainment; and his merchandising and licensing company, Lucas Licensing. Spielberg has been equally successful, forming his own production company, Amblin Entertainment, in order to extend his reach into more personal projects and produce countless features and television shows. In 1994, Spielberg, along with two other media moguls, created their own studio, DreamWorks SKG, the first new entrant in the major studio scene in over sixty years (a short-lived dream, it was sold in 2005 to Viacom, the parent company of Paramount Pictures; similarly, Lucas's empire was sold to Disney in 2012).

A concurrent trend in Hollywood has been to entrust big budget productions to auteur or arthouse directors, a practice Martin Flanagan seeks to analyse in terms of the conflicting concepts of the auteur and the blockbuster. Looking at the list of box-office hits in recent years, Flanagan finds a full range of auteur identities: veterans of New Hollywood such as Martin Scorsese, Paul Schrader, and Robert Altman; graduates of low-budget horror such as Sam Raimi, Peter Jackson, and Guillermo del Toro; innovators and documentarians such as Terry Zwigoff and Richard Linklater; and arthouse foreigners, such as Christopher Nolan and Jane Campion. Many of the largest grossing blockbuster franchises come from auteur directors: Raimi's *Spiderman* franchise (2002–2007), Jackson's *Lord of the Rings* trilogy (2001–2003), Bryan Singer's *X-Men* franchise (2000–2011), Robert Rodriguez's *Spy Kids* series (2001–2011), the Wachowskis' *Matrix* trilogy (1999–2003), and, of course, Soderbergh's *Ocean's* trilogy (2001–2007). The industry has come to see auteurs as another distinctive and thus marketable element that can be added to blockbuster appeal and used to build a franchise. In this view, the quasi-independent film festival circuit becomes a training ground from which Hollywood directors are plucked and drawn to Hollywood with the promise of bigger budgets and larger audiences. In baseball parlance, we can think of this as a farm team system; after toiling in 'the minors,' significant talent and distinction earns a director a shot at 'the majors.'

While the *Ocean's* trilogy is an obvious example of what a 'blockbuster auteur' might produce (though these films have a subversive anti-capitalist edge that we will explore in Chapter Eight), it is worth pausing to reflect upon the curious production and marketing of another of Soderbergh's larger productions: *Solaris*. In this case, Soderbergh was not the only blockbuster auteur involved in the production, as

Commenting on the difficulty of marketing *Solaris* and the use of his naked body in the publicity campaign, Clooney remarked, 'if my ass helps the film, I don't have a problem with that.'

James Cameron's Lightstorm Entertainment handled the special effects, and additional financing came from 20th Century Fox. A love letter to European art cinema, Andrei Tarkovsky's 1972 version of *Solyaris* in particular, *Solaris* is a convoluted mix of star power, art cinema, psychological drama, and special effects. One of the marketing approaches involved exploiting a brief, *risqué* scene of nudity in the film, showcasing former *People Magazine*'s 'Sexiest Man Alive' (1997 & 2006) George Clooney naked in a long shot, his bare behind on full display. Commenting on the difficulty of marketing a meandering philosophic sci-fi romance art film, Clooney claimed, 'if my ass helps the film, I don't have a problem with that.'[18] In this explicit quasi-prostitution of a star's body in order to market an art film, we see the tenuous relationship between art and commerce in Indiewood.

An analysis centered on the terms 'auteur' and 'blockbuster' is destined to be problematic, as the meanings of both terms are constantly in flux. Another auteurist dichotomy, formulated by Buckland, captures this ambivalence, classifying auteurs as either a 'classical auteur,' the 'skilled craft worker who has mastered – and indeed represents – "the tradition"', or a 'romantic auteur,' the 'lone, creative genius who works intuitively and mysteriously outside of all traditions.'[19] While Lucas and Spielberg typify the classical, Francis Ford Coppola has become emblematic of the romantic. However, Coppola himself only achieved such enigmatic status after the enormous box office success of his blockbusters *The Godfather* and *The Godfather: Part II* (1974). To consider Coppola 'outside of all traditions' would also misperceive his important economic role in American Zoetrope and the Directors Company. Coppola's complications aside, careful consideration of the economic climate in Conglomerate Hollywood would render any such nostalgic pining for a Romantic auteur figure 'existing outside of the system' highly problematic.

Directing (the) Stars: Celebrity and Authorship

> The fact that I'm not an identifiable brand is very freeing, because people get tired of brands and they switch brands. I've never had a desire to be out in front of anything, which is why I don't take a possessory credit. That's why, if I can help it, I don't like having my picture taken or doing television. I don't want to be out in front of this stuff at all.
>
> Steven Soderbergh[20]

In his 1961 critique of commercial culture, *The Image: A Guide to Pseudo-Events in America*, Daniel Boorstin offered one of the first definitions of modern celebrity: 'the celebrity is a person who is known for his well-knownness… He is neither good nor bad, great nor petty. He is the human pseudo-event.'[21] Talent or achievement have little to do with the fascination; it is not *doing* that is celebrated, but *being*. Ostensibly, a film director is known for their work, and though talent or achievement might be part of the narrative, when they reach the status of brand name, their work comes to be an expected product. With each new product, their brand is dragged through the same old sales campaign, and in an increasingly crowded entertainment market, films are publicised and sold as pseudo-events unto themselves. Adapting to this publicity-centric business climate, the contemporary director inevitably becomes involved in the management of their own films' heavily marketed pseudo-events.

The film and television industries have changed considerably since Boorstin's assessment though, from technological enhancements like cable, satellite, and the Internet, to fragmented content streams in the form of transmedia, reality TV, gossip blogs and so on. The degrees and variability of 'well-knownness' have changed in the contemporary entertainment industry, a phenomenon which Joshua Gamson dubs the 'negotiated celebration.' Quick to distinguish between performer/entertainer and star, Gamson designates the performer as both a *worker*, pertaining to their qualities and abilities, and a *celebrity*, in that 'what is developed and sold is the capacity to command attention.'[22] Increasingly, this distinction is becoming apparent in the auteur as well.

Expanding upon the romantic/classical auteur dichotomy, Matt Hills claims that the figure of the auteur produces both an 'economy of culture,' in which the power of the auteur identity is used to market the blockbuster film, and a 'culture of economy,' where the auteur works within institutional constraints in an attempt to challenge the conventions of the culture industry. Now that marketing has become as much – often more – of an economic investment than production, the name of a director is just one of many appeals made by marketers in order to promote films and maximise audiences. Just as sequels, remakes, and pre-sold properties are seen as more bankable to the studio executive, the director's name has become part of the marketing equation as an assurance of quality. The extent to which marketers will exploit previous authorial successes has reached a trivial, almost empty fruition, as *Godzilla* (Roland Emmerich, 1998) is sold as 'from the creators of *Independence Day.*'

A useful example of this 'economy of culture' can be seen in Geoff King's analysis of the ultra-high-concept *Batman* series. While the success of *Batman* (1989) and *Batman Returns* (1992) was pretty much assured with its combination of big-name stars, pre-sold comic book audience, high-budget special effects, merchandising and ancillary products, and soundtrack tie-in, Warner Bros. added a distinctive element to the two films by choosing Tim Burton as director. Burton's dark and quirky, gothic style not only complemented the material, but it widened the appeal of the film to an audience who might be averse to another big-budget, over-hyped blockbuster. Tim Burton's dramatic effect can be seen not just in these films, but on the superhero comic-book genre as a whole, which has taken a distinctly darker and more psychological turn since Burton. Notably, the franchise began to fail with the critically unfavoured Joel Schumacher behind the camera for *Batman Forever* (1995) and *Batman and Robin* (1997), but was reinvigorated – critically and commercially – with British art film director Christopher Nolan at the helm of *Batman Begins* (2005), *The Dark Knight* (2008) and *The Dark Knight Rises* (2012).

As for the 'culture of economy,' we can look at one final auteurist dichotomy, Timothy Corrigan's distinction between the 'commercial auteur' and the 'auteur of commerce,' which Hills used as the basis for his argument. Corrigan argues that the auteur's new-found marketability is a significant reversal: 'the central change in the meaning of auteurism from the sixties to the eighties' was a 'marked shift within auteurism as a way of viewing and receiving movies, rather than as a mode of production.'[23] In this analysis of auteurism, we see the rise of New Hollywood accompanied by the conception of the auteur as a commodified property, 'a *commercial* strategy for organizing audience reception... a critical concept bound to distribution and marketing aims.'[24] Historically, this idea draws an important parallel; the rise of New Hollywood in the 1960s coincided with the rise of the academic study of film, in which the auteur theory was highly regarded. This new generation of filmmakers was largely a product of film school, raised on international art cinema where a belief in the 'director-as-artist' was central. These young directors were fully aware of the auteur theory, and the industry was fully conscious of exploiting it through marketing.

As a consequence, Corrigan argues, the auteur's commercial status has been elevated to that of a star, 'a kind of brand-name vision that precedes and succeeds the film, the way that movie is seen and received.'[25] Through a torrent of advertisements, trailers, and magazine profiles, the institutional and commercial agencies at work in Hollywood have converted auteurism into an 'empty display of material surface.'[26] Such an emphasis results in a preconceived interpretation of the film as an articulation of the public image of its author. The auteur film becomes nothing more than a critical tautology, to be understood and consumed without any real interaction or effort. As an example, Corrigan shows how Spielberg, despite his earnest efforts to do otherwise, will inevitably always make 'a Spielberg film.'

Forced to negotiate this problematic celebrity, the 'auteur-star' is constantly on the verge of being consumed by their emerging star status. Corrigan detects two outcomes to this trend: the commercial auteur and the auteur of commerce. The commercial auteur includes the obvious 'superstar' directors, Lucas and Spielberg, who have achieved a considerable measure of stardom as a result of creating many beloved block-busters. A degree of high-visibility is associated with the commercial auteur, perhaps best seen in the star-turned-director, such as Mel Gibson, Robert Redford, Clint Eastwood, Sylvester Stallone, and Kevin Costner. This 'onscreen' dimension to auteurism dates back to the days of Alfred Hitchcock and Orson Welles. Corrigan even includes Woody Allen, John Sayles, François Truffaut and Bernardo Bertolucci in this designation, as all of these directors are united by a 'recognition, either foisted upon them or chosen by them, that the celebrity of their agency produces and promotes texts that invariably exceed the movie itself, both before and after its release.'[27] The grandiose image of the auteur-star is what anchors the films of these auteurs, rather than ideas, styles, themes, or modes of expression.

The auteur of commerce, on the other hand, is 'a filmmaker [who] attempts to monitor or rework the industrial manipulations of the auteurist position within the commerce of the contemporary movie industry.'[28] Corrigan chooses Francis Ford Coppola, Alexander Kluge, and Raoul Ruiz as his exemplars, formulating the auteur of commerce as a filmmaker who actively employs fissures and discrepancies in his or her work in a conscious attempt to open up a space between self-identity and auteurist-identity in order to break down the oppression of the auteur's brand name. Because films may be reduced to vehicles for directors, the auteur as brand name may threaten the film's artistic standing, moving the focus from the text to the author. Coppola's tremendous self-sacrifice of his health and finances, Kluge's fragmentation of a central, dominating auteurist agency, and Ruiz's multitude of reincarnations across cultural spaces: three different paths towards the same ends. The only way to overcome the all-encompassing weight of the branded image of the auteur, according to Corrigan, is to communicate from *within* the commerce of that image.

What Corrigan fails to consider, however, is the way the auteur must personally engage in this star-making. It is not simply a matter of the auteur's name superseding the text, or that the auteur of commerce can manipulate this image within the text, but that the auteur must also personally play the game of commanding attention. It is not just what is thrust upon the auteur, but what the auteur manufactures to have thrust upon him or herself. In an industry heavily dependent on hype and publicity, Gamson explains, 'notoriety becomes a type of capital... recognition by consumers as a brand, familiarity in itself. The perceived ability to attract attention, regardless of what the attention is for, can be literally cashed in.'[29] For Steven Soderbergh, typically taking on commercially unfriendly subject matter, any capital he can gain is valuable, and cashing in on his celebrity, and especially the celebrity of some of his more famous friends, has been a particularly lucrative form of capital.

In crafting and asserting this public persona, Soderbergh has established what has long come to be essential to every celebrity, and now every sellebrity auteur: a brand name. Elaborating on Richard Dyer's designation of stars as 'property,'[30] Graeme Turner argues for a conception of the star as a 'celebrity-commodity,' a financial asset whose commercialisation stands to make profit for a variety of interested parties. A celebrity's public persona is an integral part of this commercial value: 'as the asset appreciates – as the celebrity's fame spreads – so does its earning capacity.'[31] Turner touches on the specific importance of branding when he invokes Naomi Klein's pivotal 2001 work, *No Logo*. A striking example of our 'new branded world,' Klein attributes the introduction in 1999 of *Forbes* magazine's 'Celebrity Power 100' – which ranks celebrities according to their brand name rather than fame or fortune – as proof that 'brands and stars have become the same thing.'[32] The sellebrity auteur, then, aspires to this quality of living, breathing brand name. One of the most prominent displays of Soderbergh's brand is the promotional trailer for *Bubble*, which consists of nothing

In a rare capitalisation of his own Sellebrity Auteur status, *Bubble* was marketed as 'ANOTHER STEVEN SODERBERGH EXPERIENCE,' perhaps because he was the sole 'known' entity within the production.

more than static shots from a doll factory, a frenzied string arrangement, and a proclamation, in stark capital letters:

Star power is not to be underestimated in Hollywood; as King reminds us, 'stardom is generally considered the single most important factor in the commercial viability of many films.'[33] In the era of the package system, when most films are one-off productions, stars are the closest thing to reliable box-office potential. A recognisable brand in an already overcrowded entertainment marketplace is invaluable; it is not hard to imagine why the sellebrity auteur would want to craft his or her own star image as an assurance of economic stability, and why the industry would want to encourage and exploit just such a venture.

At the nexus of all these interrelated and correlative dichotomies – the romantic/classical, the economy of culture/culture of economy, the commercial auteur/auteur of commerce – is the contemporary director who must negotiate his or her economic situation alongside his or her star image; in other words, he or she must become a sellebrity auteur. The 'sell,' as we have seen, is simply the economic imperative of Conglomerate Hollywood. The auteur has always been constrained by the industrial nature of the system. In fact, auteur theory emerged out of an explicit acknowledgement of the industrial contexts of studio filmmaking in early Hollywood. However, the ever-increasing corporate logic of Hollywood has also forced the auteur to be actively involved in the 'business-end' of the business, lest he or she be reduced to a 'director-for-hire.' Part of this business venture is exploiting – and being exploited by – the celebrity angle of that equation.

It takes most directors years to build a brand and worm their way into public consciousness; Soderbergh, on the other hand, was thrust into the spotlight with his very first film, due to the film festival success of *sex, lies, and videotape*, followed by its surprising crossover entry into multiplexes and impressive domestic box office. Interviews and profiles immediately established Soderbergh as a 'young, new talent,' and though his subsequent films were met with different degrees of critical and commercial reception, his name remained visible. Over the past twenty years, the Soderbergh brand has been attached to Academy Award nights (*Erin Brockovich* and *Traffic*), global blockbusters (*Ocean's* trilogy), controversial business strategies (*Bubble*), and a multitude of artsy, 'Indiewood' releases and the niche marketing and publicity campaigns that accompany them. 'A clear general tendency exists,' King notes, in his analysis of Soderbergh's critical reception, 'in reviews at the relatively "serious" or "quality" end of the newspaper spectrum, to place *Traffic* and *Solaris* within the Soderbergh oeuvre.'[34] Reviews of his films often comment on his long and varied career, attempting to place the current film within that context. Even his blockbuster and genre films are often considered from an auteurist perspective, injecting a sense of novelty and malleability into his brand.

In contrast with some other more publicity-chasing directors, Soderbergh has taken some steps to keep his brand from shining too bright, such as limiting television interviews and using pseudonyms instead of listing his name multiple times in credit sequences. Paradoxically, this strategy can be seen as a brand-enhancing technique; by preventing the brand from being corrupted by pigeon-holing critics, the sellebrity

Not only does Soderbergh capitalise on his performers' stardom, but he often exploits and satirises their star image, such as the scene between Julia Roberts and Bruce Willis in *Ocean's Twelve*.

auteur is afforded more versatility in pursuing a range of projects. For this reason, we are careful not to designate these directors as mere 'celebrity auteurs' (or 'star auteurs,' like Clint Eastwood, according to Corrigan), because they are hoping to avoid the trap of being 'famous for being famous.' An important distinction, the sellebrity auteur is attempting to 'sell their celebrity,' exploiting it as capital in the complex negotiations of contemporary Hollywood financing and distribution.

A popular technique for the sellebrity auteur to achieve notoriety yet avoid the trappings of predetermined interpretation is to attach themselves to a particular celebrity in recurring projects, to the mutual benefit of both director and star. Soderbergh's relationship with Clooney, having worked with him on more than a dozen films in both a director-actor and co-producer capacity, is certainly one of the more high profile cases, but other contemporary examples abound: Martin Scorsese with Robert DeNiro, then Leonardo DiCaprio; Woody Allen and Diane Keaton; Tim Burton and Johnny Depp; Wes Anderson and Bill Murray; Pedro Almodóvar and Penélope Cruz. The director exploits and deflects the spotlight to the star, while the star absorbs the cultural capital of the director.[35] This director-star relationship is exploited by the studios as well. 'In fact,' claimes Thomas Schatz, 'the indie surge has relied heavily on the mobility of top stars [George Clooney, Julia Roberts, etc.] who are willing to work on indie projects for far less than their studio rates.'[36] Stars, directors, and studios have a stake in this elaborate game of 'well-knownness.' Soderbergh proves an especially adept player in this game, most noticeably in the way he has managed to exploit the economic and celebrity aspects of the industry in order to carve out a creative space for himself and his collaborators; paradoxically, his strategy for achieving this creative, artistic freedom is mostly economic.

Sellebrity Synthesis: Soderbergh and Section Eight

Following his Academy Award for Best Director in 2000, with both *Erin Brockovich* and *Traffic* critical and commercial successes, Soderbergh capitalised on his advantageous position within the Hollywood system by entering into a partnership with another Hollywood player whose fame and success were also starting to blossom. Fresh off his first major roles working with 'serious' directors – David O. Russell in *Three Kings* (1999) and the Coen Brothers in *O Brother, Where Art Thou?* (2000) – George Clooney was in the process of exchanging his 'television heartthrob' and 'world's sexiest man' status for some cinematic cultural capital. Soderbergh was the auteur/quasi-celebrity and Clooney was the celebrity/soon-to-be-auteur, so they joined forces and formed a production company together: Section Eight Productions.

Having met during their first collaboration, *Out of Sight*, Soderbergh and Clooney pitched their idea of a production company to Warner Bros., which was looking to increase its Academy Award-calibre output. The two created Section Eight by offering the studio a generous proposition: 'Neither of us are looking to get rich as a company, so we can bring you the lowest overhead of any company you'll ever have.'[37] With Hollywood's reliance on the blockbuster formula requiring massive capital investment for production and marketing budgets, there is a high degree of financial risk in film production. Capitalising on the desire to avoid this risk, Section Eight holds a distinct advantage over other production companies by minimising the studio's financial risk – and that of their investors – by cutting their personal fees and keeping budgets low (all Section Eight productions, apart from the *Ocean's* franchise, had budgets under $50 million, most much less). 'Because we set [Section Eight] up [ourselves],' Clooney explains, 'we're like a tenth the cost of any of the production companies at Warner Bros.'[38] With this unique economic position, Section Eight managed to establish a relatively open, creative space within a confining system. 'From the studio perspective,' King explains, 'the arrangement offered an appealing combination of the prestige and Academy Award potential brought by Soderbergh (and other upcoming directors) with the bankability of Clooney's star presence in a number of the films that… [were produced] mostly on modest budgets.'[39]

Section Eight's philosophy was simple: give filmmakers the freedom to make their own choices and protect them from studio interference as much as possible. Citing the auteur-driven days of Coppola and Kubrick in the late 1960s/early 1970s as a source of inspiration, Soderbergh and Clooney were willing to forego substantial financial returns in order to maintain as much creative control for their clients as possible.[40] While certainly not as expansive as Lucas's or Spielberg's empires, Section Eight is equally as impressive in terms of the financial and creative control it has allowed Soderbergh. *Insomnia*, by British filmmaker Christopher Nolan, was one of the first Section Eight productions and earned well over $100 million on its less than $50 million budget, a significant achievement for an 'art film.' Warner Bros. wanted a more seasoned director, but Section Eight fought for Nolan, later stepping in to defend his choice of cinematographer and editor as well. Similarly, Soderbergh struggled against studio executives on Todd Haynes' behalf, protecting *Far From Heaven* from studio tampering.[41] *Far From Heaven* would go on to be a critical darling, garnering four Academy Award nominations. Section Eight also mediated between the studio and another Indiewood director, Richard Linklater, for *A Scanner Darkly*, which encountered post-production problems on account of its intensive rotoscoping animation process.

Section Eight also cultivated a group of then-unknowns, starting with Anthony and Joe Russo (*Welcome to Collinwood*, 2002), who would later find critical success on television, with *Arrested Development* and *Community*. Soderbergh's long-time assistant director Gregory Jacobs would be given a chance at the helm of *Criminal* (2004),[42] and then *The Wind Chill* (2007), though both would fail to find an audience. Section Eight's negotiation with the studio would not always work in their favour, however; with *Rumor Has It…* (Rob Reiner, 2005), Warner Bros. fired first-time director Ted Griffin, Soderbergh's close friend and writer for *Ocean's Eleven*, though he too would later find critical success on television, with *Terriers*. Section Eight can thus be seen as a training ground for up-and-comers, including some of Indiewood and television's most creative auteurs. But the heart and soul of Section Eight was the work of its principals, Soderbergh and Clooney.

The first film of Section Eight – which would go on to become the franchise keeping the whole company afloat – was *Ocean's Eleven*. It is as if Soderbergh had studied Justin Wyatt's high concept manual from front to back; *Ocean's Eleven* is a high concept wet dream. Relying primarily on one of the most star-studded casts ever assembled in Hollywood history – including George Clooney, Brad Pitt, Matt Damon, and Julia Roberts – *Ocean's Eleven* has all the necessary ingredients of a high-concept blockbuster: a pre-sold property in the form of a remake, slick visuals set to an infectious soundtrack, a familiar crime/heist genre, witty dialogue, fashionable costumes, a glitzy setting in Las Vegas, and multiple music video montages.

Ostensibly a licence to print money, the *Ocean's* trilogy represents Section Eight's compromise between art and commerce: 'It goes back to what we're trying to do,' Clooney explains:

> which is do the films that we think are interesting and that people should see, within the structure of the studio system. And part of that means that we have to find some compromises that will help get it done… If the compromise is *Ocean's Eleven*, that's a good film and we're proud of it, so we'll do this, happily, because entertainment's a good thing.[43]

When Soderbergh followed up *Ocean's Eleven* with two very uncommercial films, he had a fallback position: 'When *Solaris* tanked in the States on the heels of *Full Frontal* tanking, I immediately called George and said, "We're going to do [the next] *Ocean's* first."'[44] *Ocean's Twelve* bought the two another series of smaller, more personal films – *Good Night, and Good Luck, Bubble, Syriana*, and *The Good German* – with *Ocean's Thirteen* the final entry, providing for Section Eight's last run: *Michael Clayton, Che*, and *The Informant!*. A sort of Hollywood contingency plan, the *Ocean's* franchise allowed Section Eight the freedom to engage in a variety of different projects, from indie to studio, low budget to big budget, arthouse to high concept.

A useful comparison to be made at this point is with Martin Scorsese, who is also notorious for engaging in the 'one-for-them, one-for-me' negotiation with the Hollywood system. Having only recently produced a blockbuster hit of the scale necessary to earn him the clout required for studios to take multiple chances on him (*The Aviator* in 2004 was his first film to gross more than a hundred million dollars domestically), Scorsese often oscillates between personal and commercial projects. The success of *The Color of Money* (1986) was followed by *The Last Temptation of Christ* (1988); *Cape Fear* (1991) proved profitable enough to permit *The Age of Innocence* (1993). In the case of *The Last Temptation*, an intensely personal and controversial project Scorsese had been unsuccessfully trying to get off the ground for more than a decade, Universal's commitment contractually required Scorsese to produce a more commercial film in return. Just as Scorsese would inject his own personal flavour into even the most commercial and mainstream of his films, Soderbergh too would leave his distinct touch on the *Ocean's* franchise.

In the context of a 'cinema as art' discourse, the *Ocean's* franchise is easily dismissible; an idea of 'pure entertainment' is certainly at the core of the series. As *Variety* succinctly summarises, 'It's the most high-end junk food imaginable, completely unnourishing and forgettable afterward, but delicious and all but impossible not to enjoy while it's in front of you.'[45] To consider the franchise 'completely unnourishing,' however, would be to miss Soderbergh's subtle, reflexive play with star culture and the notion of celebrity, as well as the films' ruminations on capital and ethics as part of a resurgent cycle of crime films (see Chapter Eight). But for the purposes of the sellebrity auteur, we can see the *Ocean's* films, and their ilk, to be a kind of Hollywood 'patronage,' in which the artist is financially supported in exchange for other commercial products. Fellow sellebrity auteur Christopher Nolan, graduate of the Section Eight school of Hollywood business, seems to be following a similar pattern, alternating his more personal, art films with a recurring blockbuster franchise: *Insomnia* was followed by *Batman Begins*, *The Prestige* (2006) by *The Dark Knight*, and *Inception* (2010) by *The Dark Knight Rises*.

Perhaps taking a cue from his partner's prolific output, Clooney also managed to write, direct, and star in a multitude of projects, starting with his directorial debut, *Confessions of a Dangerous Mind*. A hybrid spy/biopic/crime story set amidst the Cold War, its evocative colour palette and time-shifting editing structure suggests that Soderbergh may have assisted Clooney considerably with his first foray behind the camera.[46] By his next feature though, Clooney already seemed seasoned; a vigorous examination of news legend Edward R. Murrow's historic showdown with Senator Joseph McCarthy, *Good Night, and Good Luck* is directed and co-written by Clooney, and was one of the best-reviewed films of the year. Again exploiting his fame, Clooney also plays an unglamorous role as the bookish Fred Friendly, a move almost certainly motivated in part by the ability to sell the film with Clooney's visage. The poster image shows a much more attractive version of Clooney than is visible anywhere in the film; again, the promise of celebrity sex appeal is used to steal audiences for this civics lesson. Following the amicable dissolvement of Section Eight, Clooney teamed with Grant Heslov to form SmokeHouse Pictures, continuing the actor's fusion of celebrity and politics in his star image and creating a vehicle for his own brand of socially-engaged filmmaking. *The Ides of March* (2011) demonstrates this pattern, with Clooney directing, co-writing, and starring alongside Ryan Gosling in a mix of Hollywood charm and political intrigue. The son of famous TV anchorman Nick Clooney,

The Girlfriend Experience, with its provocative advertising campaign, attempted to capitalise on the built-in celebrity of Sasha Grey – a well-known pornographic actress – a curious strategy given the film's rather chaste treatment of nudity and sex.

nephew of legendary pop and jazz singer Rosemary Clooney, and a former student of journalism himself, George Clooney has successfully navigated and exploited his celebrity for an increasingly impressive career on both sides of the camera.

In addition to these profile-raising projects, Soderbergh and Clooney utilised Section Eight to finance digital experiments, including two proto-reality television series for HBO, the Washington, D.C.-set political mockumentary *K-Street*, and the quasi-documentary *Unscripted*, which followed three struggling actors in Los Angeles. Soderbergh took this digital experimentation to the industrial level when he entered into a co-production deal with Mark Cuban, owner of HDNet and Landmark Theaters, to establish the 'day-and-date' approach to releasing films to theatres, DVD, and pay-TV on the same day. This 'challenge' to the typical, tiered distribution strategy (whereby the film experiences a prolonged release through various 'windows': theatre, DVD/Blu-ray, video-on-demand/pay-per-view, premium cable, free-to-air television) drew a significant amount of attention, with the actual film (*Bubble*) seeming to matter less than the potential implications for the industry.[47] A catalysing point for the anxieties over digital distribution, opinion pieces spread through the trades and other press, with many more detractors than supporters for Soderbergh's ambitious plan to simply give viewers the option of how they would like to see his film.

Also in the mould of Martin Scorsese, Soderbergh has cultivated a persona as a film curator, historian, and impresario: assisting the funding of the restoration and DVD release of Charles Burnett's seminal film *Killer of Sheep* (1977), rescuing screenwriter Terry Southern's collected works from his family's bankrupt estate and installing them in the New York Public Library System,[48] and commenting on the significance of films such as *The Graduate*, *The Third Man* and half a dozen others on their DVD commentary tracks. Soderbergh's canonisation has continued into prestige DVD releases of his own films, with Criterion Collection releases of *Traffic*, *Che*, the overlooked, nearly-forgotten *Kafka*, and the much-maligned *Schizopolis*. This final edition seemingly speaks to the cultural capital that the director has garnered over the course of his career, something that is reflected in Soderbergh's tongue-in-cheek DVD commentary where the director, portraying an obnoxious reporter, interviews an equally obnoxious director in opposite speaker channels.

In the minefield of economics and celebrity that is contemporary Hollywood, the sellebrity auteur is a necessarily paradoxical conception that helps account for the many seemingly contradictory elements at play. Upon closer inspection, the intersection of art and commerce – whether independent versus corporate, arthouse versus mass marketed, or mini versus major – reveals itself to be a dialectical paradox in cohesion, not collision. The most visible proof of this phenomenon is evidenced in the way some of these oppositional terms have literally become conjoined, such as Indiewood, indie blockbuster, and the mini-major. Economically, we see box-office reception tied to critical reception, as well as ownership concerns tied to artistic control. With regards to the auteur, we see rigid boundaries beginning to blur: blockbuster and arthouse, romantic and classical, economy of culture and culture of economy, celebrity and artist. The sellebrity auteur, as exemplified by Steven Soderbergh, demonstrates that ideas concerning 'authorial genius' are to be located not just in the films themselves, but in the way the auteur directs both the finances and publicity of making films.

Notes

1 Quoted in James Mottram, *Sundance Kids: How the Mavericks Took Back Hollywood* (New York: Faber and Faber, 2006), xxiv.

2 This argument first appears in Andrew deWaard, 'Joints and Jams: Spike Lee as Sellebrity Auteur,' in *Fight the Power!: The Spike Lee Reader*, eds. Janice D. Hamlet and Robin R. Means Coleman (New York: Peter Lang, 2008), 345–361. Spike Lee and his production company, 40 Acres and a Mule Productions, make a fitting comparison to Soderbergh and Section Eight.

3 For a more detailed discussion of the Clooney/Soderbergh relationship see Anne Helen Petersen, 'The Rise and Fall of the $100 Million Paycheck: Hollywood Stardom Since 1990,' in *American Film in the Digital Age*, ed. Robert Sickels (Santa Barbara: Praeger, 2011), 123–42, and Thomas Schatz, 'New Hollywood, New Millennium,' in *Film Theory and Contemporary Hollywood Movies*, ed. Warren Buckland (New York: Routledge, 2009), 19–46.

4 Thomas Schatz, 'The New Hollywood.' in *Film Theory Goes to the Movies*, eds. Jim Collins, Hilary Radner, and Ava Preacher Collins (New York: Routledge, 1993), 10.

5   See Justin Wyatt, *High Concept: Movies and Marketing in Hollywood* (Austin: University of Texas Press, 1994).

6   See also David A. Cook, *Lost Illusions: American Cinema in the Shadow of Watergate and Vietnam, 1970–1979* (New York: C. Scribner, 2000). Cook describes the decade-long process where the Amercian auteur cinema was swallowed up in favour of an 'era of consensus-building "super-grosser" or "mega-hit."'

7   See Peter Biskind, *Down and Dirty Pictures: Miramax, Sundance, and the Rise of the Independent Film* (New York: Simon & Schuster, 2004); James Mottram, *Sundance Kids: How the Mavericks Took Back Hollywood* (New York: Faber and Faber, 2006).

8   Alisa Perren, 'sex, lies and Marketing: Miramax and the Development of the Quality Indie Blockbuster,' *Film Quarterly*, 55 no. 2 (2001): 30.

9   See Allen J. Scott, 'Hollywood and the World: the Geography of Motion-Picture Distribution and Marketing,' *Review of International Political Economy*, 11 no. 1 (2004): 33–61.

10 Thomas Schatz, 'The Studio System in Conglomerate Hollywood,' in *The Contemporary Hollywood Film Industry*, eds. Paul McDonald and Janet Wasko (Malden, MA.: Blackwell Publishing, 2008), 25.

11 Ibid., 14.

12 Geoff King, *Indiewood U.S.A: Where Hollywood Meets Independent Cinema* (London: I.B. Taurus, 2009), 3.

13 Ibid., 29.

14 Ibid., 141.

15 Cook also notes the new importance that 'super-agents' like Lew Wasserman at MCA, Ted Ashley, David Begelman, and Michael Ovitz in the post-studio model, where these figures were as responsible for creating these packages as anyone else. Cook, *Lost Illusions*, 20.

16 See Jon Lewis, 'The Perfect Money Machine(s): George Lucas, Steven Spielberg and Auteurism in the New Hollywood,' *Film International* 1, no. 1 (2003): 12–26; Warren Buckland, 'The Role of the Auteur in the Age of the Blockbuster: Steven Spielberg and DreamWorks,' in *Movie Blockbusters*, ed. Julian Stringer (London: Routledge, 2003), 84–98; and Martin Flanagan, '"The Hulk, An Ang Lee Film": Notes on the Blockbuster Auteur,' in *New Review of Film and Television Studies* 2, no. 1 (2004): 19–35.

17 Lewis, 'Perfect Money Machine(s),' 4.

18 Quoted in Natasha Nair, 'George Clooney Bares His Bottom In *Solaris*,' *CinemaOnline*, last modified January, 2003, http://cinemaonline.com.my/news/news. asp?search=georgec.

19 Buckland, 'Role of the Auteur,' 84–85.

20 Quoted in Ryan Stewart, 'Steven Soderbergh: The Girlfriend Experience,' *SuicideGirls*, last modified May 21, 2009, http://suicidegirls.com/interviews/Steven+Soderbergh:+The+Girlfriend+Experience/.

21 Daniel J. Boorstin, *The Image: A Guide to Pseudo-Events in America* (New York: Harper and Row, 1961), 57.

22 Joshua Gamson, *Claims to Fame: Celebrity in Contemporary America* (Berkeley: University of California Press, 1994), 58.

23 Timothy Corrigan, 'The Commerce of Auteurism: A Voice Without Authority,' *New German Critique*, 49 (1990): 44.

24 Timothy Corrigan, *A Cinema Without Walls: Movies and Culture after Vietnam* (New Brunswick, N.J.: Rutgers University Press, 1991), 103.

25 Ibid., 102.

26 Ibid., 106.

27 Ibid., 107.

28 Ibid.

29 Gamson, '*Claims to Fame*,' 62.

30 Graeme Turner, *Understanding Celebrity* (London: Sage, 2004), 5.

31 Ibid., 35.

32 Naomi Klein, *No Logo.* (London: Flamingo, 2001), 49.

33 Geoff King, *New Hollywood Cinema: An Introduction* (New York: Columbia University Press, 2002), 160.

34 King, *Indiewood*, 178.

35 Earlier star director teams such as the James Stewart/Alfred Hitchcock, John Ford/John Wayne, and the Josef von Sternerg/Marlene Dietrich pairings. Richard Dyer explores the complicated relationship in Richard Dyer and Paul McDonald, *Stars* (London: BFI 1998), 154.

36 Schatz, 'Studio System,' 34.

37 Clooney quoted in Laura M. Holson, 'Trying to Combine Art and Box Office in Hollywood,' *New York Times*, January 17, 2005, http://www.nytimes.com/2005/01/17/business/media/17clooney.html.

38 Quoted in Geoff Andrew, 'Again, with 20% more existential grief: Steven Soderbergh and George Clooney at the NFT,' *Guardian Unlimited*, February 13, 2003, http://film.guardian.co.uk/interview/interviewpages/0,,897475,00.html.

39 King, *Indiewood*, 142.

40 Soderbergh also attempted to form his own 'Director's Company' based on Coppola's model, which would have included the talents of himself, Spike Jonze, David Fincher, Alexander Payne, and Sam Mendes. But, as Waxman muses, 'Ultimately, the rebels could not muster a united front.' See Sharon Waxman, *Rebels on the Backlot: Six Maverick Directors and How They Conquered the Hollywood Studio System* (New York: HarperEntertainment, 2005), xix.

41 The story of Soderbergh's role in shepherding *Far From Heaven* can be found in Biskind, *Down and Dirty Pictures*, 428–30, 446–47, 467, and 470.

42 Soderbergh would also revive his screenwriting alter-ego, Sam Lowry, for this 2004 film.

43 Quoted in Andrew, 'Existential Grief.'

44 Ibid.

45 Todd McCarthy, 'Ocean's Twelve [review],' *Variety*, December 8, 2004.

46 Although Clooney had never directed, he assured Miramax that he could get the film made for a budget of under $30 million by using his star status and his asso-

ciation with Section Eight. He approached Miramax for funding, in exchange for the commitment to work with them at a later date, and with assurances that certain stars would appear throughout the film. Clooney called Drew Barrymore and Julia Roberts and asked them to work for union scale and begged favours of his recent *Ocean's 11* co-stars Brad Pitt and Matt Damon to make brief cameos (see George Clooney quoted in Colin Kennedy, 'O Lucky Man!,' *Empire Magazine*, March 2003). Clooney also collaborated with talented behind-the-scenes people like cinematographer Newton Thomas Sigel (whom he had worked with in *Three Kings*) and Academy Award winning editor Stephen Mirrione (*Ocean's 11* and *Traffic*) and helmed the first script written and sold by a less-famous Charlie Kaufman.

47 For an extensive history see R. Colin Tait, 'Piercing Steven Soderbergh's *Bubble*,' in *The Business of Entertainment*, ed. Robert Sickels (Westport, CT: Praeger Publishers, 2009), 179–194.

48 Southern was the screenwriter of classics *Dr. Strangelove*, (Stanley Kubrick, 1964), *The Cincinnati Kid* (Norman Jewison, 1965), *Barbarella* (Roger Vadim, 1968), and *Easy Rider*.

CHAPTER THREE

Corporate Revolutionary: Soderbergh as Guerrilla Auteur

The existence of a revolutionary cinema is inconceivable without the constant and methodical exercise of practice, search, and experimentation. It even means committing the new filmmaker to take chances on the unknown, to leap into spaces at times, exposing himself to failure as does the guerrilla who travels along paths that he himself opens up with machete blows. The possibility of discovering and inventing film forms and structures that serve a more profound vision of our reality resides in the ability to place oneself on the outside limits of the familiar, to make one's way amid constant dangers.

Solanas and Getino – 'Towards a Third Cinema'[1]

Thus far, we have outlined how Steven Soderbergh belongs to a traditional model of film authorship and auteur theory, considering his multi-faceted signature, yet also challenges this model in the instability and adaptability of this signature style across a diverse range of films. We have also explored recent economic shifts in Hollywood and the changing nature of celebrity and marketing that necessitate a reconsideration of the contemporary director as 'sellebrity auteur,' of which Soderbergh is a fitting example. However, two fully-fledged auteur analyses still do not seem to capture the full scope of Soderbergh's career and oeuvre. In addition to his traditional craftsmanship and canny financial understanding, there is a reckless and experimental edge to the director that appears in a variety of formal, industrial, philosophical, and political capacities. Our attempt to account for this 'surplus' value involves a potentially contentious utilisation, considering its context, of an overtly political praxis: Third Cinema.

A primarily Latin-American film movement with revolutionary aims of decolonisation and liberation, Third Cinema crystallised with a polemical manifesto in 1969, and includes a series of political films created by Argentinian, Brazilian, Cuban, and Bolivian filmmakers in the late 1960s and 1970s, though its definition can be

Che begins with Guevara's infamous public speech – in which he spoke at the UN in 1964 – and then back-tracks to document the successful Cuban revolution.

widened to include other members of the so-called 'Third World' in Asia and Africa. The historical, political, and cultural context of this movement is significant, as is its legacy.[2] The theory and practice of Third Cinema, oppositional to both 'First Cinema' (Hollywood spectacle) and 'Second Cinema' (European auteur film), sought to establish an alternative mode of filmmaking; indeed, 'the most compelling and significant aspect of the New Latin American Cinema movement,' in Julianna Burton's estimation, was 'its capacity to create alternative modes of production, consumption, and reception.'[3] Third Cinema also advanced the idea of an Imperfect Cinema, one that subverts cinematic code and challenges bourgeois notions of taste.

Terming Soderbergh a descendant of this movement is problematic, to say the least. Obviously, it challenges the term's original political resonances: necessary projects of post-colonial and class struggle. When applied to a white, heterosexual, wealthy North American male filmmaker by two white, heterosexual, middle class North American male authors, it is a characterisation that could be received as insensitive at best, and downright oppressive at worst. Make no mistake: Steven Soderbergh works for corporate America. And he has realised a tremendous amount of capital for it – upwards of 2 billion dollars in box-office gross. He is a part of the (neo-)imperialist 'System' to which Third Cinema stood in direct opposition. But much has changed in the conception of the 'First World' and the 'System,' and a more nuanced view of a globalised world can better appreciate the ways in which Soderbergh has also exploited his position to create challenging, flawed films that use 'guerrilla' techniques, alternative modes of production, and political themes that side with the oppressed. These films lie outside the rubric of both traditional Hollywood escapist fare and auteurist self-expression. The dialectical dynamism of Soderbergh's career includes these oppositional stances that require the critic to think beyond evaluative concerns and consider the sheer display of *difference* in much of his work. Using two of his most challenging, experimental films, *Schizopolis* and *Che*, which both involved unique filmmaking practice and were met with a mixed, confused reception, we can elaborate on Soderbergh's utilisation of an alternative technique that is indebted to Third Cinema, and points towards both an Imperfect Cinema and a Minor Cinema.

Guerrilla Cinema in Hollywood's Mist

Like many manifestos that accompany artistic movements, 'Towards a Third Cinema,' written by Argentine filmmakers Fernando Solanas and Octavio Getino, is as aspirational and suggestive a document as it is a call to arms. Though we can point to various concurrent Latin American film movements that arose within this discourse – *Grupo Cine Liberación,* Brazil's *Cinema Novo*, Cuban revolutionary cinema – the provocation of Third Cinema remains a lasting inspiration and plea for an alternative filmmaking practice. The most consistent theme in the manifesto is the need for filmmakers to combine theory with praxis to make films that stand outside of the 'First World' (Hollywood) dictum of entertainment and the 'Second World' art cinema's self-obsession. Films made to honour the legacy of Third Cinema are designed to provoke audiences, inspire thought, and foster a more informed citizenry. Though the immediate goal of Third Cinema may have been to set the stage for an emerging revolutionary consciousness in a particular post-colonial context, its spirit can be invoked more abstractly on a wider political and historical field.

Solanas and Getino provide a description of the guerrilla filmmaker, excerpted in the epigraph that begins this chapter, that we think is applicable to the filmmaking mode of Soderbergh: 'practice, search, and experimentation,' 'take chances,' and 'exposing himself to failure.'[4] For our purposes, we are abstracting the following criteria from Third Cinema theory to indicate the spirit of guerrilla filmmaking. First, the guerrilla filmmaker must be willing to experiment, adopting new forms in narrative, editing, film style, and cinematography. They should also attempt to control the means of production, utilising a 'do-it-yourself' (DIY) technique that marks them as outside of the system through this combination of experimentation and control. The guerrilla filmmaker should also be prolific, a worker whose constant labour is the primary method of ascertaining control and fostering experimentation. Finally, the guerrilla filmmaker possesses an 'image weapon' which is symbolically described in Third Cinema theory as a device to bludgeon (a rock), to cut (a machete), or to shoot (camera-gun). The tool, or apparatus, of cinema is thus a significant concern of the guerrilla filmmaker. We can now turn to how Soderbergh utilises these techniques:

Experimental: Our previous discussion of Soderbergh's dialectic signature has pointed to the formal nature of his filmmaking that alternates between a classical Hollywood polish and an experimental, chaotic streak. Highly-kinetic, handheld camera work is matched by over-saturated, bleached cinematography. His equally aggressive editing style not only destabilises the very textures of what we are seeing, but dictates the puzzling rearrangement of the stories that he tells. Soderbergh is as much the mad scientist as he is the Jackson Pollock-esque 'action painter,' mixing chemicals in a lab and throwing paint at a canvas to see what sticks. As the painter metaphor evokes, sometimes material ends up on the walls and the floor, just as chemicals in a beaker sometimes fizzle.

Means of Production: As director/producer/cinematographer/writer/editor/actor, Soderbergh certainly evokes Solanas and Getino's description of a guerrilla filmmaker who 'equips himself at all levels,' and 'learns how to handle the manifold techniques of his craft.'[5] We can even pinpoint the exact moment when Soderbergh turned away from traditional Hollywood production to achieve this self-reliance and multi-faceted technique. Following *The Underneath*, Soderbergh 'retreated to his hometown of Baton Rouge, Louisiana, and, guerrilla-style, knocked out a couple of no-budget films, the Spalding Gray monologue *Gray's Anatomy* and *Schizopolis*, a brilliant and seriously unhinged psychodrama.'[6] His subsequent Hollywood success allowed him more agency within the industry, and his deft negotiation of celebrity, public relations, and finance (outlined in the previous chapter) accrued him considerable power in his role as producer. For Solanas and Getino, the guerrilla filmmaker 'acts with a radically new vision' of the 'role of producer'; 'above all, he supplies himself at all levels in order to produce his films.'[7] Section Eight can be seen as Soderbergh's guerrilla technique to 'supply himself' with fuller access to the means of production, even finance and distribution. His ability to facilitate film production for his fellow creative partners (Clooney, Gaghan, Gilroy, Nolan, Linklater and so on) invokes Solanas and Getino's notion of the '*film-guerrilla* group,' which is 'in the same situation as a guerrilla unit.'[8] Lofty language for Hollywood production, but the similar organisational structure is apparent, however corporate the financial backing happens to be in this context.

Labour: As noted previously, with nearly thirty films in the role of director (and often cinematographer and editor as well), and another thirty as producer, Soderbergh is a cinematic labourer. To say that Soderbergh is prolific is an understatement; he has challenged himself to tackle almost every film form and genre, to assume the mantle of almost every role on set, and to tackle projects large and small in scope. The speed and consistency with which Soderbergh makes films is unrivalled in contemporary Hollywood, and elsewhere, with the exception of the 'Classical Hollywood' production-line studio system and perhaps modern-day Bollywood.[9] Soderbergh himself points to this attitude of labour when he opposes the romantic account of authorship, proclaiming 'I'm not a visionary... What I am is a dedicated, passionate craftsman who is trying to get better.'[10] The subtitle of his own book suggests he is 'the luckiest bastard you ever saw,'[11] modestly sidestepping the tireless work ethic that very book chronicles, and his extensive resume indicates. Labour itself is a key part of his creative process: 'there's no substitute for shooting'; it 'roots out preciousness... the enemy of art.'[12] Though his product is typically

Hollywood, his method is pure Third Cinema: 'constant vigilance, constant wariness, constant mobility.'[13]

Image-Weapon: The apparatus and technology of cinema has always been foundational to film movements, most notably the mobile cameras that motivated the direct, location-based technique of Italian Neo-Realism and the loose, ephemeral style of the French New Wave. Third Cinema also venerated the apparatus of the cinema, but in aggressive terms: 'The camera is the inexhaustible *expropriator of image-weapons*; the projector, *a gun that can shoot 24 frames per second*.'[14] Such militaristic language suited the revolutionary mindset, and we can consider the *digital* image-weapon to be of significant value to contemporary revolutionary struggles: user-generated footage, social networks, and mobile phones are an essential part of the protester and guerrilla's tool kit. Soderbergh, for his part, can be seen as an important 'early adopter of digital and video innovations,'[15] helping pave the way for a cinematic imaginary that includes such digital, 'amateur' imagery. Soderbergh's career parallels the history of the medium's development, from his Hi-8 video inserts in *sex, lies, and videotape*, to his emulation of the Dogme 95 mini-DV movement in *Full Frontal*, through to his digital recording of politics as they occur in real-time in *K-Street*. Soderbergh was an early adopter of the High Definition format as well, beginning with modest HD projects like *Bubble* and *The Girlfriend Experience*, before escalating to wider releases such as *Che*, *The Informant!*, and *Contagion*. Soderbergh's use of digital contributes to his harnessing of the means of production as well, as digital allows him the freedom to shoot far less expensively, personally editing and colour-correcting as he goes. Soderbergh is also among the first to use the RED One camera, a significant advancement in mobile, high quality digital camera technology that continues the evolution of the cinematic apparatus. Combined with the day-and-date release strategy he employed for *Bubble* – immediate, simultaneous distribution to theatre, DVD and cable television – Soderbergh is blazing the trail for a production and distribution process that cuts out several 'middle men' and 'gatekeepers.' The digital revolution might not have as serious political overtones as other more immediate revolutions, but Soderbergh can lay claim to a significant role in this broad paradigm shift in the means of cultural production.

Fail Better: An Imperfect Cinema

While the preceding guerrilla criteria help account for some of the outlying stylistic and formal features of Soderbergh's work, as well as his increasingly self-reliant process, the over-arching character of his perceivably 'flawed' oeuvre can also be illuminated under the rubric of Third Cinema. Solanas and Getino call for 'works in progress – unfinished, unordered, violent works,'[16] a filmmaking practice rooted in the aggressive politics of its revolutionary impulse. Another influential piece of Third Cinema criticism, 'For an Imperfect Cinema,' held the hegemonic art world and its closed, elitist regime as its target. 'Imperfect cinema,' according to Julio García Espinosa, must above all show the process which generates the problems. It is thus the opposite of a cinema principally dedicated to celebrating results, the opposite of a self-sufficient and contemplative cinema, the opposite of a cinema which 'beautifully illustrates' ideas or concepts which we already possess.[17]

This was a call for a messy cinema, an amateur cinema, a cinema that did not conform to Eurocentric notions of taste. Worried that the increasing attention Third Cinema began receiving from the 'European intelligentsia' was only an aesthetic appreciation, potentially of an exoticising nature, Espinosa cautioned against Cuban cinema aspiring to the status of technical and artistic mastery, or, 'perfect cinema.'

In order to avoid the pitfalls of this apolitical, narcissistic cinema, Espinosa proclaimed that imperfect cinema was 'no longer interested in quality or technique. It can be created equally well with a Mitchell or with an 8mm camera, in a studio or in a guerrilla camp in the middle of the jungle.'[18] Elsewhere, Espinosa expands the blended nature of imperfect cinema to include 'the documentary or the fictional mode, or both'; it 'can use whatever genre, or all genres… It can use cinema as a pluralistic art form or as a specialized form of expression.'[19] It is not the method or form that is most significant, but the intent; by dismissing the bourgeois conception of quality and taste, and embracing a relativistic formal process, imperfect cinema could 'overcome the barrier of the "cultured" elite audience'[20] in its active rejection of the confines of 'good taste.' With no desire for quality or technique, imperfect cinema would be more accurately tied to the idea of socialism as an unfinished, unending process.

Again, we can abstractly apply this technique of Third Cinema to Soderbergh's case: a series of 'imperfect' films that work to reveal process and challenge traditional systems of 'taste' and 'quality.' While it is certainly true that 'imperfection' lies in even the most acclaimed auteur, the sense of imperfection is especially true of Soderbergh's oeuvre, whose many, varied films have continued to divide audiences and critics for more than twenty years. There is the possibility that Soderbergh actually *intends* to frustrate audiences. 'I realized another thing,' he remarks, referring to his streak of poorly received films in the early 1990s, 'I was very comfortable disappointing people.'[21] Intention aside, his films have often been met with less than desirable receptions. To many critics and viewers, they are simply failures, having not fulfilled their expectations (and to be fair, the marketing of his films often promises something more 'entertaining'). But another faction of Soderbergh's reception is the continuing trope of the 'interesting failure' or 'noble failure.'[22] There is an almost begrudging respect for simply *trying* something different, especially in a multiplex-environment reliant on blockbuster formulas, tent pole releases, and focus groups. Experimentation is rare in conglomerate Hollywood, but critical appreciation of it is even more rare, beyond reluctant acknowledgement.

If we are to consider experimentation a critical category worth evaluating, which seems necessary even beyond the confines of considering an 'imperfect cinema,' then as critics we would have to delve into 'failure' more delicately. All too often in film studies, failure – whether critical, financial, or otherwise – has occluded a sober view of a credible film canon. Films that initially fall outside of the purview of 'success' are often ignored entirely, and directors are excluded from a larger discussion of film history regardless of the industrial, economic, or personal factors that may have influenced their status as auteurs. Meanwhile, the new economics of authorship ensure that savvy directors who can immediately fashion for themselves a brand and series of recognisable directorial tics will earn themselves a place in the new conglomerate Hollywood.

Rarely making easily digestible films and refusing to make so-called 'Oscar-bait' or 'quirky indie fare,' Soderbergh's willingness to take creative risks results in his films often being characterised as impenetrable. In the popular press, Soderbergh is described as 'scientific,' 'cold,' and 'clinical'; he is likened to a mad scientist or an academic. The labyrinthine nature of *Schizopolis* is 'self-referential in ways that hold dim academic interest without otherwise engaging attention';[23] the formal and narrative experimentation of *Full Frontal* is a 'two-hour masturbatory exercise.'[24] The considerable technical achievement of *The Good German* is merely 'an exercise in sleight of hand,'[25] while *Che* 'reeks of authenticity but also self-indulgence.'[26] The derogatory outpouring is endless, but these quotes, almost back-handed compliments, indicate the confused nature of such criticism. It is as if they recognise the creativity on display but are unable to rectify that artistry with their 'job,' which is, ostensibly, recommending palatable movies.

For Soderbergh, the challenge of appreciating experimentation, and thus failure, go hand in hand, as his most 'imperfect' experiments are also those most deemed failures in the larger critical sphere. *Schizopolis* and *Che* are the most demonstrative of 'guerrilla' and 'imperfect' tendencies, and it is no coincidence that they were met with the biggest critical backlash. These are films that fulfill Solanas and Getino's requirements for Third Cinema, '*films that the System cannot assimilate and which are foreign to its needs.*'[27] Oddly enough, both films were immediately disparaged at their Cannes debut, and the narrative of their failure was already set. In key reviews, critics seemed more preoccupied with telling the story of their debut screenings, than reviewing the films. Janet Maslin's review of *Schizopolis* echoes the bourgeois tenor of these sentiments, highlighting that although the film was '[s]hown under ideal circumstances to an eager group of international cineastes,' it 'still managed to excite jaw-dropping indifference.'[28] The story of the film's reception also includes exaggerated claims of audience walk-outs, though Soderbergh recalls that '[o]ut of the approximately 850 in attendance, about 50 of them walked out in the first thirty minutes when they discovered it was weird and had no stars in it.'[29] Reaction to the Cannes screening also caused Harvey Weinstein to retract his initial offer of $1 million, sight unseen, to buy the film outright.

As for *Che*, key figures of the Hollywood press corps seem to have constructed the story of its reception in advance, with the common thread of comparing it to other notorious Cannes flops. A 'fiasco' is more likely to describe an event, rather than an evaluative term for a piece of art, but it is the lasting sentiment for the debut of *Che*, along with being compared to other infamous Cannes duds such as *The Brown Bunny* (Vincent Gallo, 2003) and *Southland Tales* (Richard Kelly, 2006).[30] Todd McCarthy's scathing *Variety* review offers much of the same, suggesting that 'it will be back to the drawing board for *Che*,' despite it being 'intricately ambitious' and 'defiantly

With *Schizopolis*, Soderbergh gained the confidence to experiment with cinematic convention, as seen in his character's bizarre transformation from Fletcher Munson into Dr. Jefferey Korcheck in this sequence.

nondramatic.'[31] Again, a begrudging respect earned Benicio Del Toro the Best Actor award, but the film failed to pick up a major distributor, and continued to confound critics once it play in limited release.

Commercially, these films fared even worse. *Schizopolis* was released on only two screens, with its total revenue amounting to just over $10,000. Against the film's $275,000 budget, this was a box-office disaster, and Soderbergh's original plan for a sequel, entitled *Neurotica* or *Son of Schizopolis*, was shelved. Despite the film's attempt to be (and critics' understanding of it as) a 'midnight film,' *Schizopolis* was the victim of conflating historical trends and a categorical difficulty. Since it only played for two weeks in only two theatres, it was never able to gain the momentum that cult films usually attain, and consequently went unseen anywhere in the world. His lone attempt at comedy up until that time, Soderbergh's 'serious' reputation was in no way changed, and the film remains a largely unseen, aberrant intervention. *Che* was released at a moment when, according to producer Laura Bickford,[32] seven out of ten independent distributors had gone under, exacerbating *Che's* potential to recoup its budget. Despite costing nearly $80 million to produce, it failed to attract a major distributor, making it extremely difficult for the movie to be released theatrically. The two-part 'road-show' format (a brainchild of Soderbergh) recouped a domestic total of less than $2 million.

Despite their initial drubbing in the popular press and at the box office, both films contain a great deal of value, particularly for a broader analysis of Soderbergh's career. We can, therefore, view each of these films as provocations and experiments, each of which pushes at the boundaries and solidifies Soderbergh's preferred style as a one-man-filmmaking machine, as he incorporates nearly all of the major creative roles into his persona. Much of this technique of trial and error emerged from Soderbergh's own encounter with unemployability and failure. This is particularly true of the years from 1994 to 1998, when he shot *Gray's Anatomy* and *Schizopolis* with donated film stock and thus learned to be diligent and economical with the means he had at his disposal. While it is clear that Soderbergh's earlier projects expressed these desires (as seen in his experiments with colour in *Kafka* and *The Underneath*), these attempts were ill-suited to the conventional narratives that the director tried to shoehorn them into.

With *Schizopolis,* Soderbergh liberated himself from ill-fitting Hollywood conventions and grabbed the reins as cinematographer, editor, director, composer, and actor, trying anything and everything that he wanted to do with a script, a camera, and an editing bay. To wit, this bizarre film is as innovative as it is tedious to watch. Nevertheless, *Schizopolis* should be viewed as the piece that rejuvenated the director's creativity in the face of his frustrations with Hollywood's narrative filmmaking. More importantly, he discovered a method with this movie that allowed him to work under his own terms. With *Schizopolis,* Soderbergh gained the confidence to try things and fail (sometimes spectacularly), linking him to a much larger tradition of experimental, student, and guerrilla filmmaking traditions rather than his indie and Hollywood roots. Refining and mastering his signature styles of cinematography, editing, and directing, *Schizopolis* was a laboratory where Soderbergh experimented on himself, along with his friends and family, and devised the formula that he would then more successfully apply to all of his subsequent works. It is also the film with which Soderbergh officially embraces the mandate of DIY, experimenting with guerrilla filmmaking techniques.

By the time he gets to *Che*, he is able to take to the jungles of Spain and counter the traditional form of the historical epic/biopic with a small crew and a digital camera. Soderbergh takes Guevara's first-hand accounts of the successful Cuban and failed Bolivian revolutionary efforts to create a self-interrogating document of success and failure, similar to his own dialectical patterns. Refusing to shoot a standard biopic, Soderbergh attempts to de-mythologise Guevara in order to focus 'on events or situations that we felt humanized him that were eye-level.'[33] Devoid of any showy scenes, Soderbergh's use of a documentary aesthetic is important to the way this verisimilitude develops; the direct, raw quality of the RED One camera contributes to Soderbergh's desire to create 'a procedural about guerrilla warfare.'[34]

Production-wise, the camera allowed the small crew to shoot two films in 78 days, utilising a symmetrical 39 days per shoot. The average film aims to shoot around a page of script per day, amounting to an approximately ninety-minute finished film. When we consider the four and a half hour long running time of *Che* – shot, edited, and released within less than a year (with three days remaining to get it to the Cannes festival) – this is a Herculean task. Comparing *Che* to another epic, Michael Cimino's infamous debacle *Heaven's Gate* (1980), serves up an interesting parallel. Both filmmakers set out to make historical films about epic subjects with a wide scope and a unique visual signature. Whereas Cimino went at least $30 million over budget (more than $100 million by today's standard), according to Bickford, 'Steven likes to say we had enough money to make one movie and we made two, which is true.'[35] Where Cimino attempted to contain his outsized personality into the epic form, there is very little trace of Soderbergh in his film. Soderbergh was not aiming for a poetic historical biopic in the vein of David Lean's *Lawrence of Arabia* (1962) or *Doctor Zhivago* (1965), but rather something that better suited his subject matter. In essence, it is the present-ness that is so remarkable about the film, rather than its mythologisation of its subject matter.

Che also exhibits all aspects that we have outlined for Soderbergh's filmmaking practices, but this time they are contained within a single piece, rather than over the course of several films. The first part, which was far better received than the second, highlights the signature stylistics that we have thus far described as uniquely Soder-

berghian. Based primarily on Che's journals, the story is told in flashback, moving between the staggered times and spaces as varied as Guevara's address to the United Nations, the jungles of Cuba and the streets of Mexico before the revolution. Soderbergh's typical fragmented structure is utilised here as a means to negotiate the varying accounts of the revolution from the different historical vantage points that Che was writing from. This also partly accounts for the shift in tone between the films, as the second part was largely drawn from Guevara's first-hand account of his failed venture in Bolivia. Each part of the film contains a mirror image within its formal and narrative structure.

Soderbergh's filmmaking follows a similar trajectory. As we have argued, his career is a pattern of dialectical choices which often seem counter-intuitive, but never-theless inform the larger trajectory of his cinematic oeuvre. In this instance, Soderbergh juxtaposes

Che Part II – The Argentine begins with the long, slow decline of Guevara's failed Bolivian campaign, ending with the adoption of the protagonists' POV as he dies.

success and failure within the same film, necessitating that we investigate *Che* as the culmination of the director's career to date. His decision to film in Spanish, rather than English, is a significant decision considering the economic implications. Soderbergh's inclusion of *cinéma vérité* tropes and insistence that 'authenticity trumps everything'[36] marks the filmmaker's belonging to the larger tradition of realism. In this case, the anti-commercial choice is not solely an artistic one, but one that attempts to capture, in retrospect, the complexities of a significant man without resorting to the typical clichés found in historical epics. Soderbergh's refusal to play by the rules for the film, eschewing the use of generic and storytelling clichés, is only one of the many ways that the film conforms to the guerrilla aesthetic. The speed with which the movie was made, the harnessing of the means of production, and its manufacture outside of the Hollywood system are other notable qualifications.

Both films are excellent examples of Soderbergh's 'guerrilla' filmmaking. Though they stand almost a decade apart, they nevertheless reveal particular patterns that cover many of his so-called 'failures.' Both also mark the endpoints of frustrating periods in the filmmaker's career, summarising the artistic trajectory and innovative storytelling and visual practices, as well as coming at personal low points in Soderbergh's life. Though these films may never be recognised for the potential that they have unleashed in the larger context, ultimately, by way of their guerrilla tactics and aesthetics, they are instrumental in unleashing a wave of unharnessed potential energy, the likes of which have yet to be realised or understood. While this may seem hyperbolic, to say the least, it nevertheless adheres to the aspiration of Third Cinema that, by way of its opposition to the mainstream, enlarges the scope of the political sphere. 'Such works cannot be assessed according to the traditional theoretical and critical canons,' Solanas and Getino proclaim. 'The ideas for *our* film theory and criticism will come to life through inhibition-removing practice and experimentation.'[37] By this standard, the failures of *Schizopolis* and *Che* are a success.

Soderbergh: Towards a Minor Cinema

Ultimately, we do not wish to designate Soderbergh as a direct descendant of Third Cinema, which would be an affront to the cultural and political specificity of the film movement, as well as a reduction of Soderbergh's complex filmmaking practice. Instead, by using 'guerrilla' and 'imperfect' criteria to show how surprisingly applicable its tenets are to Soderbergh's practice, we merely wish to highlight the considerable *difference* visible in his work. Following this purposefully provocative suggestion, we can settle on a more accurate designation, it too based on experimentation, opposition, and political motivation: Minor Cinema, following Gilles Deleuze and Felix Guattari's *Kafka: Towards a Minor Literature*.[38]

The concept of a 'minor literature' is proposed by Deleuze and Guattari to denote the use of a major language from a marginalised or minoritarian position with the intention of 'deterritorializing' the major language. Minor literature is inherently and thoroughly political: 'positively charged with the role and function of the collective, and even revolutionary, enunciation.'[39] Applying this conception to a Minor Cinema is not such a big leap, and has been attempted sporadically by critics.[40] However, these applications have been on behalf of 'minor languages,' such as Queer Cinema, considering the major language to be the established codes of cinema itself. A true application of Deleuze and Guattari would have to be someone speaking in/through the 'major' language of cinema, i.e. Hollywood.

If resistance to a dominant model from within that dominant model is indicative of a minor cinema, then our delineation of Soderbergh's multi-variant 'classical'/'chaotic' signature is enough to warrant consideration under Deleuze and Guattari's rubric.[41] His tendency to 'rip apart' the time and space of his narratives through editing is of particular interest to a notion of 'deterritorialization.' The formal 'resistance' on display in Soderbergh's films is one qualifier of minor cinema, the overtly political subject matter that takes the side of the 'oppressed' in many of his films is another: a class-action lawsuit against corporate malfeasance (*Erin Brockovich*), the 'War on Drugs' (*Traffic*), the failed representation of mixed-race couples (*Full Frontal*), governmental lobbying (*K Street*), journalistic accountability (*Good Night, and Good Luck*), geopolitical power structures and the petroleum industry (*Syriana*), corporate circumvention of the law (*Michael Clayton*), complicity in war crimes (*The Good German*), one of the most notorious anti-imperialist thinkers and revolutionaries of the twentieth century (*Che*), the financial crisis of 2007–2008 (*The Girlfriend Experience*), and conspiracy to fix global prices (*The Informant!*). The bureaucratic nightmare of Soderbergh's *Kafka* indicates a minor cinema, naturally.

In addition to overt politics, we might also consider Soderbergh's minor cinema from the standpoint of a uniquely American cinema. Hollywood's hegemony is often deplored from a global perspective, with a cultural imperialist argument in tow, but its dominance over its domestic market is largely a foregone conclusion. For many, American cinema simply *is* Hollywood, and the lack of alternatives is considered only in so much that 'independent' films struggle on the margins of this system. An alternative system is rarely proposed, and historically, any such occurrence has been quickly subsumed (e.g. Blaxploitation). Soderbergh's insistence on regionalism within his films, then, speaks to this ability to communicate a minor language from his Hollywood megaphone. His interest in realistic depictions of site-specific locales can be seen as part of his attempt to create a less dominant and more intimate American cinema. For instance, the 'fly-over' states rarely receive much screen time in Hollywood films, and when they do, it is often at the expense of a 'backward,' 'rural' stereotype. Soderbergh, however, delicately explores an unlikely working class friendship in a Belpre, Ohio, doll factory in *Bubble*, and his hometown of Baton Rouge, Louisiana, is rendered as lonely and alienating in *sex, lies, and videotape* and *Schizopolis*. Other less prominent American locales include a ghostly Austin, Texas, in *The Underneath*, scenes of urban plight in Detroit and Cincinnati, in *Out of Sight* and *Traffic*, respectively, and Decatur, Illinois, whose residents and accents become part of the satire in *The Informant!*.

As opposed to the flatness of a standard American dialect, found in the typical Hollywood fare, Soderbergh's characters present us with a heavily accented cinema.[42] This is certainly true of *King of the Hill*, where the characters speak in Missouri accents, just as the characters in *The Underneath* speak in a distinctly Texan drawl. As *Schizo-*

polis is shot in Soderbergh's hometown, using his friends, his family, and their houses as settings, this regionality presents its unique character on a micro level. *The Limey*'s Wilson is the most pronounced here, as his heavily-accented cockney speech is regional to the point of being all but unrecognisable as English to those Americans who hear him.[43] Soderbergh's work in other languages is also important here, especially in films where regional difference is still important. In *Che*, the differences between accents in Latin American dialects is part of the way that the film resists the dominant mode of filmmaking, in addition to the fact that it was shot almost entirely in Spanish, despite being originally funded as an English-language film. In a cultural industry that thrives on the homogeneity of characters, types, and locations, where everyone is supposed to look the same way and speak with the same accent, Soderbergh's regional, accented cinema presents an America that is far more diverse and unique than is indicated by its primary media industries and centres of media power.

The final component of minor literature according to Deleuze and Guatarri is that 'everything takes on a collective value.'[44] As we will demonstrate in the final three chapters – with analyses of the crime film, the heist film, and the global social problem film – Soderbergh emphasises ensemble casts as protagonists, whose class and social status are on the other side of power. Furthermore, most of his characters are underdogs in opposition to institutional-scale power: multinational corporations, bureaucracies, and national governments. Thus, the audience is presented with surrogates for their collective desires to right the injustices in the larger context of institutional indifference. Though 'Hollywood liberalism' is often – and rightfully – decried as self-serving and self-righteous, we can, at the very least, credit Soderbergh with a willingness to tackle or question some of the main ideological threads in American society, marking his politics as outside of the mainstream. We have already elaborated on how his films deviate wildly from Hollywood's formal and narrative hallmarks, and we can further assert that his resistance to closure, the happy ending, and the marriage plot themselves constitute a political act of resistance against normative ideology.

Having traversed Third, guerrilla, imperfect, and minor cinema, following a trek through Hollywood finance, celebrity, and publicity, subsequent to an analysis of cinematography, editing, performance, and production, we believe we have offered a variety of means to account for the multiple 'Soderberghs,' some of whom seem to contradict the work of others. As Deleuze and Guattari would have it, Soderbergh is 'a sort of stranger within his own language.'[45] Perhaps we can assert that *Schizopolis*, with its multiple incarnations of the director within the film, as well as a DVD commentary which features the director as an obnoxious interviewer questioning a self-important director figure, reveals some of the major tensions between the many hats that Soderbergh wears, and the multiple (and perhaps schizophrenic) methods necessary to address such a complicated subject. As we turn more directly towards the textual content of this chameleon-sellebrity-guerrilla, we ask that the reader continue to consider how Soderbergh as artist, mogul, and 'revolutionary' exists within each of these films, and how his distance from or closeness to the centre of filmmaking power marks him at different times as insider and outsider, sellebrity and guerrilla, as well as practitioner of the major and minor modes of contemporary American cinema. In reference to Third Cinema's insistence on flexibility, Paul Willeman makes a claim that equally applies to the auteur status of Soderbergh: 'an all-encompassing definition [would be] impossible… even undesirable.'[46]

Notes

1   Fernando Solanas and Octavio Getino, 'Towards a Third Cinema: Notes and Experiences for the Development of a Cinema of Liberation in the Third World,' in *New Latin American Cinema*, ed. Michael T. Martin (Detroit: Wayne State University Press, 1997), 48.

2   See *New Latin American Cinema*; Mike Wayne, *Political Film: The Dialectics of Third Cinema* (London: Pluto Press, 2001).

3   Quoted in Michael T. Martin, 'Introductory Notes,' *New Latin American Cinema*, 27.

4   Solanas and Getino, 'Towards a Third Cinema,' 48.

5   Ibid., 50.

6   Dennis Lim, 'Sight Seeing: Steven Soderbergh Loosens Up,' in *Steven Soderbergh: Interviews*, ed. Anthony Kaufman (Jackson: University Press of Mississippi, 2002), 108.

7   Solanas and Getino, 'Towards a Third Cinema,' 50.

8   Ibid., 49.

9   There are exceptions, of course, such as Rainer Werner Fassbinder, who made 40 feature films, as well as television and theatre productions, in just over 15 years.

10 Quoted in John H. Richardson, 'The Very Boring Life Of Steven Soderbergh,' *Esquire*, August 1 2002, http://www.esquire.com/ESQ0802-AUG_SODER-BERGH.

11 Steven Soderbergh, *Getting Away with It*, 216.

12 Richardson, 'Life Of Steven Soderbergh.'

13 Solanas and Getino, 'Towards a Third Cinema,' 51.

14 Ibid., 50.

15 Everett M. Rogers and F. Floyd Shoemaker, *Communication of Innovations: A Cross-Cultural Approach* (New York: Free Press, 1971).

16 Ibid., 49.

17 Julio Garcia Espinosa, 'For an Imperfect Cinema,' trans. Julianne Burton, *Jump Cut* no. 20 (1979): 24–26, http://www.ejumpcut.org/archive/onlinessays/JC20folder/ImperfectCinema.html.

18 Ibid.

19 Quoted in Paul Willeman, 'The Third Cinema Question: Notes and Reflections,' *New Latin American Cinema*, ed. Michael T. Martin (Detroit: Wayne State University Press, 1997), 227.

20 Espinosa, 'For an Imperfect Cinema.'

21 Quoted in Richardson, 'Life Of Steven Soderbergh.'

22 Anne Thompson, 'Cannes: Che Meets Mixed Reaction,' *Variety*, May 21, 2008, http://weblogs.variety.com/thompsononhollywood/2008/05.html.

23 Janet Maslin, 'Schizopolis,' *New York Times*, April 9 1997.

24 Rick Groen, 'Your Time Is Up: Steven Soderbergh,' *The Globe and Mail*, August 24, 2002, R8.

25 J. Hoberman, 'Nostalgia Trip,' *The Village Voice*, December 5, 2006, http://theen-velope.latimes.com/news/la-et-che1–2008nov01,0,4392866.story.

26 Peter Howell, 'Che: A Revolution is Not a Slumber Party,' *Toronto Star*, February 20, 2009, www.thestar.com/article/590412.

27 Solanas and Getino, 'Towards a Third Cinema,' 42.

28 Maslin, 'Schizopolis.'

29 Soderbergh, *Getting Away with It*, 46.

30 'Is *Che* This Year's *Southland Tales*?', *New York Magazine*, May 22, 2008, http://nymag.com/daily/entertainment/2008/05/is_che_this_years_southland_ta.html.

31 Todd McCarthy, 'Che,' *Variety*, May 21, 2008.

32 'Making Che.' *Che*. Supplementary DVD Material. 2008.

33 Ibid.

34 Quoted in Mark Olsen, 'Soderbergh Takes a Revolutionary Approach to 'Che,'' *LA Times*, October 31, 2008, http://theenvelope.latimes.com/news/la-et-che1–2008nov01,0,4392866.story.

35 'Making Che.'

36 Ibid.

37 Solanas and Getino, 'Towards a Third Cinema,' 49.

38 Gilles Deleuze and Félix Guattari, 'Kafka: Towards a Minor Literature,' trans. Dana Polan, in *Theory and History of Literature* 30 (Minneapolis: University of Minnesota Press, 1986).

39 Deleuze and Guattari, 'Kafka,' 17.

40 See Patricia White, 'Lesbian Minor Cinema,' *Screen* 49, no. 4 (2008): 410–25; Ka-Fai Yau, 'Cinema 3: Towards a "Minor Hong Kong Cinema,"' *Cultural Studies* 15, nos. 3+4 (2001): 543–63.

41 Since we're already borrowing post-colonial terminology, we will steal another, although we use the term in a far more literal sense than Naficy does in his seminal work. Hamid Naficy, *An Accented Cinema: Exilic and Diasporic Filmmaking* (Princeton: Princeton University Press, 2001).

42 Ivo Ritzer also makes this connection of Minor Literature to Kafka. For an in-depth analysis see Ivo Ritzer, 'Philosophical Reflections on Steven Soderbergh's Kafka' in *The Philosophy of Steven Soderbergh*, eds. R. Barton Palmer and Steven Sanders (Lexington, KY: University Press of Kentucky, 2011), 145–58.

43 To the point where Yaphet Kotto, the DEA agent that Wilson speaks to, says: 'There's one thing I don't understand. The thing I don't understand is every moth-erfuckin' word you're saying.'

44 Deleuze and Guattari, 'Kafka,' 17.

45 Ibid., 26.

46 Willeman, 'Third Cinema Question,' 231.

PART TWO

HISTORY, MEMORY, TEXT

CHAPTER FOUR

Searching Low and High: *The Limey and the Schizophrenic Detective*

Ann, you don't even know who I am. You don't have the slightest idea who I am. Am I supposed to recount all the points in my life leading up to this moment and just hope that it's coherent, that it makes some sort of sense to you? It doesn't make any sense to me. You know, I was there. I don't have the slightest idea who I am and I'm supposed to be able to explain it to you?

Graham, *sex, lies, and videotape*

Tell me. Tell me about Jenny.

Wilson, *The Limey*

Having so far examined authorship in three different auteur analyses, we now turn to closer textual analysis of Soderbergh's work by focusing on the central character and plot archetype that animates most of his films: the detective. Soderbergh uses the detective character outright in many films – the titular insurance worker in *Kafka*, the police detective in *Out of Sight*, the investigative lawyer in *Erin Brockovich*, the FBI team in *The Informant!*, the epidemiologist who searches for patient zero in *Contagion*, the spy in *Haywire* – while other films overtly employ the viewer as the detective to unravel the film's plot: the bank heist in *The Underneath*, the psychological confusion in *Schizopolis*, the increasingly elaborate heists in the *Ocean's* trilogy, the working-class whodunit in *Bubble*, the mental motivations of Spalding Gray in *And Everything Is Going Fine*, and the psychopharmacological mystery in *Side Effects*. This interplay between the various levels of detection – character, plot, viewer – in conjunction with the formal and stylistic method with which the films present this enigma, accounts for much of how Soderbergh structures his films.

The Limey, *Solaris*, and *The Good German* are emblematic of these concerns. All three of these films utilise the MacGuffin of a murder mystery to propel the plot forward into an intimate character study. In *The Limey*, both Wilson and the spec-

Other detectives in Soderbergh's films include: the title character in *Erin Brockovich* (Julia Roberts); Dr. Erin Mears (Kate Winslet) as one of many 'medical detectives' investigating and controlling the viral outbreak in *Contagion*, and Charles Whitacre's (Matt Damon) would-be spy in *The Informant!*.

tator are wed in their twin desires to solve the mystery of who killed his daughter Jenny and also to negotiate the film's postmodern, splintered narrative. In *Solaris*, the detective work depends on revisiting the site of Kelvin's trauma through psychoanalysis. Finally, *The Good German* binds the spectator to the protagonist Jake to decipher the intertextual codes and histories within the movie. With a Soderbergh detective film, one does not simply watch a suspenseful mystery unfold; one becomes implicated in the very problem at hand.

Soderbergh's film detectives follow the basic structure of the genre, but with several modifications. On top of solving a central mystery, these detectives must also negotiate their own symptoms that emerge over the course of these stories. They are, in Slavoj Žižek's view, the postmodern *noir* detectives as seen in films such as Alan Parker's *Angel Heart* (1987) and Ridley Scott's *Blade Runner* (1982).[1] According to Žižek, these detectives become progressively involved in the narrative to the point where they ultimately uncover their own central role within the case; the 'final outcome is that he himself was from the very beginning implicated in the object of his quest.'[2] In other words, Wilson, Kelvin, and Jake are all charged with the tasks of uncovering their own culpability or responsibility regarding an even bigger crime. Soderbergh's films doubly-code this passage, charging each detective to interpret 'symptomatic "clues" in order to 'reconstruct the "primal scene" of the crime.'[3] In effect, the detective performs the function of the psychoanalyst, as both are charged with uncovering sites of trauma, and the personal moment of crisis often uncovers a societal or collective trauma as well.

In the case of Wilson, his detective work involves reconciling the film's odd fusion of past and present. This means that Wilson needs to navigate through *The Limey*'s schizophrenic structure while attempting to achieve equilibrium by settling the score of his murdered daughter. Similarly, *Solaris* seems to have been designed specifically for the psychologist Kelvin's reconciliation of his own trauma, rather than the rumination of larger existential questions, as seen in Tarkovsky's original film. Finally, *The Good German* offers a stark re-visioning of history and the history of film. As the narrative reveals previously censored details of America's recruiting of ex-Nazi scientists for its rocket programme at the advent of the Cold War, it too revisits a 'primal scene' of historical trauma, presenting a candid look at the roots of current geopolitical trauma by uncovering the sins of the father, as it were.

In each case, the viewer is introduced to a violently destabilised diegetic world, wherein the detective is called upon to re-establish order. Thus, for Wilson, he must embrace that he is at the centre of the mystery and transform the film's fractured narrative into a linear pattern. For Kelvin, this means fully embracing his 'symptom,' in Žižek's terms, to the extent of repeating his wife's suicidal act and reconciling the trauma of her death. With Jake, Soderbergh achieves something much more subtle. Instead of leading us through the protagonist's subjective journey, Soderbergh presents us with the opportunity to objectively view the documents of history, as seen in the films of the 1940s, 1950s and beyond, and uses Jake as a tool not only for us to consider the historical details of the moment that these early films omitted, but why revisiting this particular moment through various intermedia is so important to our present understanding of history. These detective films do not just present mysteries for the detective, then, but also the viewer, who is charged with solving both the formal construct and the traumatic core.

Watching the Detectives

Many of Soderbergh's protagonists are seemingly untethered to a linear or teleological progression; they resemble Kurt Vonnegut's protagonist Billy Pilgrim from *Slaughterhouse-Five* – 'unstuck in time.'[4] More to the point, they follow the logic of the schizophrenic subject, either by way of their navigation through an increasingly fragmented world, or by the scars they bear of a schizophrenic consciousness. *Schizopolis*, with its multiple protagonists portrayed by the same actor (Soderbergh) is one such example; *The Informant!* presents another, wherein the protagonist Mark Whitacre 'has a mental illness that prevents him from assembling the pieces of his past into a coherent internal pattern.'[5]

Following Fredric Jameson, we might say that Soderbergh and his protagonists are trapped within the limitations of postmodern storytelling techniques. Correspondingly, a film like *The Limey* may be seen as an attempt to 'determine new types of syntax' as well as Soderbergh's effort to cope with the 'problem of the form' and the new 'spatial logic' of the contemporary subject.[6] These films reveal as much about our contemporary attitudes towards the past as they do about the present. Each features characters that find out that if they had only dealt properly with their trauma when it occurred, their realities, and ours, would be very different than they are today. This journey takes place on the level of narrative and form, complicating the generic traits of the detective film by fusing both of these issues together.[7]

After killing a warehouse full of thugs near the beginning of *The Limey*, Wilson screams 'tell him I'm fucking coming!' pushing the film into the second act and introducing the mystery of Jenny's death from Terry Valentine's perspective.

Just as Graham (James Spader) in *sex, lies, and videotape* struggles to understand the present impact of his past traumas, Soderbergh's protagonists move through their memories, battling with the ghosts that still haunt them. These characters question the validity of their own memories, trying to make sense of their lives and to heal old wounds. Often, these issues are presented via postmodern aesthetics that embody psychoanalytic and intertextual characteristics. Subjective flashbacks allow Soderbergh's characters to revisit and confront their traumatic moments. *The Underneath* features Soderbergh's first attempts to create a visual language that resembles the non-linear processes of memory. This film seamlessly shifts between past and present by using green and yellow hues to identify different memories and time periods, following the whims of the filmmaker. Soderbergh would later develop these experiments more coherently, commanding these thematic, cinematographic, and aesthetic characteristics most prominently in *The Limey, Solaris*, and *The Good German*.

These three films best represent Soderbergh's mediations on postmodern schizophrenic narratives, trauma, and intertextuality. They also present the director's ongoing efforts to represent the elusive logic of a character's thoughts onscreen. Soderbergh, his protagonists, and his audiences all seek the same thing – a lost object that contains the moment when it all went wrong, and the fantasy fulfillment of fixing earlier mistakes. Wilson, Kelvin, and Jake all get this opportunity, which stems from the recognition of their responsibility in each of these cases. It is only by way of their remembering correctly that they move on and heal themselves. For Žižek, engagement with trauma (whether personal or historical) is never a choice between 'remembering' or 'forgetting.' Rather, we revisit 'traumas that we are not ready or able to remember' for fear that they will 'haunt us all the more forcefully.' In order for us to 'really forget an event, we must summon up the strength to remember it properly.'[8] Seizing this opportunity, Soderbergh's narratives engage with a larger notion of historical memory which is set alongside previously repressed memories.

As historical films, *The Limey*, *Solaris*, and *The Good German* are bound together by the following stylistic and thematic traits. First, they are governed by an overwhelming awareness of narrative schizophrenia, expressed via pastiche and non-linearity. Second, each of these movies reflexively provides socio-historical commentary from a later point in history, and Soderbergh's attitude towards the past is filtered through his stylistic emulation of an earlier moment such as the Classical and New Hollywood eras, as well as the French New Wave. Third, Soderbergh's protagonists are charged with solving a mystery, whether these events are personally traumatic, or involve them in larger historical events, such as the Potsdam conference in *The Good German*. Finally, all of these works wrestle with the legacy of cinematic nostalgia. As movies they express an awareness of and a desire to appropriate a missing past, as well as a concerted effort to view, if not correct, the mistakes that took place in the past. Our analysis of *The Limey* will explore how the film embodies the two major traits of postmodernism – schizophrenia and nostalgia – and how these elements are both resolved by the use of the detective figure/function.

Temporal Schizophrenia

The Limey begins with a blistering montage of hundreds of shots and narrative fragments, taking us from Wilson's initial touchdown at LAX airport, to his motel room, through his initial encounter with Eduardo Roel (Luis Guzmán), to his purchase of a gun and bullets, and finally to the warehouse where he will get information surrounding his daughter's mysterious death. The narrative information is piled on with the appearance of each successive image. This sequence establishes that the film's temporally schizophrenic structure is tethered to a particular consciousness, and for Geoff King, shows us Soderbergh's 'understanding of the nature of human consciousness.'[9] R. Barton Palmer echoes this sentiment, stating that the 'editing patterns of the film… reflect the double movement of consciousness' that is an 'accumulation process' of 'recollection images … increasingly enriched by introspection.'[10] The goal of the film, it would seem, is to untangle this fractured narrative and to restore linearity at the end.

In this way, the narrative logic of the sequence follows Soderbergh's earlier experiments in *The Underneath*, where each temporality within the film is coded with its own colour. Soderbergh deliberately uses art film narration in *The Limey* to re-code the typical narrative of the detective film. As we will explore further in chapter seven, the crime film has often been the site of Hollywood's absorption of art cinema's techniques. Viewed in this light, *The Limey*'s opening sequence provides us with some cues not only to the form of the film itself, but how the narrative will be staged. Foremost, it is the utterance of a voice (who we learn to be Wilson some moments later) against the black background that cues us as to what the narrative will investigate: 'Tell me about Jenny.' A simple request that will require a complex formal structure and character study to unravel.

The Limey is Soderbergh's first film to successfully employ all of the aesthetic and narrative features that he had been developing up until this point in his career, allowing him the 'opportunity to try out ideas that occurred to [him] during previous [*sic.*] film

The Limey begins with a blistering montage of hundreds of shots and narrative fragments, establishing that the film's temporally schizophrenic structure is tethered to Wilson's memories and recollections.

Out Of Sight, but that [he] couldn't find a place for.'[11] Wilson's thinking follows its own patterns rather than the standard narrative trajectories of Classical Hollywood; it meanders, it lingers on other events of the past, it imagines, it projects backwards and forwards. In short, it is a schizophrenic narrative, as suggested by Jameson's description of postmodern subjectivity. In an oft-cited passage, worth recalling, Jameson notes the increasingly 'schizophrenic' structure of the postmodern era, particularly related to public and private histories, which convey

> ...a new depthlessness, which finds its prolongation both in contemporary 'theory' and in a whole new culture of the image or the simulacrum: a consequent weakening of historicity, both in our relationship to a public History and in the new forms of our private temporality, whose 'schizophrenic' structure (following Lacan) will determine new types of syntax or syntagmatic relationships in the more temporal arts...[12]

The Limey is a curious beast under this rubric, as it certainly exhibits a schizophrenic structure, yet is wholly consumed with its relationship to history. It is worth returning to Ramírez-Berg's alternative narrative structures to look beyond this traditional 'post-modern' explanation for these effects, with factors that point to the 'schizophrenic':

> Outside of the world of film, many possible contributory factors might have helped to shape this surging trend in unconventional narration: the frag-menting 'postmodern' condition and its revolt against master narratives, the ubiquity of shorter narrative media forms such as music videos; video games… the branched experience of surfing the net; and hypertext linking that might include text, image, video and sound.[13]

As products of a 'schizophrenic' age that has excelled far beyond Jameson's now two decade old prescription, the emphasis on fragmented, non-linear editing, particularly in *The Limey*, seemingly embodies Jameson's warning of 'depthlessness' in its surface-traveling form, yet also communicates something about this very schizophrenic depth-lessness.

Questioning this schizophrenia, Soderbergh adopts the detective genre in order to doubly-infuse the film with narrative and formal questions. On the one hand, the spectator is invested in the 'whodunnit' element of the story, but with the emergence of more complex storytelling structures, the viewer is similarly interested in 'how' the story is going to be told. The complex, schizophrenic story structure is as mysterious and perplexing as the main thrust of the narrative. *The Limey* presents us with two parallel sets of questions from the outset. Who is Wilson? What is he doing in America? How many different time frames are recalled? How do we differentiate between them? Why is the narrative structured the way it is?

The film's excessive subjectivity provides our first cue, as we realise that we are tethered, for better or worse, to Wilson's recollections. Though we do not know where or when they are taking place, we soon understand that part of the detective story is bound to the film's narration, and the other is tied to the narrative operations. The haunting voice-over set against the black screen that begins the film cuts to a rack focus shot of LAX, and the soundtrack plays 'The Seeker' by the Who ('They call me The Seeker / I've been searching low and high / I won't get to get what I'm after / Till the day I die'). As a haggard Terence Stamp steps into focus, the sound and picture combine to announce that Wilson is the detective, the seeker, and the protagonist in the movie. We are presented with a traditional detective tale, one of the most standard Hollywood tropes, yet we are also presented with some unconventional elements that we cannot initially understand. Wilson's 'Tell me about Jenny' is actually from the film's climax, rather than the beginning, and the rushing of ocean waves heard on the soundtrack are also flashing forward to the final scene of the film, unbeknownst to the viewer.

The fundamental characteristic of the detective film is the interplay between story and plot information, as elements of the crime plot are withheld from the viewer in order to create mystery and suspense. In the case of *The Limey*, the dual structure of Wilson's investigation is compounded by its non-linear structure, and so the viewer's investment is not only *how* the story is formally assembled and reassembled, but also *where* and *when*. Multiple, staggered narrative ellipses dictate the film's formal, schizo-phrenic logic. When the mystery is finally 'solved' at the end of the film, the viewer discovers that the film has been an extended flashback, stretching back over some forty years' worth of unstable memories. Moreover, the mystery roots the story back to a 'primal scene' of history, presenting the viewer with a point where if only Wilson had decided differently, his daughter might still be alive.

The formal construction of *The Limey* offers viewers several additional problems, especially in the film's opening moments, which present a series of radically different spaces and times. Edward Branigan's 'Levels of Narration' explains how this works, describing how it is possible for a film to present different levels of authorship within these various levels.[14] In the case of this film, the multiple narrators range from studio authorship (Artisan Entertainment as proprietor), Steven Soderbergh's authorial presence, a quasi-omniscient narrator within the film, and Wilson, whose subjective, unreliable recollections dictate the substantial logic of the film. Not only are there differences between the authorial presence of Soderbergh and Wilson, the narrator within the diegesis, there are also subjective, internal focalisations, such as those that occur within Wilson's projected memories, which compete for dominance within the film.

Wilson's levels of narration shift between 'objectivity' and 'uncertainty,' reflecting the viewer's own confusion as to where (and when) the narration is coming from. Branigan's framework allows us to view and analyse narrative issues in *The Limey* which are 'alternated, overlapped,' or 'otherwise mixed, producing complex descriptions of space, time, and causality.'[15] This explains the various ways that a character can present an objectively rendered recollection of events without relying solely on traditional point-of-view shots. In the film, this onscreen effect is similar to a novelist's first-person narrator, who was there at one point, but may have a different recollection of the events as they are being written. Soderbergh's modification takes 'objectivity' and 'uncertainty' a step further, by presenting many competing temporalities and sound bridges within scenes and destabilising the spectator's assurance as to when and where they are occurring. The film pushes at the boundaries of just how much manipulation these levels of narration can bare:

> The text must, to a greater or lesser degree, inscribe – make explicit and defi-nite – its own spatial, temporal and causal coordinates for at least *some* of its levels of narration. This enables the spectator to judge how knowledge may be acquired by a 'person': an author, narrator, character, or observer, and ulti-mately the spectator himself or herself.[16]

The oscillations between Soderbergh, Wilson, narrator, and viewer are key to the way *The Limey* functions; the (con)fusion between each of these figures underscores the film's fragmented, schizophrenic logic.

Soderbergh goes to great lengths to show Wilson thinking in his respective locales. Though it is not immediately recognisable where he is and what he is thinking about, these shots cue the viewer to the introspective nature of the text, drawing the spectator into the formal mystery of the film's narrative schema. These various shots of an inert Wilson also demonstrate his changing attitude within the unfolding narrative, as sometimes the shots of him on the plane show him smiling, or images of him in the hotel show him resolute. Following this logic, these inserts of Wilson (when it is revealed that he is leaving LA rather than travelling to it) serve the same function as the overt voiceover narration that marks detective films like *Double Indemnity* (Billy Wilder, 1944). Using *Citizen Kane* as another precedent for this kind of flashback structure, Branigan suggests that the attitude of the flashback's narrator brings his own unique perspective to the events that are being depicted, and this is precisely what occurs in *The Limey*.[17] The unfolding narrative in *The Limey* can be both simultaneously objective and personal, possessing the reminiscent qualities of Wilson's narration (as the implied author) while still objectively showing his travels within the film. As a result, the film's narrational flashback structure allows the viewer '"objective" glimpses of the events upon which the recollection is based but mixed with the character's desires and fears,' what Branigan calls 'free indirect discourse.'[18]

Only at this later vantage point can we see that the narrative moves between Wilson's subjective recollections and the normal work of the diegetic narrator, who presents certain details of the narrative that Wilson is not privileged to. One example of this action is the entire Terry Valentine plot, where the character is privileged with his own aesthetic and cinematographic style, existing wholly apart from Wilson's perceptions of the investigation story. Because Valentine's plot is rendered objectively, it must be the work of the diegetic narrator, along with some authorial flourishes from Soderbergh. As the narrative unfolds, the plot's resolution will come when these disparate narrative strategies intersect.

The aesthetics of this narrative strategy also suggest that Soderbergh has an even more sophisticated version of memory in store for his spectator, particularly as it is controlled by Wilson's stream-of-consciousness and memories. Correspondingly, the viewer is privy to flashbacks, flash forwards and projected renditions of reality, as imagined by Wilson. Occasionally, this pattern conforms to the Classical Hollywood style, where Wilson's glance-object-cut moves to the name on the envelope that he holds. Soderbergh then takes this subjectivity to a new level, as Wilson free-associates the name Eduardo Roel to their initial meeting. Even more complicated are Wilson's projected memories that accompany Roel's narration. When Eduardo (Luis Guzmán) says, 'I felt like she was watching my back,' the accompanying visuals show an image of Jenny, rendered in extremely 'flared,' bluish, handheld cinematographic style, arguing with some thugs in a warehouse. This is an 'impossible' shot insofar as we are unable to ascribe it to the POV of any character within the film, as its portrayal as a memory would indicate. Also, it is soundlessly rendered as a medium close-up of Jenny and Eduardo, making it even more difficult for a particular character to own. This effect also occurs in Wilson's projection backwards to a young Jenny on the beach as well as to the image of a burning car in the film. In each of these instances, it is impossible to tell where the narrative information is coming from, particularly within the destabilising and confusing opening moments of the film. In each of these short shots, the aesthetic is messy and stained, and the images are overwhelmed by an excess of natural light that fills the camera. These images follow a decisive visual style and pattern, differentiating them from other sequences, but not until the final scene is the reason given for such a discrepancy. Appropriately, considering the prominence of recollection for both the narrative and the protagonist, the film's formal and aesthetic meaning does not fully resonate until you watch it a second time.

Wrestling with Nostalgia

> Did you ever dream about a place you never really recall being to before? A place that maybe only exists in your imagination? Some place far away, half remembered when you wake up. When you were there, though, you knew the language. You knew your way around. That was the Sixties. [pause] No. It wasn't that either. It was just '66 and early '67. That's all there was.
>
> Terry Valentine, *The Limey*

Terry Valentine's evocation of a 'half-remembered' place 'that only exists in your imagination' prompts our examination of the film's overwhelming tone of nostalgia. A central trait of postmodernism, we should recall that nostalgia is the 'chief symptom of a society that has forgotten how to think historically,'[19] and that a significant portion of this film is devoted to reconciling the past in the present. As opposed to many other nostalgia films, which set their films in the actual past, this film is unique insofar as it grapples with the legacy of the past from the perspective of the present, while also integrating moments of history. This film is an unconventional rendition of the Freudian 'return of the repressed,' pitting two international movie icons, Terence Stamp and Peter Fonda, against one another, and exploiting their association with important moments of 1960s' film history to negotiate the legacy of the 1960s in the present day. In Soderbergh's words, it is thus a 'simple revenge film with a lot of '60s' baggage.'[20] If only it were that simple. Instead, Soderbergh presents two 1960s icons, 'Captain America vs. Billy Budd,' who are not only *doppelgängers* of sorts, but also literally wrestle at the film's climax in a battle between 'bad guy and worse guy.'[21] In effect, the legacy of the 1960s and its failure to live up to its utopian politics is rendered bare.

In a variety of ways – thematic, aesthetic, political, industrial – Soderbergh has sought to recapture the late 1960s' and early 1970s' era of Hollywood filmmaking, relaying the shifting styles, histories, and sights of that era, yet careful to avoid the excesses of the period. The projection of loss has less to do with a particular worldview or ideology as it does with a missing locality, a fixed space that was unequivocally 'national' and stood apart from the multinational chains and globalised franchises that saturate contemporary America. Thus, these films truly express the urgency of nostalgia's original definition – a painful psychological and physiological condition attributed to a person's 'missing homeland' and their irrepressible desire (not to mention their inability) to return there.[22] According to Jameson, directors in the postmodern era 'have nowhere to turn but to the past' which expresses itself through 'the imitations of dead styles, speech through all the masks and voices stored up in an imaginary museum of a now global culture.'[23] The 'nostalgia film' is the chief object of this phenomenon, as it 'restructure[s] the whole issue of pastiche and project[s] it onto a collective and social level.' *The Limey*'s references and allusions, then, might be seen as a 'desperate attempt to appropriate a missing past,' which is now 'the emergent ideology of a generation.'[24]

In the intervening years of Jameson's writing, this 'emergent ideology' has certainly established itself, and pastiche is an increasingly central component of cultural logic. However, having largely come to terms with the inherent intertextuality of art and the creative possibilities of rewriting, remixing, and reconstituting, contemporary critics and audiences are now much more prepared to accept pastiche not just as mere imitation, but as a practice in and of itself. Often, we evaluate and enjoy based on the skill of such imitation. Soderbergh is a fitting example; Michael Valdez Moses accounts for his 'originality' as consisting of

> recycling, reiterating, repeating, and remaking the works of his cinematic predecessors… Soderbergh can metaphorically be said to channel the voices of the dead (those of his predecessors); he first absorbs and then entirely refashions their cinematic visions until he can claim them as his own.[25]

King echoes this idea of a skillful intertextuality when he notes the significance of concluding *The Limey* with a scene from another film (*Poor Cow*); the integration of the protagonist's nostalgia with the director's expresses a 'kind of second-order nostalgia that seems a fitting note on which for Soderbergh to finish.'[26] At this second level, nostalgia becomes something much more than just wistful desire.

Just as the film is not merely an embodiment of schizophrenia but speaks *through* it, and concerning it, *The Limey* is a nostalgia film that speaks through and concerning the language of nostalgia. The film exhibits a certain reverence for the era it emulates, certainly, but there is also a mournful tone undercutting the outright nostalgia. In the evocative Cliff Martinez score, in the sad state of its older male characters, in the ironic juxtapositions of its 1960s' popular music selections – this is not mere homage. Valentine in particular plays a pivotal role in this critical nostalgia. Ostensibly the antagonist of the narrative, Valentine is afforded many of the same sort of narrative and cinematographic embellishments that Wilson is afforded within the film, albeit in a slightly different fashion. Similar to Wilson's introduction, which utilises a sound bridge, Wilson yelling 'Tell him I'm fucking coming!' cuts abruptly to Valentine's question: 'tell *who* I'm coming?' Valentine is then privileged with a parallel montage to Wilson's. The scene begins with a long shot of a young woman in a bathing suit as she walks through an extremely bright Hollywood Hills mansion. The camera pans in order to follow her as she walks to the pool past Valentine's many framed gold records. As she dives in, the camera finds Valentine, who is speaking softly on his cordless phone. Throughout the visual imagery, the soft strumming of a guitar has been building: the Hollies' 'King Midas in Reverse.' Suddenly, and seemingly without motivation, the film devotes itself to images of Valentine edited to the rushing pattern of the music. The viewer is presented with a montage of Valentine's image on a billboard, Valentine driving an expensive car along the coast, Valentine flossing his teeth, and Valentine speaking to his very young new girlfriend: 'He's King Midas with a curse /

Ostensibly the antagonist of the narrative, Valentine is afforded many of the same sort of narrative and cinematographic embellishments that Wilson is afforded within the film, including a parallel montage.

he's King Midas in reverse.' Unbeknownst to the viewer, many of the shots come from later moments in the film, impossibly condensed within the chorus of the song, and relaying a great deal of narrative information.

The sequence evokes a parallel narrative, not only linking Valentine to Wilson by introducing them both with music from the 1960s – and that both of their occupations exploited the music business (Valentine was a 'promoter,' Wilson was imprisoned for stealing receipts from a Pink Floyd concert) – but fusing them together by way of their 'past-ness.' Fonda is as iconic as Stamp, particularly considering his role of 'Captain America' in *Easy Rider*, referenced in a later scene when Valentine drives up the coast to the sounds of Steppenwolf, evoking a decidedly nostalgic use of his image. Valentine becomes less of an antagonist, in the traditional sense, than a sub-protagonist who is privileged with his own set of narrative, aesthetic, and montage tropes. That Wilson will eventually see himself in the visage of Valentine's betrayal and realise his complicity in his daughter's death, while wrestling with his double on the beach, completes the parallel. A final, doubly intertextual insert twists the nostalgia: the clip from *Poor Cow* shows a young Terence Stamp quietly strumming on a guitar, singing Donovan's song 'Colours.' Wilson had actually been humming the tune throughout the film, but only at the end of the film, by way of a different film, do we comprehend its meaning: the lyrics are 'reminds me of the time / of the time / when I was loved.' The various aesthetic, narrative, performative, and intertextual uses of nostalgia are wed together in an uncomfortable, unsettling union.[27]

Ultimately, the ending of *The Limey* suggests the possibility of being able to navigate out of our present-day historical crisis. By employing the postmodern detective story, Soderbergh offers several uniquely rendered solutions to the problems of the narrative. What begins as a straightforward revenge story slowly emerges as a tale of self-reflection, reconciliation, and friendship. The open-ended montage at the end of the film suggests several other possibilities for the postmodern detective, provided that he acknowledges his central role at the core of the film's problem. When Wilson finally confronts Valentine, he realises that it was his initial past performing petty crimes, and Jenny's reaction to finding out her father's secret, that caused Valentine to believe she would turn him in, leading to her accidental death. At that point, the film shifts gears, becomes more contemplative, and rather than exact his revenge, Wilson is shown saying goodbye to his new friends and returning home to England. The Donovan song takes this unity a step further, describing Stamp's reminder of the time that he 'was loved' and evoking a parallel universe where if he had only done the proper thing in the first place, Jenny would have been saved the fate she encounters at the hands of Valentine. In this sense, the film not only embraces the qualities of schizophrenia and nostalgia in order to interrogate their function, it also subverts one of the great guilty pleasures of Hollywood, and its audience: revenge.

Notes

1   Slavoj Žižek, 'The Thing that Thinks: The Kantian Background of the *Noir Subject'*, in *Shades of Noir: A Reader*, ed. Joan Copjec, (London: Verso, 1993), 199–226.
2   Ibid., 200.
3   Ibid., 222.
4   Kurt Vonnegut, *Slaughterhouse-Five; or, The Children's Crusade, a Duty-Dance with Death* (New York: Delacorte Press, 1969), 1.
5   David Sterritt, 'Schizoanalyzing the Informant,' in *The Philosophy of Steven Soderbergh*, eds. R. Barton Palmer and Steven Sanders (Lexington, KY: University Press of Kentucky, 2011), 213.
6   Fredric Jameson, *Postmodernism, or, the Cultural Logic of Late Capitalism* (Durham: Duke University Press, 1991), 25.
7   For an outline of the detective film form, see David Bordwell, *Narration in the Fiction Film* (Madison, WI: University of Wisconsin Press, 1985).
8   Slavoj Žižek, *Desert of the Real!*, 22.
9   Geoff King, 'Consciousness, Temporality, and the Crime-Revenge Genre in *The Limey'*, in *The Philosophy of Steven Soderbergh*, eds. Palmer, R. Barton and Steven Sanders (Lexington, KY: University Press of Kentucky, 2011), 95.
10 R. Barton Palmer, 'Resnais Meets Film Noir,' 71.
11 Soderbergh quoted in Ann Hornaday, 'Stamp of Approval,' *Sunday Herald*, October 31, 1999.
12 Jameson, *Postmodernism*, 6.
13 Ramírez-Berg, 'Tarantino Effect,' 6.
14 Edward Branigan, *Narrative Comprehension and Film* (London: Routledge, 1992).
15 Ibid., 161.
16 Ibid., 172.

17 Additionally, Branigan states that flashbacks can contain more than one voice controlling the attitude of the scene, or rather, that 'Thatcher's flashback represents at least an implied authors view of the reporter Thompson's view of Thatcher's view of Kane.' Ibid., 173.

18 Ibid.

19 Jameson, *Postmodernism*, 1.

20 Soderbergh quoted in Scott Kelton Jones, 'Straight Man: Joking Around, or Not, with *Limey* Director Steven Soderbergh,' in *Steven Soderbergh: Interviews* (Jackson: University Press of Mississippi, 2002), 122.

21 Ibid.

22 See Linda Hutcheon, 'Irony, Nostalgia and the Postmodern,' Accessed May 12, 2009. http://www.library.utoronto.ca/utel/criticism/hutchinp.html; and Svetlana Boym, *The Future of Nostalgia* (New York: Basic Books, 2001). Hutcheon argues about the relationship between postmodernism and nostalgia, explaining how it is nostalgia (rather than irony) that has come to be understood as characteristic of the era. She makes the important distinction between the etymology of the term (a physiological condition demarcating separation from a missing homeland) while applying it to contemporary (postmodern) situations. Boym offers a retrospective on the issue of nostalgia taken from the perspective of the post-Soviet sphere. She offers a counter to Fukuyama's 'End of History' writings by arguing for the existence of n*ostalgie*, or for communism in the post-communist world.

23 Jameson, *Postmodernism*, 17–18.

24 Ibid., 19.

25 Michael Valdez Moses, '*Solaris,* Cinema, and Simulacra,' in *The Philosophy of Steven Soderbergh*, ed. R. Barton Palmer and Steven Sanders (Lexington, KY: University Press of Kentucky, 2011), 283.

26 King, 'Consciousness, Temporality, and the Crime-Revenge Genre,' 104.

27 In an interesting display of what might be dubbed 'meta-meta' filmmaking, Soderbergh and Dobbs are seemingly paying homage to their own earlier collaboration, when they quote *The Limey* in *Haywire*, which share many similar qualities, including a dark confrontation in a hilltop manor and a final beach fight where the antagonists both twist their ankles within rocks.

CHAPTER FIVE

Returning to the Scene of the Crime: Solaris and the Psychoanalytic Detective

Earth. Even the word sounded strange to me now… unfamiliar. How long had I been gone? How long had I been back? Did it matter? I tried to find the rhythm of the world where I used to live. I followed the current. I was silent, attentive, I made a conscious effort to smile, nod, stand, and perform the millions of gestures that constitute life on Earth. I studied these gestures until they became reflexes again. But I was haunted by the idea that I remembered her wrong, and somehow I was wrong about everything.

Chris Kelvin, Solaris

Having considered how *The Limey* absorbs and aestheticises the operations of history and memory within its formal and narrative structure, and how the process of 'remembering correctly' functions within Soderbergh's conception of schizophrenia and nostalgia, we can continue our exploration of the role of the detective in Soderbergh's oeuvre. *Solaris* takes the process of memory details and negotiation of personal histories one step further, not only immersing the spectator in the character's memories, but allowing the characters to actually interact directly with these recollections, as a result of the planet Solaris's psychological effects on the inhabitants of the orbiting space station. In effect, both the protagonist and the viewer are required to return to the scene of the psychoanalytic crime.

Soderbergh's *Solaris* differs from Tarkovsky's film (1972) as well as the original science fiction novel by Stanislaw Lem (1961), on account of its mostly psychological narrative and its expression of three separate but interrelated traumas. The first of these is on the level of character, as the protagonist Kelvin must come to terms with his wife's suicide by delving deeply into his own complicity with this traumatic act, a narrative arc emphasised by formal and stylistic embellishments. The second is Soderbergh's artistic trauma as he copes with the fact of his 'belatedness' and his personal engagement with a larger canon of film history, particularly as he seeks to 'remake' one of the classics of art cinema, while folding in the influence of another, Stanley Kubrick's *2001: A Space Odyssey* (1968). The third is a negotiation of a much larger, societal trauma, a result of the production of *Solaris* and a release in the wake of the events of 9/11, one of the first films dealing with loss and reconciliation in the uncertain years following the attack on the World Trade Center. Thus, the mournful tones, gloomy palette, and various narratives of loss in *Solaris* are woven together into a complex tapestry of trauma, one that both the detective and the viewer are charged with unravelling.

Temporal and Psychological Trauma

The protagonist of *Solaris* is a psychologist, which foregrounds the narrative's concern with the unconscious and prompts the viewer and critic to a psychoanalytic reading of the film. The patient who is subjected to an intense traumatic event, as formulated by Freud and others, bears damage to their psyche and is doomed to repeat the repressed symptoms that erupt unexpectedly in everyday life. Kelvin is initially presented as an empty shell of a man, clearly having undergone something so traumatic that it has shattered his psyche. The narrative arc of the film will thus trace Kelvin's therapeutic journey, tied to the science fiction mystery of the planet Solaris. Ultimately, the resolution of Kelvin's issues and the solving of the Solaris mystery amount to the same thing. Thus, Kelvin functions as both detective and psychologist for the viewer by

presenting two interrelated questions. In his role as the former, we seek to understand what is going on in the space station orbiting Solaris, and in the case of the latter, we seek to understand how Kelvin's psyche will be affected by the planet's unique powers.

Like *The Limey* before it, the film opens with a voice whispering over a black screen. As it speaks – 'Chris, what's wrong, don't you love me anymore?' – there is a slow fade-in to Kelvin going through the motions of his present-day life, establishing the terms of his haunted, everyday reality. Several short scenes show Kelvin running therapy sessions, listening half-heartedly to conversations, travelling absent-mindedly on subway trains, and making lonely dinners for himself in his bare, futuristic

In *Solaris*, all of the scenes on Earth are rendered in gloomy sepia tones, while the rain which accompanies all of his actions reflects Kelvin's (George Clooney) bleak outlook.

home. Fittingly, all of the scenes on Earth are rendered in gloomy sepia tones, and the rain which accompanies all of his actions reflects Kelvin's bleak outlook. Shot after shot shows Kelvin's lonely existence on Earth, revealing that he is obviously living through trauma, but does not reveal why. The opening sequence thus punctuates the apparent meaninglessness and abstraction that Chris is feeling on Earth.

The film's first incitement to action occurs when a military officer interrupts Kelvin's dinner, claiming that Kelvin is uniquely qualified to explain the strange phenomena that are occurring near the planet Solaris. According to a video message from his friend Gibarian (Ulrich Tukur), Kelvin 'needs' to come to the space station Prometheus, because the planet will 'help' Kelvin, if only he gives himself over to its power. Kelvin quickly boards a space flight and is seen docking with the station, a sequence featuring some astonishing special effects. Kelvin arrives to discover that there are even deeper mysteries occurring on the vessel. His friend Gibarian has committed suicide and the doctor in charge, Gordon (Viola Davis), has locked herself in her cabin. The only reasonable person on board seems to be the computer engineer, Snow, (Jeremy Davies) who cryptically claims that 'I could tell you what's happening, but I don't know if it would really tell you what's happening.'

Already a hybrid of the science-fiction and detective genres, the film then proceeds to enter the realm of the 'fantastic,' presenting a haunted world which has one foot in reality and another in fantasy. There is also the element of the uncanny, or Freud's *Das Unheimliche*,' which involves a paradoxical encounter with that which is both familiar and foreign. The planet Solaris appears to have the ability to read the dreams of its visitors and project them in their waking life, reproducing painfully real facsimiles of departed loved ones. The characters thus interact with their Freudian symptoms, a literal 'return of the repressed.' This is one of the more horrific aspects of the film, as the various ghosts exhibit unhealthy, obsessive attachments to their subjects, which in Gibarian's case, eventually drives him to suicide. True to Tzvetan Todorov's characterisation of the fantastic, it is never clear to the characters or the viewer whether these apparitions are real or imagined, though the traumatic effect of their occurrence is very much real.[1]

When Kelvin sleeps for the first time on the space station, he dreams of the day he first met his wife Rheya, now dead, thus revealing the object of his trauma. Evocative ambient tones fill the screen, and Kelvin's sleeping face is juxtaposed against the shimmering planet. Kelvin flashes back to a familiar train car, catching the eye of a woman who is holding a door knob in the seat across from him. Later that evening, meeting by chance at a formal event, they smile at each other in shared amusement as they recognise the strange coincidence. As he approaches her, she says, 'Don't blow it,' and their dialogue overlaps shots of the pair getting into an elevator and then going in to Kelvin's apartment. Curiously, this memory blurs into a dream, and as the action crescendos to a kiss, Kelvin imagines that Rheya is also present in the cabin of the space station. Their lovemaking wraps around the recollection already in progress, which is skilfully cut together using match-on-action cuts as their bodies move together. When the music fades out and the omnipresent hum of the space station fades in, Kelvin awakes from these vivid dreams as a hand crawls over his shoulder, pulling him towards it. Impossibly, a third version of Rheya is present. Horrified, Kelvin slaps himself repeat-

Using skillful editing, Soderbergh presents several timelines; here we see shots from a flashback to the days Kelvin first met and courted his wife, as well as her present-tense reappearance on the space station.

edly while shouting, 'how are you here?'

This elongated passage sets up the psychoanalytic narrative as well as establishing the rules that govern the film, defining the intrinsic structure of the plot which shifts between dreams, memories, and Kelvin's symptoms in the present-tense of the story. Ultimately, the *planet* acts as Kelvin's psychoanalyst. As he lies on a bed that resembles the analyst's couch, the film's shot/reverse-shot patterns between Clooney's face and the planet puts these images in dialogue with one another, and sets up the analyst's study of his dreams. Like a psychotherapist, the planet draws out traumatic material through dream work and associational imagery, then literally conjures up Kelvin's symptoms for him to interact with. Thus, Solaris and Kelvin work together in order that he can face Rheya's centrality in his trauma, relive his past, and remember it correctly.

At the heart of Kelvin's trauma lies the realisation that he was responsible for a chain of events that ended both his relationship with Rheya and her life. As the flashbacks gradually reveal, Kelvin's mistake was projecting on to Rheya who he thought she was, rather than recognising her manic-depressive personality, marked by extreme highs and lows. Likewise, Rheya's misrecognition of Kelvin's personality – her belief that his atheism and the prospect of fatherhood were oppositional concepts for him – led her to mistakenly believe that Kelvin would want her to abort their baby, from which Rheya never recovers. Fittingly, the key scene here provides us with the image of a doorknob and a symbol plucked from Kelvin's subconscious to decipher as a psychotherapist would in dream analysis. Rheya's doorknob can be seen as the *objet fixé* that Kelvin misunderstood as the essence of her personality.[2] The decline of their relationship is a result of Kelvin's inability to understand, or 'enter into' Rheya's true essence – her manic-depressive personality – married to his mistaken belief that he can 'fix' her. In effect, Kelvin 'blows it' from the very beginning.

Kelvin's crime, then, was not only that he remembered Rheya incorrectly, but in a way, never really knew her in the first place. When he later declares that he was 'wrong about everything,' it implies that what initially attracted him to her was that she satisfied his projected needs, but that who she was and who he thought she was turned out to be entirely separate things. This important line not only reveals Kelvin's eventual realisations, but defines the subjective nature of his haunting by Rheya on the space station. In other words, unless Kelvin can fix his flawed memories of her, Rheya is doomed to repeat her suicidal behaviour as he is equally doomed to witness it. The audience, Kelvin, and Rheya become increasingly aware of the true circumstances behind these traumatic events. These flashbacks resemble appointments to the therapist as each are prompted by shot/reverse-shot patterning, in which Kelvin encounters his repression through repetition, eventually resulting in the release of his symptoms. Each flashback pushes Kelvin and the viewer closer to the root of his trauma.

When the film finally catches up to this central event – the revelation that Rheya's depression caused her to misunderstand Kelvin's intentions, leading to an abortion and a suicide – Kelvin returns to the scene after clearing his head, discovers her body, and internalises the traumatic event. This moment is played out through some very intricate editing, presenting a series of shots from different temporalities that fuse Rheya's memories with Kelvin's as she becomes privy to information that had previously been withheld from her and the audience. When Kelvin says, 'I came back for you. I came back that day. I'm sorry,' both sets of viewers realise that if only Rheya had waited, Kelvin could have saved her life. The 'just a moment too late' of this situation is the staple of melodrama, but the psychological trauma also reverberates. Rheya asks whether she is really herself, and in this moment he replies, 'all I see is you.' The effectiveness of the scene is a result of Kelvin and the viewer's shared realisation that the facsimile of Rheya is doomed to repeat her suicidal tendencies on the ship *because* Kelvin has remembered her that way. As a result, Kelvin is forced to come to terms with his memories, coloured as they are by his sense of loss, and find a way to perceive Rheya differently. In Dominick La Capra's terms, Kelvin must 'act out'[3] the events of the trauma through 'performativity.'[4]

Compounding the revelation and negotiation of this trauma, the film presents the viewer with an ambiguous ending that can be interpreted in various ways. The climax of the film occurs when Rheya stops acting like Kelvin's ideal, and more like the suicidal woman that he remembered her being. After several failed attempts to kill herself, she convinces Gordon to vapourise her using a portion of the space station's power, leading to the station's free fall into the planet. In the film's penultimate sequence, Kelvin decides to repeat Rheya's suicidal gesture, remaining on the station to meet with his demise. His reconciliation of his traumas means identifying himself fully with Rheya's impulses in addition to recognising and embracing her 'true' suicidal and depressive tendencies. Solaris the psychoanalyst allows Kelvin the opportunity to confront his moment of trauma and to re-imagine his constructed version of Rheya through his new experiences with her and, most importantly, to repeat her suicidal gesture. The paradox here is that only by re-enacting her suicidal gesture (i.e. sacrificing himself) can he actually resolve his traumatic issues. Thus, he moves finally from the side of the subject to the side of the object, and realises that Rheya's final (suicidal) sacrifice is also an invitation in itself.

In addition to this psychoanalytic interpretation, the realm of modernist science fiction writing offers another perspective, particularly with the fixture of sci-fi that

Brooks Landon calls the 'conceptual breakthrough.' According to Landon, this ending is characterised as the 'challenging and overthrowing of an established paradigm,' suddenly offering the audience 'a radically new way of thinking.'[5] In *Solaris*, the viewer is suddenly led to believe that the reality that Kelvin enters at the end of the film is one that his sacrificial act has produced. The conceptual breakthrough thus occurs at three levels: first, it is experienced by the characters; second, it is expected of the audience to participate and come up with their own explanation for the events happening; third, the ending comes up with a final, scientific and rational explanation, which refuses the mundane and produces an entirely new outcome for the narrative.

Similar to *The Planet of the Apes* (Franklin J. Schaffner, 1968), in which Charlton Heston's character Taylor discovers the ruins of the Statue of Liberty and realises that he was on Earth all along, *Solaris* presents a narrative revision in which Kelvin discovers in flashback that he stayed on the space station, and despite having ostensibly returned home, it is clear that he remains on the planet. The film depicts this conceptual breakthrough as Kelvin seemingly returns to the routine of his mundane life, in a scene which mirrors the opening montage. But Soderbergh's version is much more subtle than Tarkovsky's closed, unambiguous ending. Instead of zooming out to reveal that Kelvin is on the planet (as in the original film, where Tarkovsky actually shows a small house on the planet), the conceptual breakthrough here is that Earth, as Kelvin remembered it, has been reproduced entirely, and that not only is Rheya there, but he has seemingly inherited her regenerative powers. Cutting his finger again, as in the film's first scene, he watches it heal before his eyes. This is the moment that Kelvin experiences the conceptual breakthrough, followed by the audience who must put together the pieces, to arrive at the final, rational resolution: Kelvin has remained on Solaris.

This ambiguous about-face at the end may account for the ambivalent reaction to the movie's final ending, as it is not clear whether Kelvin and Rheya's reunion is a good or a bad thing. Rheya's unnerving stare directly at the camera at the film's ending evokes the final scene of Hitchcock's *Psycho* (1960), where Norman Bates's seemingly innocuous incarceration actually leads to an even more unsettling ending; rather than having to 'act out' as Mother Bates, he has identified even more fully with her and absorbed her into his psyche. Similarly, in *Solaris*, we are either witnessing Kelvin's final moments within his own dream/consciousness, where he has been afforded certain powers (as exhibited by his healing knife wounds), or his consciousness has fused with the planet (or whatever other interpretation you prefer), but it is left to the audience to decide the cost of choosing to stay in this dream-state rather than returning to Earth, and whether living in the perpetual present is necessarily a good thing. Is Rheya's final gaze into the audience comforting or horrifying?

Anxiety of Influence: Nostalgia, Trauma, and Belatedness

Picking up where our discussion of nostalgia in the previous chapter left off, *Solaris*'s status as a remake of a European art cinema classic suggests that Soderbergh is grappling with the postmodern trauma of his own 'belatedness.'[6] The director's recombination of previous cinematic material, in addition to his engagement with the legacy of past filmmakers, can be seen as a comparable level of 'revisiting the scene of the crime.' Just as Harold Bloom's 'Anxiety of Influence' (1973)[7] (also assuming the language of psychoanalysis, and the Oedipus complex in particular) asserts that poets inevitably confront the legacy of former poets, film directors must grapple with the 'Fathers' of classical cinema, including, but not limited to: Ford, Hawks, Lang, Murnau, Ozu, Hitchcock, Welles, Kurosawa, Fellini, Bergman, Godard, etc. Contemporary directors must contend with an added level, engaging with these previous directors in addition to wrestling with the giants of New Hollywood: Scorsese, Altman, Kubrick, Coppola, and others.

Soderbergh's struggle in *Solaris* is less about remaking the Tarkovsky film than coping with the legacy of filmmaking within the Hollywood renaissance and engaging directly with a second (or perhaps even third) wave of American filmmaking. In this way, we should see the references within this film as pointing directly to the 1970s' auteurs and their influences, as well as European art cinema. At the same time, as Michael Valdez Moses argues, Soderbergh does bring something new to the table, by way of his intricately interwoven pastiche of many different canonical films and genres, as well as his utilisation of contemporary technologies to do so.[8] Reading the film at this level means analysing it through the lens of what King calls 'second-order nostalgia.'[9] In this sense, we can see that Soderbergh is not even trying to grapple with modernist ideas of film, but with the most recent iteration of generational clash.

Just as the American and French New Wave quoted the generation of Hollywood filmmakers before them, Soderbergh liberally quotes whole sequences from Kubrick's *2001*, in addition to borrowing from the art direction, *mise-en-scène*, and set designs from Ridley Scott's *Alien* (1979) and *Blade Runner*. This suggests that Soderbergh is doing something altogether different than merely remaking Tarkovsky's original film. The director's collaboration with James Cameron on this film adds to the hybridity, as Cameron himself could be seen as one of the pivotal filmmakers who fashioned the postmodern science-fiction film with *The Terminator* (1984) and *Aliens* (1986). With the weight of Cameron's Lightstorm Entertainment production company behind him, Soderbergh was afforded the technological and financial opportunities that computer-generated imagery requires.

The docking sequence in *Solaris* is the most striking example of how this second-order nostalgia aided by digital imagery functions within Soderbergh's films: a literal returning to the *scene* of the crime. Though Kubrick's original docking sequence in *2001* features a waltz by Strauss as its reference point (evoking high culture and thus fixing it as a modernist enterprise), Soderbergh's reference is Kubrick's film, bringing the tension between modernism and postmodernism to the fore. Though the film emulates the sequence precisely, including its shot lengths, match-on-action cuts, and even the orange reflections of machinery onto Kelvin's helmet, there are a few essential modifications and, dare we say, improvements. In this case, *Solaris* certainly benefits from the application of digital effects, as the result is surely a more striking image than Kubrick's in terms of pure aesthetics.[10] Soderbergh's sequence also differs in its use of ambient noise in Cliff Martinez's evocative, electronic score, more befitting of the

Just as the American and French New Wave quoted the generation of Hollywood filmmakers before them, Soderbergh liberally quotes whole sequences from Stanley Kubrick's *2001*, in addition to borrowing from the art direction, *mise-en-scène*, and set designs from Ridley Scott's *Alien* and *Blade Runner*.

cold alienation of the scene.[11] In effect, what Soderbergh's sequence evokes is a mediation, much like Kelvin's own, of the historical trauma of cinema history, and his own compulsion to repeat, restage, and 'act out' the symptoms of his own cinematic psyche.

Ultimately, *Solaris* reveals Soderbergh's own trauma within a larger canon of filmmaking, most visible in the pure gall of restaging two veritable cinematic classics. The negative reception of the film illuminates this tension, divided as it was between critics who faulted Soderbergh for a lack of originality and those who criticized him for not staying true to the Tarkovsky original. His references to these earlier films are a significant mediation, dictating the limit of the contemporary director to engage with the previous generation of filmmakers. For a film set in the future, *Solaris* is equally as concerned with the past. Soderbergh's film is not only projecting forward to a vision of the future, but back to specific aesthetic and narrative referents, as envisioned by these predecessor films. There is something substantially different occurring when Soderbergh references a film that is specifically dealing with the historical crisis that accompanies postmodernism. Retracing these patterns in film history allows us to correlate relationships to an earlier moment of genre revisionism that occurred in the 1970s. Once again, it is worth remembering that these films and their directors, including Kubrick, Altman, Penn and Polanski, all re-worked classical genres and dealt with issues of nostalgia by setting their films – such as *Bonnie and Clyde* (Arthur Penn, 1967) and *Chinatown* (Roman Polanski, 1974) – in the pre-World War II era. As Polanski's film marks a return to history in a particularly problematic moment of crisis (that of postmodernism), the film attempts to re-work and re-inscribe contemporary history within its cinematic frame.

As Jameson states, contemporary filmmakers have no choice but to engage within the larger reflexive practices of a self-aware generic model. Unlike the modernist filmmakers (Kurosawa, Hitchcock, Bergman, Fellini) who are defined by the autonomy of their artistic visions, the contemporary director can only work within generic frameworks. This idea is complicated further when considering contemporary filmmakers operating past 1990, who grapple with these same issues of influence, but within an even shallower pool. It is worth asking whether contemporary filmmakers such as Soderbergh have no choice but to refer only as far back as this initial moment and whether they are reflecting on reflection, or whether the new digital era allows them new opportunities to recreate these works. As *Chinatown* reflexively positions itself as an explicitly metageneric text, it mediates the 1930s' hard-boiled film noir mode through the historical subjectivity of a politically-charged 1970s' moment. *Solaris* occupies a similar role, foregrounding the distance between the sci-fi films of the 1970s and 1980s while presenting a reflexive mediation on the genre.

Additionally, we can see these references as an attempt by the director to heal old wounds by returning to them and by negotiating with the traumatic transition (encounter) between modernism (Tarkovsky, art cinema and so on) and postmodernism. In this sense, critic Rick Groen accurately captures the tension of Soderbergh's filmmaking when he states that the 'director who put truth under a newfangled microscope in *sex, lies, and videotape*,' and was 'instantly heralded as a sharp chronicler of today and a bright hope for tomorrow,' is actually 'himself a reluctant modernist, a captive of his time and his press.'[12] This idea highlights the tension and trauma between Soderbergh's intentions and his output. It would appear as though he is indeed Groen's 'reluctant modernist,' but one who is either blessed or doomed to haunt the earlier moment of American cinema by utilising the tools and technologies only afforded to today's filmmaker.

Revisiting the Trauma of 9/11

To analyse a film within the era that it is produced is a risky prospect. It would be unwise to speak with any certainty as to why *Solaris* experienced such an ambivalent response or why it provoked such negativity from established critics.[13] Nevertheless, our analysis of the psychoanalytic nature of *Solaris* prompts us to attempt a cursory examination of Soderbergh's film as one of the first post-9/11 texts, which is an equally difficult task as strictly reflectionist textual analyses of films are almost always problematic. Nevertheless, it is worth asking, at least to some degree, whether *Solaris* belongs to an even larger wave of films which deal specifically with protagonists moving through the steps of trauma and interacting with them accordingly, and whether the film's release only a year after 9/11 might partially account for its weak reception.[14]

Solaris is one of the first Hollywood films to negotiate the larger trauma of 9/11 within a diffused cultural space. Following this logic means asserting that films are necessarily products of larger, cultural trends and patterns, reflecting what Fredric Jameson calls 'The Political Unconscious' (1981).[15] In other words, films operate somewhat like the dreams of a society, reflecting their symptoms, concerns, and most often, their fears. As a post-9/11 film, *Solaris*'s story of an individual coming to terms with trauma provides an opening to view the larger issues of a society, particularly as it copes with the open wound of a traumatic event. In describing the group therapy sessions that Kelvin leads at the beginning of the film, Moses rightly asserts that *Solaris* provides 'a small and easily overlooked hint at what might be the most proximate historical cause of our current discontents.'[16] Soderbergh himself states that '[t]he implication is that these people are undergoing grief counseling due to some recent cataclysmic event.'[17] Though Moses is careful to assert that the film is not necessarily '*about* the events of 9/11,' he does state that 'it's not too much of a stretch to suggest that the cataclysmic event…is meant to resonate with an audience still traumatized by the terrorist attacks in New York and Washington.'[18] Expanding on Moses' assertion means situating *Solaris* at the vanguard of films that deal obliquely with this larger societal trauma.

Gilles Deleuze has argued that film is a historical record which contains the preoccupations of a particular society at a particular time. In this view, each film is a 'crystal' which freezes the moment in history: 'what we see in the crystal is time itself, a bit of time in its pure state.'[19] Similarly, Jameson has stated that film 'allows us to grasp mass culture not as empty distraction, or "mere" false consciousness' but rather, as 'a transformational work on social and political anxieties which must then have some presence in the mass cultural text in order to be 'managed' or repressed.'[20] *Solaris* opens up a space for commemoration and narratives that translate individual traumas into larger ones. Fittingly, Moses has suggested that *Solaris* is Soderbergh's attempt to negotiate a collective psychic wound, as the various characters all struggle to make sense of their lives in the shadow of a collective traumatic event. This accounts for Soderbergh's emphasis (unlike Tarkovsky's) on Kelvin's earthly life with Rheya, his engagement with an earlier moment of filmmaking, and his placement of healing on a collective, rather than individual level. A historical turning point such as 9/11 represents a 'break with the past' which is 'bound up' with the torn memory of the previous era.[21]

Solaris, then, absorbs all of this material, including the ambiguities which followed the disaster, and presents them in a narrative that contains an equally fractured, somewhat unsatisfactory resolution to what was then too fresh a wound to process. Upon reflection nearly a decade later, these tensions and heartbreaking details seem more relatable, whereas upon the film's release this negotiation may have still been too soon. The legacy of 9/11 is still a delicate subject, but documents such as *Solaris* provide the opportunity to cinematically revisit the scene of that traumatic crime.

Notes

1   Tzvetan Todorov, *The Fantastic; A Structural Approach to a Literary Genre* (Cleveland: Press of Case Western Reserve University, 1973).

2   See Jacques Lacan and Jacques-Alain Miller, *The Seminar. 11, The Four Fundamental Concepts of Psychoanalysis* (New York: Norton, 1998). Within the context of Lacanian psychoanalysis, the *objet fixé* here should be seen as the thing in Rheya that is 'more-than-herself,' or rather, the object that Kelvin, as her lover-to-be, fixates on in his subsequent perceptions of her. In this vein, Lacan states that 'the unconscious was invented' so that 'we could realize that man's desire is the Other's desire.' And that 'love' is dependent entirely on the misrecognition of the desired object (4).This reading is justified through its presence in his memory *before* he sees her face, and must be read as the *objet a* that Kelvin misreads as her

essence. Returning to our discussion of the lovers' meeting in Kelvin's dream, this encounter inches us closer to his repetition of the original site of his trauma, his misrecognition of Rheya's essence in the first place. Additionally, the scene echoes Lacan's description of the waking and dreaming life of the subject. It resembles the dream work of psychoanalysis, where 'the encounter, forever missed, has occurred between dream and awakening, between the person who is still asleep and the person who has dreamt merely in order not to wake up' (59).

3   Dominick La Capra, *History and Criticism*, (Ithaca: Cornell University Press, 1985), 245.

4   Ibid., 246.

5   Brooks Landon, *Science Fiction After 1900: From the Steam Man to the Stars* (New York: Twayne Publishers, 1997), 33-4. Thanks to Eliot Chayt for this insight.

6   See David Bordwell, *The Way Hollywood Tells It: Story and Style in Modern Movies*, (Berkeley, CA: University of California Press, 2006), 26. Bordwell refers to 'belatedness' as intertwined with his recitation of 'allusionism,' and states that belatedness has always been a feature of Hollywood, but that 'after the early 1960s, most filmmakers became painfully aware of working in the shadow of enduring monuments.'

7   Harold Bloom. *The Anxiety of Influence: A Theory of Poetry*. New York: Oxford University Press, 1973.

8   Moses, '*Solaris,* Cinema, and Simulacra,' 282.

9   King, 'Crime-Revenge Genre,' 104.

10   Obviously, it is unfair to compare two images more than thirty years apart, and Kubrick's is certainly the more 'innovative' of the two.

11   Again, this is another unfair comparison and evaluation, as Kubrick was after something else entirely in his use of Strauss, but for the sake of argument, we can at least consider Martinez's score as more diegetically befitting of the scene.

12   Rick Groen, 'Soderbergh's Arc of Triumph,' *The Globe and Mail*, March 23, 2001.

13   For an excellent account of *Solaris*'s critical reception and some of the issues regarding its marketing, see Geoff King, 'Some Kind of Hybrid' in *Indiewood*,179–86.

14   We can also see Soderbergh's *Solaris* as a film that likely anticipates more recent capitulations of a similar story. The increased emphasis on characters living through their memories was featured prominently in two major films of 2010 – *Shutter Island* (Martin Scorsese) and *Inception* – highlighting the centrality and overarching theme of trauma writ large in popular cinema. We might go so far as to assert that had *Solaris* come out in 2010, it would have found better company, and perhaps, a more friendly critical reception.

15   Fredric Jameson. *The Political Unconscious: Narrative As a Socially Symbolic Act* (Ithaca, N.Y: Cornell University Press, 1981).

16   Moses, '*Solaris,* Cinema, and Simulacra,' 298.

17   Soderbergh quoted in Moses, Ibid.

18   Ibid.

19   Gilles Deleuze. *Cinema 2: The Time Image* (London: Continuum, 2005), 79.

20   Jameson, *Signatures*, 25.

21   Deleuze, *Cinema 2*, 7.

CHAPTER SIX

The (Bl)end of History: The Good German and the Intertextual Detective

The true picture of the past flits by. The past can be seized only as an image which flashes up at the instant when it can be recognized and is never seen again... For every image of the past that is not recognized by the present as one of its own concerns threatens to disappear irretrievably.

Walter Benjamin[1]

In an interview given a few years before beginning production on *The Good German*, Soderbergh relates his formal and stylistic promiscuity to his desire to make an innovative 'leap' within the medium of film. Soderbergh is searching for 'another level,' and one idea he has is to tell a story spanning the entire twentieth century, and then

> ...cut it up into ten ten-minute sections. You pick a year from each of those decades. In each year, let's say the 1903 decade, you shoot in the aesthetic of *The Great Train Robbery*. In the teens, you shoot in the style of D. W. Griffith. In the twenties, you shoot in the style of the silent films. Each section is done in the aesthetic of that period.[2]

Four years later, the trans-historical spirit of just such a formal undertaking would be realised with *The Good German*. If Soderbergh were to have continued that train of thought for his dream project, listing styles according to decade, surely he would have chosen the sultry film noirs of the 1940s.[3] *The Good German* certainly focuses its brazen pastiche on 1940s-era film noirs such as *Casablanca* (Michael Curtiz, 1942) and *The Third Man*, but like the noirs themselves, the cinematic lineage goes back further, and continues down the line as well. Film noir is intimately tied to German Expressionism, so perhaps we can assume Soderbergh would have chosen this style for the 1920s and 1930s, before returning stateside for the noirs. From there, *The Good German* skips over to the 1970s for a neo-noir, *Chinatown*, which is itself nostalgically set in the 1930s. The penultimate stop on Soderbergh's history travelogue is the

1990s, in which *Schindler's List* (Steven Spielberg, 1993) would reinvigorate the use of black-and-white cinematography within Hollywood and begin a minor resurgence in Holocaust memorial, affixing it (some would say appropriating it) as a key site for American trauma and rebirth. Spielberg himself would use a multitude of forms, styles, and genres in his self-described 'authentic'[4] portrayal of the 1940s, so perhaps we can imagine that when Soderbergh arrived at his tenth decade and tenth style, the first of the new century, he chose *neo-meta*. This decade would be *The Good German*.

Midway through the film, there is a brief exchange between Jake (George Clooney) and Levi (Dominic Comperatore), a disabled Jewish Holocaust survivor and shop owner. 'What happened to you?' asks Jake, to which Levi responds: 'An experiment, to see if you can transplant a bone from one man into another. It turns out you can't… How about a camera? Rolleiflex. The old ones used to turn the image upside down in the viewfinder. Little mirror sets it right.' This offhand comment is of little relevance in the film's plot, but is an explicit, literal embodiment of the central intertextual tension in the director's work: Soderbergh's philosophy of history is predicated on polyphonic mediation. Levi's suggestion to 'turn the image upside-down' in order to '[set] it right' operates on two levels. Formally, Soderbergh emulates and simulates myriad cinematic styles and forms, the 1940s' film noir of Michael Curtiz in particular, 'transplanting' these cinematic methodologies from one era into another. Thematically, Soderbergh performs a deft intertextual and intermedial negotiation of mediated history. Levi's innocent sales pitch – 'How about a camera?' – has been the prolific American film-maker's continual refrain for nearly thirty films over the past twenty years. Soderbergh, occupying the role of director of photography, as well as director and editor, presents the 'POV of a DOP'[5] in a distinctly intertextual assemblage of style, theme, and philosophy. *The Good German*, a morality play about historical guilt, is experienced as a multiplicity of mediation; Soderbergh is not just shining a light into the abyss of American war crime complicity, but taking his camera with him and editing the footage together into a non-linear, intertextual blend of history itself.

Francis Fukuyama's unfortunate declaration of 'The End of History' (1992) was premature, to say the least; rather than a 'triumph' of liberal democracy at the end of the twentieth century, might we instead ponder the 'triumph' of information communication technology, digital networks, and vast cultural industrial production? Ours is an era of unparalleled access to the documents and artifacts of history, as well as the means to interact with them in art and culture. Surely the end of history is yet to be written, but the writing of history itself has morphed, taking on the form of polyphonic dispersion: The Blend of History. Benjamin's famed angel of history – for whom a storm 'irresistibly propels him into the future to which his back is turned, while the pile of debris before him grows skyward'[6] – is now thrust forward by the last century's gramophone records, magnetic tapes, magazines, videotapes, and film reels. The new century brings digital debris, and the angel of history is awash in a sea of ones and zeroes. Nevertheless, the angel of history as a metaphor is limited by its linearity. Time itself may be a physical, linear constant, but history certainly is not; it is a variable, a battleground, a montage. Rather, Benjamin's lasting insight comes in an earlier thesis, quoted in the epigraph, in which he proclaims the true picture of history to be a

Midway through *The Good German*, Levi (Dominic Comperatore), a disabled Jewish Holocaust survivor offers Jake (George Clooney) a camera, noting its defect, 'The old ones used to turn the image upside-down in the viewfinder. Little mirror sets it right.' This exchange acts as a metaphor for the film itself, an attempt to reverse historical perception using cinematographic means.

momentary flicker, evoking the apparatus of cinema. But how can it 'threaten to disappear irretrievably' if it only ever appears but for a brief moment? Perhaps Benjamin had it backwards and we should 'turn the image upside-down in the viewfinder' to rewrite his maxim: every image of the present that is not recognised by the past as one of its own concerns threatens to reappear *ad infinitum*.

A Cinema of Cinema: Steven Soderbergh as Intertextual Auteur

Not since the self-righteously self-reflexive days of the French New Wave has there been a provocateur of *ciné-écriture* quite like Steven Soderbergh. While Quentin Tarantino may hold the crown as postmodern poster boy and master of *playing* homage, his collage-by-numbers approach remains fixed on the surface, content to merely steal and remix with an unmatched panache. Soderbergh, on the contrary, plunges into the depths of technologically mediated subjectivity, projecting his stories from behind the camera and *through* the camera. Quite literally, as the cinematographer on many of his films, Soderbergh's visions are textbook examples of 'form = function.' Often explicitly embodied in a diegetic camera, the recurring motif of mediation and cinematic subjectivity is seen throughout the entirety of this camera man's oeuvre. Crime themes are prominent through Soderbergh's body of work, as is a preoccupation with history and memory across his films; intertextual reflexivity is another through line.

In *sex, lies, and videotape*, Soderbergh's preoccupation with the camera is channelled through the character of Graham, a traumatised Gen-Xer who convinces women to confess their sexual histories on videotape. Utilising a cross-medium flashback structure, the film juxtaposes grainy videotape with polished film, accompanied by a frenzied soundtrack overlaying dialogue with disjunctive aplomb. *Full Frontal*, billed as the 'spiritual sequel' to *sex, lies, and videotape*, would rekindle this dichotomy while pushing the meta to its limit: converging stories set in Hollywood reveal the film-within-a-film structure to be contained within yet another film. Pairing together two of his later outings, we get sex, lies, and digital videotape in the form of *The Girlfriend Experience*, a cerebral yet intimate experimental film featuring adult film star Sasha Grey, and *Che*, a 258-minute bio-epic shot on the 'revolutionary' RED One digital camera. Other formalist provocations of mediation include remakes that are more akin to remixes – *The Underneath*, *Solaris*, *Ocean's Eleven* – and adaptations that bear little resemblance to their source material – *Kafka*, *King of the Hill*, and *Traffic*. Transtextually, Soderbergh will borrow a character, such as Ray Nicolette (Michael Keaton) from *Jackie Brown* (Quentin Tarantino, 1997) who reappears in *Out of Sight*, or borrow footage from another film, such as the aforementioned use of a young Terence Stamp in *Poor Cow* for *The Limey*. Stamp then reprises his role from *The Limey* briefly (and bizarrely) in *Full Frontal*. The star text of his celebrity actors are fair game for satire, most visible in the *Ocean's* trilogy. And Soderbergh can even be seen to experiment with the medium outside of the text itself, considering *Bubble*'s unique distribution strategy which saw it released in three different formats simultaneously. In a multitude of ways, Soderbergh is pushing at the boundaries and malleability of the text.

For this reason, in our final exploration of the detective figure caught up in issues of history and trauma, we have isolated the intertextual detective, whose case to solve inevitably encounters the power of mediation on the process of history and memory. Our two previous detectives, Wilson and Kelvin, already contain elements of this character and form, as we discovered through tracing the influences of their cinematic nostalgia. Needless to say, one of the central ongoing preoccupations throughout Soderbergh's work is the unique power of temporal and subjective mediation, particularly as it pertains to historical trauma rendered through cinema. What would the result be, then, when this time-travelling 'Man with a Movie Camera' set his sights and fixed focal-length lenses on the twentieth century's most pivotal trauma, the Holocaust?

Adapted from the 2006 novel by Joseph Kanon, *The Good German* is set in Berlin during the Potsdam negotiations immediately following the Allied victory in the European theatre of World War II. Jake, a war correspondent previously stationed in Berlin, returns to Germany to cover the conference and seek out his lost love, the German Jew Lena (Cate Blanchett), who is currently being prostituted by Tully (Tobey Maguire), an American racketeer soon found murdered. The titular 'Good German,' Lena's husband Emil (Christian Oliver), holds the proof that a German scientist being granted amnesty by America is a war criminal, having employed slave labour at Camp Dora in order to produce the V-2 rocket. Jake is drawn into the American cover-up, as they race to capture the German scientists for Operation Overcast/Paperclip before the Russians can. The plot appears to refer to the lives of Arthur Rudolph and Wernher von Braun, German scientists who were successfully expatriated to America to work for NASA, but who never stood trial for their complicity in the Mittelbau-Dora/Mittelwerk concentration camps. Guilt is a thematic motif both on an individual level, as revealed in Lena's personal tale of survival and betrayal, as well as collectively, as the American whitewashing of war criminals is rendered bare.

Before considering how *The Good German* blends so many forms, styles, and genres, we might first analyse the peculiar production manner Soderbergh used to create the film. Not content to merely set the film in the 1940s, Soderbergh sought to produce the film as if he were actually in the 1940s, using only the equipment that would have been available to him on a studio backlot at the time: fixed focal-length lenses, boom mics, rear projection, and incandescent lighting. The luxuries available to contemporary filmmakers – zoom lenses, wireless mics, computer-generated imagery, complex lighting rigs – were forbidden on set, and as a result, Soderbergh forced himself to explore the constraints of the Classical Hollywood style. The lack of wireless mics, for example, meant that actors had to clearly enunciate and crisply deliver their lines, resulting in very direct, presentational performances unlike the intimate, Method-influenced acting popular in current American cinema. Limiting himself to camera techniques of the time, Soderbergh shot with a single camera, often eschewing close-ups and reverse shots for master shots that create a different dynamic for staging and character interaction. Shorter lenses, which mean a wider field of vision, emphasise this more theatrical space, as does the stiff, disciplined camera movement. The opening credit sequence of the film uses archival footage, mugging for the camera, film production clapboards, and a visible projector gate to *frame* this film as an exercise in formalism.

Add soft-edged wipe cuts and a 1.85:1 ratio (1.33:1 on DVD, representing Soderbergh's original vision) to this list of archaic production techniques and *The Good German* is a curious beast in a contemporary multiplex; the initial intent for the film was even more bizarre. According to Kenn Rabin, archivist for the production, the 'original plan for the film was that every shot would be digitally placed over archival footage. So that literally, the film would be "shot" in 1945 Berlin; the actors would be green-screened over archival [footage].'[7] Budgetary constraints prevented

The film's title sequence blends archival footage and scenes from other films, including footage Billy Wilder shot for *A Foreign Affair*, into its recreation of postwar Berlin.

such a (potentially disastrous) undertaking, relegating archival use to rear-projection scenes, but the 'millions of feet of archival footage' Rabin found were assembled into a computer database, virtually constructing a version of Berlin-in-ruins that Soderbergh and his crew, particularly the art department, could study and emulate. The advantages of modern day technology were not completely renounced,[8] but rather *blended* together in a technical hybrid of past/present and fact/fiction. A testament to this unique blend, what little archival footage was actually utilised for rear-projection scenes in *The Good German* included unused location film shot by Billy Wilder for *A Foreign Affair* (1949), a film noir about a *femme fatale* (played by Marlene Dietrich, a clear source of inspiration for Cate Blanchett's sultry, deep-voiced Lena) suspected to have ties to Nazi war criminals in postwar Berlin.

Which brings us to the key intertexts of *The Good German*: the film noir classics *Casablanca* and *The Third Man*. Soderbergh is not so much slyly nodding to *Casablanca* as he is wildly waving his arms in homage. The promotional poster for *The Good German* is a direct recreation of the poster for *Casablanca*, replacing Humphrey Bogart and Ingrid Bergman with George Clooney and Cate Blanchett, just as the film does. Beyond this mere paratextual homage, however, lies a far deeper engagement with the Michael Curtiz classic. One of, if not *the* most iconic scene in Hollywood history, the conclusion to *Casablanca* is lifted by Soderbergh for his own finale, complete with rainy runway setting and identically framed getaway plane: 'Blanchett is wearing an Ingrid Bergman cloche hat and Clooney is desperately trying to think for the both of them.'[9] But whereas *Casablanca* ends on a timeless romantic note of

The final scene of the film brashly invites comparison to *Casablanca*; whereas that film ends on a timeless romantic note of patriotic sacrifice, *The Good German* ends on Jake's (George Clooney) horrified response to Lena's (Cate Blanchett) revelation that she turned in twelve Jewish people to the Gestapo in order to survive.

patriotic sacrifice, *The Good German* ends on Lena's sombre confession: she identified twelve Jewish people to the Gestapo in order to survive. Tully foolishly contributes to the burgeoning criminal underworld, Jake inadvertently participates in the American whitewashing of suspected war criminals, and Lena cooperates with the Nazis; the problems of three little people do amount to a hill of beans in this uncensored world of postwar moral relativism.

While the film does share numerous formal similarities with Hollywood studio productions of the 1940s, *The Good German* also deviates from this style in certain ways we can attribute to the influence of another key intertext: the 1949 British noir *The Third Man*. Unlike the softer three-point lighting of *Casablanca*, *The Third Man* is rendered in heavy chiaroscuro, with high contrast between its rich blacks and blasted whites, with cast shadows the size of buildings. We can trace this influence back to a longer lineage of other urban-based black-and-white films: the *Kammerspiel* movement classic *The Last Laugh* (F. W. Murnau, 1924), the late German Expressionist grit of *M* (Fritz Lang, 1931), and the war-ravaged Italian Neo-Realism of *Rome, Open City* (Roberto Rossellini, 1945), to name but a few of the seminal texts. The extreme canted angles of *The Third Man* (and German Expressionism before it) are seen in *The Good German* as well; a particularly poignant composition has Lena at a low, canted angle with the camera tracking back and framing her against an enormous poster of Stalin.

But the influence of *The Third Man* is felt in more than just cinematography. There is the setting, a postwar Vienna divided into four districts, one for each occupying power, just as Berlin is in *The Good German*. A key location – the dramatically-lit labyrinthine sewer system – is borrowed for Emil's hideout. But most significantly, we have the character of Holly Martins (Joseph Cotten), the writer of pulp western novels, who arrives in Vienna and is enmeshed in a convoluted mystery when attempting to seek out an old friend, just as Jake, a journalist, arrives in Berlin and is led astray searching for Lena. A diverse range of media is encountered by each media practitioner: Holly attends a play, listens to a lecture, sneaks into a cinema, watches a slideshow, listens to a jukebox, and is the special invited guest to a book club, while Jake listens to a radio broadcast of the peace conference, learns about Hiroshima through a newspaper, is offered a camera, and watches a newsreel of Stalin, Truman, and Churchill. There is even a rendezvous at the '*kino*' (cinema). Careful attention is paid in each film to point out the constant mediation that is at play; Holly renders this self-reflexive motif explicit when he proclaims that he is writing a new book, a murder mystery called 'The Third Man,' which will 'mix fact and fiction.'

A third man of a different sort is also detectable within Soderbergh's trans-historical mash-up. While few reviews of *The Good German* fail to make the connection to *Casablanca* and *The Third Man*, another key intertext has, to our knowledge (and Google's), been completely missed: *The Devil Makes Three* (Andrew Marton, 1952).[10] Consider this familiar plot: American soldier returns to bombed-out German city after the war to seek out woman who has become jaded barmaid at sleazy nightclub selling her 'company' in order to survive. In this case, the woman, Wilhelmina (Pier Angeli), is the only survivor of a family of 'good Germans' who saved Capt. Jeff Eliot (Gene Kelly) when his plane was shot down over Munich. A hint of moral relativity and the complexity of war are glimpsed when Wilhelmina expresses hatred towards the Americans, who were the perpetrators of the air raid that killed her family. The film is then pushed into action mode when a gang of Nazis on motorcycles attempt to revive the Third Reich by retrieving 'Nazi Booty,' and Gene Kelly must save the day and win the girl, with nary an opportunity to sing or dance. Still, *The Devil Makes Three* is an intriguing postwar film, not least because its climactic chase scene is filmed inside the ruins of The Berghof, Hitler's house in the Alps.[11] Without knowing if the strangely similar plot set-up was a conscious theft or not, one wonders if Soderbergh perhaps sought to pay tribute to this odd, forgotten film and historical document.

We catalogue this multitude of references and homages in *The Good German* not to engage in some parlour game of intertextual source finding, but in an effort to map the multi-meta-generic structure of the film which is at the root of Soderbergh's philosophy of history. How appropriate then, that the final key intertext at play is *Chinatown*, a film seen by both John G. Cawelti and Fredric Jameson as the marker of a new breed of genre film. For Cawelti, it is the exemplary case of 'generic transformation' and 'generic exhaustion,'[12] while for Jameson it represents a debilitating 'metageneric production.'[13] It is fitting that noir is used as the site for this generic discussion, for noir remains a contested term, its constitution as style, genre, or mode never finalised, its formulation already at a distance, its discovery a retroactive act by French critics. For Richard Gilmore, in his exploration of *Chinatown*, this means that 'American film noir was always neo-noir.'[14] *The Good German*, then, in also naming its protagonist Jake, and also marring him with a symbolic facial wound, can only be seen as a reflection of a reflection of a reflection – 'neo' three times removed. Forget it Jake, it's Chinatown in postwar Berlin too. And as Lena's *femme fatale* informs us, for our purposes referring to the meta-generic abyss the film finds itself in: 'You can never really get out of Berlin.'

Beyond Pastiche: Broken Mirrors and Montage History

In a promotional interview for *The Good German*, Soderbergh wonders what films of the 1940s would have looked like if filmmakers in Hollywood had not been constrained by the Hays Code. If they were granted the creative freedom to explore sexuality and violence, how different would their depiction of the war have been? This is the central pivot point of *The Good German*, which recasts this Classical Hollywood 1940s' visual style with contemporary permissiveness: Tully aggressively engages in graphic, rear-entry sex with Lena, Jake is savagely beaten on numerous occasions, and crude language is used throughout the film. 'It will be interesting,' Soderbergh ponders, 'to see if people can wrap their minds around the *blending* of these two ideas.'[15] If box office and critical reception is any indication, the answer is a resounding no, but the historical intervention remains. *Casablanca* was received as blatant propaganda immediately upon its release, seen as a way to bolster support for America's entry into the war less than a year previously; *Variety* dubbed it 'splendid anti-Axis propaganda.'[16] A simplistic tale at such a time is understandable, but what about that *other* contemporary black-and-white Hollywood Holocaust film that pastiches film noir?

A veritable academic cottage industry has arisen since the release of *Schindler's List* to decry and condemn the social and historical irresponsibility of Spielberg's opus. We need not rehearse such criticisms here, save the simple fact that Spielberg is unable to present the Holocaust as anything but spectacle. Because Spielberg is so enchanted with the power of his own cinema, he renders the Holocaust as a struggle between two powerful German men, shot in beautiful chiaroscuro, relegating the Jewish people to the role of extras in this Manichean battle between good and evil. This is history devoid of any nuance, perpetuating the reductive myth of the Good War, but because Spielberg is a master of emotional manipulation, *Schindler's List* is the recipient of countless awards and is used as teaching material in classrooms. *The Good German*, on the other hand, is a cold, methodical lesson in mediated history, and lacking any emotional chemistry between its characters, it is unsurprising that the film failed to attract an audience.

In addition to its confusing formal structure and alienating performances, *The Good German* is also unsettling in the way it pokes and prods at some sacred objects in American history. Not only does the film suggest that American interests in the postwar setting resulted in the active support of morally reprehensible figures, it uses one of the most cherished scenes in one of the most beloved American films to do so. As opposed to *Casablanca*'s timeless conclusion, *The Good German* actually allows the character of Lena to get away with her shocking complicity in the Holocaust, fleeing the scene of the crime. And unlike *Chinatown*, in which Noah Cross (John Huston) simply aims to control the water supply of California, in postwar Berlin, the Americans seek to control the supply of weapons-producing scientists by any means necessary. Undermining the central mythology of triumphant post-World War II Americana and contesting the legacy of the 'Greatest Generation' is not exactly feel-good multiplex fare. As it implicates the American spectator with this ugly truth, *The Good German* leaves a bad taste in the viewer's mouth. Rather than caressing the scar of World War II, as Spielberg does, Soderbergh pours salt in the wound.

The popularity of *Schindler's List* lies not only in its innocuous, fairy tale method of storytelling, but its meta-cinematic method of filmmaking as well. Conflicting elements of film noir, Italian neo-realism, and newsreel documentary constitute its style, but generically, recent critics have reinterpreted it as everything from a 'historical epic'[17] to a 'repurpos[ing]' of the biographical film as a modernist form'[18] – even a horror film.[19] If we pair *Schindler's List* along with the other hugely popular historical film of the 1990s – Oliver Stone's *JFK* (1991), a conflation of fact and fiction and media representation at breakneck speed – then we witness the ascendancy of the 'postmodern history film'[20] to the mainstream. In coining this term, Robert Rosenstone accounts for how film perceives 'history as vision,'[21] an audio-visual rendering not comparable to that of the written word. This postmodern form of delivery 'changes the rules of the historical game,'[22] but those rules have now been set for at least a decade, if not considerably more. If our conception of history is heavily shaped by cinematic representation, especially popular postmodern incarnations such as *Schindler's List*, then *The Good German* remains a sober reminder that there is a heavy price for such unquestioned mediation.

To be clear: Soderbergh does not reside in some trivial, self-reflexive, postmodern hall of mirrors; he operates in the long, labyrinthine, endless maze of history, which after a century of increasingly rampant audio-visual production, is now littered with the refuse of countless broken mirrors. Soderbergh is less interested in telling a postmodern historical story than he is curating its multiple refractory transmissions. By conflating elements of the cinematic 1930s, 1940s, 1950s, and 1970s, and contrasting it with the historical *uber*-text of the 1990s, *The Good German* does not present different times in history, or history's progression, but history *as* time: a temporal simultaneity and collapse. Unfortunately, the critical reception of the film has for the most part inaccurately reduced *The Good German* to mere pastiche and empty style, rather than the neo-meta utilisation of pastiche and style to channel the multiplicity of cinematically mediated representation. Perhaps, *in time*, this historical injustice will be 'set right.'

Après nous, le deluge.

These are the final foreboding words of '*Casablanca*: Cult Movies and Intertextual Collage,' Umberto Eco's tongue-in-cheek lament for the innocence of unbridled, unconscious archetypal thievery.[23] *Casablanca*, according to Eco, is not content with employing a select few archetypes, it uses them all: 'it is not *one* movie. It is 'movies.''[24] In the wake of *Casablanca* and its intertextual ilk, cinema is bound to an extreme awareness in which both filmmaker and audience are conscious of such intertextual reworking. Soderbergh is no doubt a sterling example of the 'semiotically nourished authors working for a culture of instinctive semioticians.'[25] *The Good German* would perhaps be more appropriately titled *Casablanca 2.0*, updated with more explicitly graphic software and deprogrammed of its Hays Code. Along with the rest of Soderbergh's body of intertextual work, it shows that Michael Curtiz's iconic classic (and the type of meta-film it represents) is not just all movies, but all *future* movies as well. We need not mourn this loss of originality; rather, we should consider it as historical instruction. Let us revisit our rewritten Benjaminian aphorism and consider Soderbergh's proposition: every image of the present that is not recognised by the past as one of its own concerns threatens to reappear *ad infinitum*. How about a camera?

Notes

1 Walter Benjamin, 'Theses on the Philosophy of History,' in *Illuminations* (New York: Schocken Books, 1968), 255.

2 Richardson, 'Life of Steven Soderbergh.'

3 *The Good German* would be Soderbergh's sixth (neo) noir, following *Kafka*, *The Underneath*, *Fallen Angels* (television), *Out of Sight*, and *The Limey*, or seventh if you also count the debut film of his apprentice George Clooney, on whom he no doubt had considerable influence, *Confessions of a Dangerous Mind*.

4 Quoted in James Russell, *The Historical Epic and Contemporary Hollywood: From Dances with Wolves to Gladiator* (New York: Continuum, 2007), 78.

5 Point of View of a Director of Photography.

6 Benjamin, 'Philosophy of History,' 258.

7 Quoted in Sheila Curran Bernard, *Documentary Storytelling: Making Stronger and More Dramatic Nonfiction Films* (Burlington, MA: Elsevier, 2007), 325.

8 The film was not actually shot on black-and-white film stock either. Photographed on colour stock, the footage was digitally altered to match the grainy black-and-white archival footage.

9 J. Hoberman, 'Nostalgia Trip.'

10 Our thanks to Keir Keightley for this insight.

11   Frank Miller, 'The Devil Makes Three,' Turner Classic Movies Website, accessed January 14, 2009, http://www.tcm.com/thismonth/article.jsp?cid=154952&mainArticleId=154931.

12   John G. Cawelti, '*Chinatown* and Generic Transformation in Recent American Films,' in *Mystery, Violence, and Popular Culture* (Madison, WI: University of Wisconsin Press/Popular Press, 2004), 198.

13   Jameson, *Signatures*, 84.

14   Richard Gilmore, 'The Dark Sublimity of *Chinatown*,' in *The Philosophy of Neo-Noir*, ed. Mark T. Conard (Lexington, KY: University Press of Kentucky, 2006), 119.

15   'Interview with Steven Soderbergh about 'The Good German,'' The Good German Website, last modified October, 2006, http://thegoodgerman.warnerbros.com.

16   'Casablanca,' *Variety*, December 2, 1942, http://www.variety.com/review/VE1117487980.html?c=31.

17   Russell, *The Historical Epic*.

18   Robert Burgoyne, *The Hollywood Historical Film* (Malden, MA: Blackwell, 2008), 103.

19   Caroline Joan Picart and David A. Frank, *Frames of Evil: The Holocaust as Horror in American Film* (Carbondale: Southern Illinois University Press, 2006).

20   Robert A. Rosenstone, *Visions of the Past: The Challenge of Film to Our Idea of History* (Cambridge, MA: Harvard University Press, 1995), 12.

21   Ibid., 15.

22   Ibid.

23   Umberto Eco, '*Casablanca*: Cult Movies and Intertextual Collage,' in *Travels in Hyperreality* (San Diego: Harcourt Brace Jovanovich, 1986), 197–212.

24   Ibid., 208.

25   Ibid., 210.

PART THREE

CRIME, CAPITAL, GLOBALISATION

CHAPTER SEVEN

Genre and Capital: New Crime Wave in the 1990s

> Maurice 'Snoopy' Miller: You ain't never shot a gun before, have you?
> Jack Foley: Not until recently, no.
> Maurice 'Snoopy' Miller: You nervous?
> Jack Foley: A little, yeah.
>
> *Out of Sight*

In this final section, we will turn from the detective character as a structuring element towards larger configurations of genre. This chapter will explore the major resurgence of crime films in the 1990s and Steven Soderbergh's participation in this larger trend. The crime film and its many iterations/sub-genres are Soderbergh's default mode, and most of his films are inflected with criminals, detectives, or a combination of both. We will investigate his role within the larger moment of the indie cinema/crime film resurgence while emphasising how his contributions are emblematic of the cycle, yet also distinct. In opposition to the traditional historical account of the indie movement, we will argue that any cultural renaissance that occurred within this era was quickly subsumed within an even larger wave of generic filmmaking. Crime was the theme that most indie filmmakers employed, if only to prove themselves as masters of this particular form.

In the 1990s, the indie film boom quickly turned to a massive generic explosion, where Hollywood's 'graduating class' wore their influences on their sleeves, becoming, in John Pierson's view, 'Sons of *Mean Streets*.'[1] The moody, introspective films that marked the early indie moment (and which *sex, lies, and videotape* set the stage for in 1989) had already transformed by 1992, when Sundance and multiplexes were dominated by crime films from first-time filmmakers such as the Hughes Brothers,

Quentin Tarantino, Bryan Singer, and Robert Rodriguez, as well as both P. T. and Wes Anderson. Though the major films of this moment are generally attributed to Tarantino and his ilk, Soderbergh is equally as influential a figure within the 1990s' proliferation of the crime film, or as we would designate his contribution more accurately: the *anti-crime film*. Soderbergh's unique artistic and auteurist preoccupations within this genre will be outlined below with a close reading of *Out of Sight*.

From Indie Innocence to Crime Wave

Now that the enthusiasm for the American indie cinema moment in the 1990s has waned, and the (gun) smoke has cleared, it is much easier to see that the romantic version of the story – recounted as a heroic narrative of 'Outsiders,'[2] 'Rebels,'[3] 'Mavericks,'[4] and others – did not quite 'redefine' cinema as much as these authors would have you believe. In fact, the moment that indie cinema was named, the process of subsumption by corporate transnationals was nearly complete; the 'indie' label was already being marketed as a mark of distinction. Accordingly, the films and their narratives moved towards this model as well. Indie film changed from slow, talky dramas in which protagonists contemplated their existential dilemmas – e.g. *Slacker* (Richard Linklater, 1991), *Passion Fish* (John Sayles, 1992), *Bodies, Rest, and Motion* (Michael Steinberg, 1993), *Clerks* (Kevin Smith, 1994), and *Sleep With Me* (Rory Kelly, 1994) – to the crime genre, ushering in a veritable 'crime wave' that more accurately characterises indie filmmaking in the 1990s. Steven Soderbergh is an important figure in this transition, as almost every one of his films, save his first two existential features, involves the idea of crime in one form or another.[5] Though the Sundance Film Festival initially served as a showcase for rising independent directors and challenging arthouse fare, by the mid-1990s, following the success of *Reservoir Dogs* and others, many first- and second-time directors were operating strictly within the crime genre.

'Crime film is the most enduringly popular of all Hollywood genres,' Thomas Leitch reminds us, 'the only kind of film that has never been out of fashion since the dawn of the sound era seventy years ago.'[6] We should add that nearly every significant cinematic renaissance – from Hollywood's postwar *film noir* in the 1930s, to the French New Wave in the 1950s, to the 'Movie Brat' New Hollywood of the 1970s, to the emergence of ultra-violent Hong Kong cinema in the late 1980s – begins with a flurry of bullets that mark the arrival of the crime genre. Not only does the crime film never sleep, but it knows no boundaries either, emerging in different times and places, sometimes as an international deviation, as in the French New Wave, and sometimes as a parallel development, as in the case of the Hong Kong crime wave and the rise of American indie cinema.

The 1990s' Crime Wave had been percolating for a few years, with the neo-noir era of the 1980s, as well as some significant contributions from an earlier generation of 'indie' auteurs such as Jim Jarmusch (*Down By Law*, 1986), and the Coen Brothers (*Blood Simple*, 1984; *Raising Arizona*, 1987; *Miller's Crossing*, 1990). Although critics such as David Desser generally cite *Pulp Fiction* in 1994 as the zero point of this cycle of films,[7] there can be no doubt that the crime wave had already gathered much momentum by that point. Beginning with Scorsese's *Goodfellas* (1990), we can trace this path to include many of indie cinema's 'rebels' and 'mavericks,' adopting the crime genre within either their breakout or sophomore films: *Boyz n the Hood* (John Singleton, 1991), *Reservoir Dogs*, *El Mariarchi* (Robert Rodriguez, 1992), *Menace II Society* (Albert and Allen Hughes, 1993), *Mi Vida Loca* (Allison Anders, 1993), *The Usual Suspects* (Bryan Singer, 1994), and *Shallow Grave* (Danny Boyle, 1994). Following the enormous success of *Pulp Fiction*, the crime wave picked up steam with *Se7en* (David Fincher, 1995), *Hard Eight* (P. T. Anderson, 1996), *Bottle Rocket* (Wes Anderson, 1996), *Bound* (Andy and Larry Wachowski, 1996), *Cop Land* (James Mangold, 1997), *Lock, Stock and Two Smoking Barrels* (Guy Ritchie, 1998), *Three Kings*, and *Memento* (Christopher Nolan, 2000).

The crime wave was not only reserved for the new indie class though, as directors who established themselves in the 1980s joined in the crime spree too: Tony Scott's *True Romance* (1993), Oliver Stone's *Natural Born Killers* (1994), Spike Lee's *Clockers*, Michael Mann's *Heat* (1995), the Coen Brothers' *Fargo* (1996), Mike Newell's *Donnie Brasco* (1997), and Jim Jarmusch's *Ghost Dog: The Way of the Samurai* (1999). 'Survivors' from the 1970s, or 'careerists' if we're being generous, also took part in the crime resurgence (though some never left), and made some of their best films: *Silence of the Lambs* (Jonathan Demme, 1991), *Carlito's Way* (Brian De Palma, 1993), *Casino* (Martin Scorsese, 1995), and *L.A. Confidential* (Curtis Hanson, 1997). Some directors found their groove and kept on working within this genre, as was the case with Tarantino (*Jackie Brown*, 1997), Stone (*U-Turn*, 1997), and the Hughes brothers (*Dead Presidents*, 1995; *From Hell*, 2001). Considering the calibre of films and directors on display here, it seems reasonable that once the romantic narrative of a 'rebellious indie' streak is replaced with the facts of its corporate reality, and only the films and directors remain, we will instead remember American film from the 1990s largely for its common preoccupation: crime.

One of the lingering difficulties in genre analysis is attributing causes to the emergence of a particular genre or cycle of films. Though these claims are difficult to prove, many scholars[8] assert that particular genres emerge in particular eras as reflections of certain issues within that society. The social problem film achieved wide popularity during the era of the New Deal, for example, and the conspiracy film struck a chord during the height of Watergate and the Vietnam War. In the case of the 1990s' crime wave, Leitch suggests that 'deepening divisions in audiences' attitudes towards violence, criminals and the law… produced a rich array of contradictory films with contradictory responses.'[9] Globally, there was no shortage of violent conflicts, including the first Gulf War that began the decade, the conflict in former Yugoslavia from 1991–1995, as well as the Rwandan genocide. Domestically, an increase of racial tensions and the rise of an independent, militia mentality came to a head in the 1992 LA riots, the 1993 Waco standoff, the capture and conviction of the Unabomber, and the Oklahoma City bombing in 1995. Economically, the first signs of globalisation were marked in 1989 with the collapse of the Berlin Wall and accentuated more fully by the signing of the NAFTA agreement, signalling the breakdown of the final borders to international trade and the beginning of the end in terms of American dominance in manufacturing.

Yet for all this crisis, there was no overwhelming and unifying theme that galvanised the culture in the 1990s. As opposed to the cinemas that arose out of the Cold War in the 1950s and Watergate/Nixon in the 1970s, films in the 1990s are notable less by a reaction to their eras than an immersion within the larger fusion of high and low culture and the ascension of a complex global culture. Into this volatile yet fragmented history moved the crime film which, according to Leitch, operates directly on the 'audience's ambivalence.'[10] Similarly, Nicole Rafter claims that crime films enable the viewer 'to dwell, if only for an hour or two, in a state of happy hypocrisy."[11] Thus, when Henry Hill (Ray Liotta) speaks to the audience at the beginning of *Goodfellas* and proclaims that for as long as he could remember, he 'always wanted to be a gangster,' he is only echoing our own sentiments. The crime film is a fantasy projection for ambivalent times.

Lacking any direct cultural or political impetus, it is easier to assume that many of the canonical crime filmmakers in the 1990s merely sought to emulate an earlier model provided by the filmmakers they idolised. The emergence of postmodernism, useful here only insofar as it indicates the degree to which film suddenly became far more accessible and audiences far more semiotically literate, is illustrated in someone like Tarantino's intertextual film collages borne out of his B-movie education at the video store. That a prevailing tone of nostalgia pervades most of these crime films – many of the protagonists live by an outdated 'code,' wear anachronistic clothing, or seem to exist in a parallel, yet highly-stylised universe – solidifies the genre as a formal echo, rather than a socially or culturally motivated response. Just as the 1970s' films such as *Chinatown* and *The Godfather* projected backwards to the 1930s and 1950s for their settings, the 1990s' films seemed to be referencing an earlier moment as well, echoing Scorsese, Altman, De Palma, and others.

What marks the 1990s' wave as distinct is the manner in which filmmakers seemingly absorbed any and all of these influences and represented them atemporally; the influence of Godard and Kurosawa is as important as Wilder, Hitchcock, and Scorsese. Perhaps most striking about these films is just how completely fluent they are in earlier cinematic genres, and the sheer comprehensive weight of references that comprise them. The crime film is one of the most influenced and influential of all genres, where the giants of filmmaking all offered some of the most beloved movies of all time, and where each director attempts to better the last by planning a more elaborate heist and cinematic experience. The crime film operates like a template that many nascent directors explore before making their way into more artistic fare. The trajectory of crime films and their influence can be traced from John Huston, Billy Wilder, and Alfred Hitchcock influencing the young idealists who would become the French New Wave, as their enthusiasm for the B-pictures of minor studios and their consumption of the entirety of Hollywood wartime output helped to produce the early films of the *Nouvelle Vague*. In this vein, we ought to remember that these early films were the result of the *Cahiers du cinéma* critics' 'obsession with American films.'[12] When Jean-Luc Godard, François Truffaut and Jean-Pierre Melville began to make films, they turned to the American B-genres, and the crime film in particular. The outward (and international) influence of this moment is significant, as both Quentin Tarantino and John Woo have waxed poetically and enthusiastically upon Melville's *Bob le flambeur* (1956) and *Le Samourai* (1967) as seminal influences on their respective filmmaking practices.[13]

Appropriately, Leitch distinguishes the crime film as a 'genre that is not a genre, even though an enormous audience recognizes and enjoys it.'[14] He also acknowledges that it is not necessarily the strongest of genres, but is better defined and analysed as a collection of sub-genres (the caper, the gangster, the thriller, and so on), each of which contributes to the larger idea of the crime film. The genre's enduring popularity, according to Nicole Rafter, 'lies in the way [it] provide[s] a cultural space for the expression of resistance to authority,'[15] corresponding to Leitch's assertion that crime films 'always depend on their audience's ambivalence about crime.'[16] Though many genres show signs of self-reflexivity, the crime film is inherently self-reflexive as each film builds on an acknowledgement of the last. This is especially true of the heist film that must resolve a *filmed* problem (how will the criminals pull off the heist?) as well as a *film* problem (how do the filmmakers differentiate this film and heist from the others?) in such a way as to evoke sympathy for the protagonist and sufficiently entertain the viewer.

In the American context, we should also consider the relationship between the New Hollywood moment and its echo, indie cinema. As enacted by Peter Biskind in *Easy Riders, Raging Bulls* (1998), among other sources, 1970s' filmmaking has been mythologised as the last time that the creative forces in Hollywood dictated the terms of production.

> The thirteen years between *Bonnie and Clyde* in 1967 and *Heaven's Gate* in 1980 marked the last time that it was really exciting to make movies in Hollywood, the last time that people could be consistently proud of the pictures they made, the last time the community as a whole encouraged good work, the last time there was an audience that could sustain it […]. The New Hollywood lasted barely a decade, but in addition to bequeathing a body of landmark films, it has a lot to teach us about the way Hollywood is run now, why today's pictures, with a few exceptions, are so unrelievedly awful, why Hollywood is in a perpetual state of crisis and self-loathing.[17]

Correspondingly, Thomas Elsaesser, Alexander Horwath, and Noel King have all suggested that the 1970s represented the 'Last Great American Picture Show.'[18] While genre revisionism is one of the acknowledged features of the era, the sheer array of crime films and the parallels between the 1970s' and 1990s' films has yet to be fully investigated.

Thus, we should recall that some of the most significant films of the New Hollywood era set the standard for crime genre renaissance: crime films are important sites for auteur experimentation. The list of canonical crime films from this era is as well-rehearsed as it is impressive, as Arthur Penn's *Bonnie and Clyde* (1967), Dennis Hopper's *Easy Rider*, Alan J. Pakula's *Klute* (1971), William Friedkin's *The French Connection* (1971), Mario van Peebles' *Sweet Sweetback's Baadasssss Song* (1971), Don Siegel's *Dirty Harry* (1971), Gordon Parks's *Shaft* (1971), Francis Ford Coppola's *The Godfather*,

George Roy Hill's *The Sting* (1973), and Martin Scorsese's *Mean Streets* (1973) were only some of the major films to emerge from the early period of this film renaissance. In Thomas Elsaesser's view, the 1970s' protagonist within each of these films represented the 'unmotivated hero' who reflected the era's 'state of crisis and self-doubt.'[19] Other critics have noted the resurgence of 'hyper-masculinity'[20] and the homosocial bonding of street toughs such as the characters in Scorsese's *Mean Streets*. Indeed, the 1990s' generation of filmmakers would seemingly return to this hypermasculine language, recreating the exclusively male (and often white) gangs to the exclusion of women. As the decade wore on, audiences got to revel with psychopaths and serial killers, hip gangsters and petty criminals, and watch increasingly violent spectacles. The lone exception is Soderbergh, whose protagonists' value systems stand at odds with the typical violent, stylised crime protagonist of the genre. Offering hopeful rather than hopeless prognoses of the era, Soderbergh's criminals inhabit the values of honour, labour, camaraderie, philanthropy, and usefulness in the face of overwhelming odds. In this sense, value, loyalty, and inclusion mark Soderbergh's crime films as espousing a veritable 'Soderberghian ethics.'[21]

Soderbergh's Anti-Crime Spree

Soderbergh was and continues to be an active participant in this crime wave, but his films open fissures within the genre and stand in stark opposition to many of the other crime films of the era listed above. Containing ruminations on social class, necessity, and oppression, the 'Soderberghian ethics' on display in his crime films are less often about theft, revenge, or gangsterism than they are friendship, camaraderie, and love. Furthermore, Soderbergh's movies are provocations against the universal conceptions of public law and private morality, complicating the binaries between right and wrong, offering subtle shifts and engaging protagonists that we do not want brought to justice. In this sense, they are more accurately designated as *anti-crime* films. However, these films still very much relish in the pleasures of the crime film: the rebellious charisma, the thrill of the chase, the forbidden desire, the powerful lawlessness. Soderbergh's crime dialectic embraces this paradox, and attempts to have its criminal cake and eat it too.

A close look at Soderbergh's oeuvre reveals that crime is a running preoccupation, extending to films that he writes and produces as well. We can subdivide his crime works as follows:

Heist: *The Underneath, Out of Sight, Welcome to Collinwood, Ocean's Eleven, Ocean's Twelve, Ocean's Thirteen*
Conspiracy: *Kafka, Traffic, Erin Brockovich, K-Street, Good Night, and Good Luck, Syriana*
Detective: *Fallen Angels, The Limey, Solaris, Bubble, Contagion, Side Effects*
Espionage/Spy: *Confessions of a Dangerous Mind, The Good German, Haywire*
Grifter/Con Men: *King of the Hill, Criminal, Michael Clayton, The Girlfriend Experience, The Informant!, Magic Mike*

All of these works are bound by their shared questioning of the hazy distinction between public law and private morality, as well as their innovative visual, narrative, and editing styles.

True to form, Soderbergh's crime films actually offer sophisticated critiques of the ideological and formal values of the genre. Rather than embodying the ideological characteristics of capitalism and success (as suggested by Robin Wood's essay 'Ideology, Auteur, Genre'),[22] Soderbergh's crime films counter this perception by serving up alternative value systems within them. Soderbergh's protagonists negotiate the moral grey zone formerly occupied by Robin Hood and other crusaders who exist outside of the law but who nevertheless straddle the lines of necessity, morality, and codes of honour. Their petty crimes are set against the overwhelming indifference of contemporary corporate capitalism. Early protagonists like Aaron (*King of the Hill*), Michael (*The Underneath*), Wilson (*The Limey*), and Jack Foley (*Out of Sight*) are just as likely to steal out of the necessity of their personal, economic, or social setting as they are to represent the 'get rich quick' values of 1980s' protagonists like Gordon Gekko (*Wall Street* [Oliver Stone, 1987]) or Tony Montana (*Scarface* [Brian De Palma, 1983]). In most cases, class (and often poverty), rather than greed, plays an important role in the characters' motivations, which is an important (and perhaps responsible) counterweight to an era marked by Mickey and Mallory (*Natural Born Killers*), Hannibal Lecter (*The Silence of the Lambs*) and Tommy DeVito (*Goodfellas*). Often enough, Soderbergh's criminals are set against their desire to do right by their families or to win back love, as in *Ocean's Eleven*.

Soderbergh's protagonists face tough ethical dilemmas. In this vein, while Graham from *sex, lies, and videotape* may not be the first person that we would characterise as criminal, his unique fetish lies on the other side of the 'traditional' moral compass. Furthermore, he can be linked to the long tradition of 'drifter' characters from *film noir*, who could just as easily be seduced by the *femme fatale* as saved by them, as Graham encounters. As a lawyer, John (Peter Gallagher) is supposed to stand on the side of the law, but rather suggests the opposite side of the moral compass. Though Graham's behaviour is unusual, John's is abhorrent, to the point that even Cynthia (Laura San Giacomo) suggests John is the bad guy, by the very nature of his sleeping with his wife's sister, despite the ironic fact that Cynthia is said mistress.

Kafka produces another surprising take on the relationship between licit and illicit, as the protagonist author ends up questioning whether the behaviour of the official government is moral or even legal. As Kafka travels to the castle, his realisation is vividly captured as the film itself shifts to startling colour. That the government is practising horrible experiments on those whom it considers 'radical' is yet another example of this shifting perspective. Here, Kafka may be on the wrong side of the law, but this does not mean that he is not in the 'right.' This shifting moral compass is also visible in Soderbergh's next film, *King of the Hill*, where young protagonist Aaron (Jesse Bradford) begs, borrows, and occasionally steals in order to make it through the Great Depression. Once again, the ethical dilemma of the protagonist is sidestepped by a more important imperative – survival – rather than obeying the rules as they stand and letting the bank repatriate all of his and his family's belongings. More to the point, having witnessed the depth and weight of Aaron's suffering, it is near impossible for the viewer not to hope that Aaron will go and steal something to eat.

Soderbergh's first attempt at a *noir* style (*The Underneath*) offers a different take on what had previously been considered a form that had a distinctly moral component. In most films of the initial cycle, order returns when the protagonist dies and the couple's moral transgression is punished when they die in each other's arms. This is exactly what occurs in the earlier version of the film, *Criss Cross* (Robert Siodmak, 1949), which Soderbergh re-wrote in 1995. In this version, instead of the couple dying, they are separated ambivalently, suggesting that the *femme fatale* will face justice without being killed, and without bringing Michael (Peter Gallagher) down with her in her vicious plot. Michael lives, and the film ends with the police chasing Rachel (Alison Elliott).

Out of Sight's Jack Foley robs banks, but without the use of weapons, and only targets places that are insured. For Foley, loyalty trumps greed, as seen in his past and present relationships in the film, such as with his partner Buddy (Ving Rhames) and his love interest Karen Sisco. Paradoxically, Foley's attempt at robbery ends up protecting his friends and even the object that he was going to rob, despite the fact of his being left to face the consequences. This also applies to *The Limey*'s Wilson, whose red-hot appetite for murderous revenge is tempered by the friendships that he develops near the end of the film. After refusing to kill Terry Valentine, and accepting his culpability in his daughter's death, the film ends with a series of images of Wilson saying goodbye to his newly constituted 'family,' who mediate his revenge and teach him something more important.

The class composition of the title character in *Erin Brockovich* is significant, as her status as struggling single-mother dictates that she needs to bend the rules and use her feminine wiles in order to overcome her disadvantaged status. *Traffic* offers a whole wealth of criminal characters, each of whom represent only one facet of the extremely complicated network of drug traffickers, consumers, police, and politicians. In each case, the film is careful to demonstrate that morality is fluid and subjective, and that everyone has their motivations, good and bad, for involving themselves in this world. We will discuss *Ocean's Eleven* in the next chapter, but it is worth mentioning briefly that despite the gang's theft of almost $200 million in the film, their likability, camaraderie, and savvy business sense mark them as some of Soderbergh's most enjoyable criminal protagonists.

While Soderbergh's protagonists are definitely criminals, their particular brand of criminality stands in opposition to other films within this era: Ray Liotta's Henry Hill in *Goodfellas*, who ends up ratting out the mafia personalities who raised him; Tim Roth's Mr. Orange in *Reservoir Dogs*, whose betrayal leads to the death of all but one of his fellow thieves; the viciousness and deplorable nature of Woody Harrelson's and Juliette Lewis's Mickey and Mallory in *Natural Born Killers*. Soderbergh's characters are affable, if not downright pleasant in comparison. For the most part these figures live by an alternate code, which eschews violence and rewards loyalty. In an era marked by the excessive cinematic violence often embodied by the nihilistic killing sprees of Mickey and Mallory or ultra-violent 'Mexican stand-offs' (a showdown resulting in everyone shooting each other to death rendered in stylistic slow motion) in Tony Scott, Robert

Rodriguez and Quentin Tarantino films, Soderbergh's non-violent criminals tend to be polite robbers rather than brutal gangsters.

Moreover, Soderberghian values of friendship, love, and loyalty to one's comrades can be seen as wildly opposite to the protagonists gracing the screen several years earlier. This is certainly the case in *Out of Sight*, but also extends to *The Limey*, where Wilson's revenge stops slightly short of killing the man responsible for his daughter's death. The blurred lines between lawful and criminal activity in *Traffic* can also be seen as opposing this trend, particularly as characters are nuanced and treated in a non-judgemental manner. As the narrative works its way through the many facets of the drug trade, the treatment of Michael Douglas's drug czar and his daughter Caroline's (Erika Christensen) addiction is one of the more interesting elements of this film, especially considering that neither exists within the terms of a Manichean universe – a revelation for an American movie primarily concerned with depicting the world of narco-trafficking and the abject failure of America's 'War on Drugs.' *Traffic* is Soderbergh's most complex, multi-faceted and even-handed crime film, one which offers dozens of perspectives as we are presented with the political, local, and personal components of an institutional and transnational problem.

This theme of overcoming social stigma extends to Julia Roberts's portrayal of Erin Brockovich, whose quest for justice for the 'little guys' is initially motivated simply by her need to get a job to support her children. Wilson's stay in America relative to his initial objective becomes softened when he learns about his daughter through his encounters with her friends. That one is a woman and the other a Latino man is significant to the issues of representation within Soderbergh's films. By no means does this present a flawless view of a society unhindered by racism, but the bonds of love and friendship that cross these boundaries are a common occurrence within Soderbergh's crime films. The ultimate translation of this ethos extends to the gang in *Ocean's Eleven*, whose loyalty to each other is as important to them as the money that they will receive from their collective criminal effort.

In many cases, the protagonists are set against institutions that are bigger than themselves, calling into question the size of their crimes by comparison. In *The Girlfriend Experience*, Chelsea, the escort is on the wrong side of the law, but on the right side of the moral spectrum. As one commodity among many others in the hyper-capitalist setting of New York City at the height of the financial crisis, the moral dimension of prostitution is not called into question, but rather how it affects the protagonist in this raw character study, and how it compares to more perverse forms of exploitation. *The Informant!* offers something altogether different. The real-life story of Charles Whitacre and his fabulous scam is set against the backdrop of a completely corrupt system in which he is only a minor player. The audience, then, is forced to call into question the scale of individual misgivings in comparison to a transnational corporate crime that robbed millions of people across the globe. Similarly, in *Haywire*, the protagonist is technically on the wrong side of the law, but only because that line keeps shifting throughout the course of the film.

Up until this point, we have only considered the criminal plots of Soderbergh's anti-crime films and the protagonists who embody his Soderberghian ethics. But an essential countervailing element to these traits is the formal and stylistic innovation which makes these anti-crime stories so enjoyable to watch. This is where Soderbergh revels in the pleasurable opportunities afforded by the crime film, and where the paradox of the anti-crime film is established. We can analyse this function in one of Soderbergh's most beloved films, the intrinsically enjoyable caper film *Out of Sight*.

Out of Sight in Deep Focus

Widely received as Soderbergh's 'return to form,' *Out of Sight* is a significant film in Soderbergh's canon for several reasons. First, it marks the filmmaker's embrace of the mainstream, following his struggling, esoteric years in the mid-1990s. Second, it spurred the formation of his fruitful partnership with George Clooney. Third, *Out of Sight* allowed Soderbergh to incorporate the experimental techniques and stylistic features that he had been developing with *Schizopolis* into a generic form. But for our purposes here, *Out of Sight* marks the beginning of the filmmaker's most productive relationship with the crime genre, and is the film where everything 'clicks' for Soderbergh; he is able to merge his artistic, commercial, and guerrilla traits within a single film, as well as solidify his long-term relationship with the crime genre.

The full spectrum of Soderbergh's crime/anti-crime nature is present in *Out of Sight*. On the one hand, it is the story of the gentleman criminal protagonist, charming his way through bank robberies, while on the other, it presents a detective who has to chase him. While we have explored the director's relationship with the detective film in the previous section, the presence of both narratives, as well as the dual emphasis on pursuer and pursued is interesting insofar as it maps the trajectory of Soderbergh's career from this point forward. What marks this film as uniquely Soderberghian are his aesthetic signature stylistics, his characters' ethical impulse, and his slickly edited narrative.

Out of Sight belongs to the rare subset of crime films that appeals to adult sensibilities rather than primarily youth audiences. The brief string of Elmore Leonard adaptations in the 1990s (including *Jackie Brown* and *Get Shorty* [Barry Sonnenfeld, 1995], in addition to *Out of Sight*) are emblematic, as they did not contain the same youthful spirit of rebellion as many of their cinematic peers; rather, they involved middle-aged adults weighing decisions that would affect the rest of their lives. These choices involved second-chance romances and lasting friendships set against the backdrop of crime.[23] *Out of Sight* follows this trajectory, privileging the romantic element over the crime story. The chemistry between the two leads – rising stars Jennifer Lopez and George Clooney – is palpable. At the same time, Soderbergh reaches into his tool kit to formally enhance the already considerable onscreen chemistry.

Though the film marks Soderbergh's return to the studio system, it is undoubtedly an auteur work. This is evident from the very first frame, as a long shot of a blurry street gradually comes into focus. The camera continues to pan left to an office building, then abruptly zooms as Jack Foley (George Clooney) makes his way out of the door frame. In the same continuous take, he angrily rips his tie from his collar

Though the film marks Soderbergh's return to the studio system, it is undoubtedly an auteur work containing signature flourishes in the cinematography and editing, in this case jumbled narratives, distinct colour palettes, and freeze-frames.

and throws it to the ground. The scene freezes midway through this action, and the title credit appears in frame left. The take continues, panning along with Clooney as he makes his way into a nearby bank. This simple series of actions, rendered in one continuous long take and involving many rack focuses, reframings, and freeze-frames marks the marriage of what we have previously described as Soderbergh's experimental, chaotic style to the Hollywood genre picture.

With regards to cinematography, the director delineates the sunny climes of the film's initial Florida setting with soft oranges and subtle reds, before juxtaposing this against the chilly backdrop of Detroit rendered with a harsh, bluish filter. There is also a surplus of signature out-of-focus, off-centre framings and handheld camera movements. But it is the editing that most marks the unique style of *Out of Sight*, and it is embodied in a single sequence that is both the film's most memorable scene and also its most unconventional.[24] Jack meets Karen in her hotel bar and the two begin to speak over a shared glass of bourbon. Instead of using Hollywood's typical shot-reverse shot pattern, the sequence subtly gives way to Soderbergh's auteurist flourish and the displacement of time and space. Their conversation dissolves into sound bridges, and Soderbergh uses associational editing to flash forward to Karen's hotel room at a later time. These brief shots are soundless, and a match on the action of the bar scene, beginning when the characters first touch. When Jack's fingers reach for Karen's hand, the narrative flashes forward to his touching her hand on her leg in the hotel room, eventually leading to a soundless, slow-motion rendering of their love scene.[25] Along the way, Soderbergh accentuates the tactile nature of this scene by continuing the wide array of freeze-frames within the film, all of which, ahem, culminate within the scene.

Staggered temporalities are used across the entire plot structure, not just isolated scenes. This editing pattern not only represents Soderbergh's larger concern with telling stories in a non-linear fashion, but also conforming to the mode of storytelling that came to dominate the crime genre in the 1990s. In *Out of Sight*, this phenomenon occurs from the very beginning of the film, which we later discover is not only a flash-back, but only a fragment of a flashback; the second time we revisit the scene, this time in full, the viewer is given added context. While this is not entirely different than other films within this genre (with *Reservoir Dogs* serving as the quintessential example of films that begin *in medias res*), what is different in this case is that it is unclear to the viewer until much later in the film that this is a flashback at all. This 'hidden flashback' (for lack of a better term) conforms to the larger signature editing stylistics of Soder-bergh, who would continue this experimentation in later films such as *The Limey*, *Ocean's Twelve*, and *The Girlfriend Experience*. *Contagion*, for example, is a linear film to all intents and purposes; however, the story's first scene is not shown until the plot's final scene, revealing the corporate culpability at the heart of the pandemic. *Haywire* also suspends the audience's expectations at the end of the film, withholding violence in a similar fashion to *Out of Sight*, and possibly offering even more pleasure from the imagined outcome.

Thus, the editing structure is not employed as mere hip stylisation, but as a method of restricting and revealing the range and depth of character information so as to complicate the viewer's understanding of the central relationship. On the one hand, the romance plot between Karen and Jack is told in a mostly linear fashion, while at the same time, flashbacks concerning Jack's exploits in prison gradually bring us back to the point in the story where the film began. We grow to understand that Jack's desire to do one last score is motivated both by his need to assert his male utility and enact revenge on Richard (Albert Brooks) for his humiliating job offer, while simultaneously securing enough money so that he can leave his criminal life behind. This is revealed to the spectator in the film's final flashback, where we understand that Jack tried to go straight, but was rebuffed by Richard, whose previous offer of a job with his company ended up being a square gig as a security guard. In this sense, the viewer learns of the circumstances surrounding Jack's getting caught the last time, as well as their compre-hension that he is not a 'bad guy' by any means.

It is more than just 'likable criminals' that distinguishes Soderbergh's films from others in the 1990s' crime wave though; it is that his criminal protagonists are set against larger, more nefarious institutions. This occurs to a limited degree in *Out of Sight*, with Richard's towering financial office, and extends to a wider scope with the large-scale indifference to human suffering as a result of corporate malfeasance in such films as *Erin Brockovich*, *Syriana*, *The Informant!*, and *Contagion*.[26] George Clooney often plays characters with this oppositional stance, who through their ingenuity and friendships attempt to rob from people who 'deserve it,' rather than from innocent bystanders. In *Out of Sight*, Foley is a bank robber who has never used a gun in any of his heists, embodying a new form of 'charming criminal,' and representing a kind of thief who is more concerned with stealing a woman's heart than money. His best friend and partner, Buddy Bragg (Ving Rhames) is another example of this good criminal/bad criminal dichotomy, which faces 'good' bad guys off against 'bad' bad guys, or bad guys against even worse guys.

In *Out of Sight*, Foley is a bank robber who has never used a gun in any of his heists, embodying a new form of 'charming criminal,' and representing a kind of thief who is more concerned with stealing a woman's heart than money.

The bad guys, in this case, are very bad indeed. This film makes a point of explicitly juxtaposing Jack's charming, thinking man's thief against the inarticulate and brutal would-be gangster 'Snoopy' (Don Cheadle). Snoopy's cold-blooded killing throughout the film is clearly positioned against Foley's 'gentleman-robber' code. In this film, Jack's loyalty to partner in crime Buddy is only eclipsed by Buddy's need to confess his crimes to his sister after every heist. Additionally, that the partners only rob from banks is important, as it demonstrates their desire not to harm anyone, but rather to only steal from insured sources. As such, their robberies are essentially 'victimless' crimes, particularly as Foley charms the female bank tellers while robbing them.

Soderbergh's treatment of on-camera violence is also significant, as it stands in stark contrast to the explicit, if not gratuitous violence of his peers such as Tarantino and Stone. One such example occurs in a brief, yet highly effective scene. Here, hapless (and harmless) stoner carjacker Glenn (Steve Zahn) realises that he has moved from Foley's gang into another, more dangerous crowd of criminals, led by the greedy Snoopy. In order to show his loyalty to them, the gang forces Glenn to shoot someone who owes them money. As opposed to the infamous car scene in *Pulp Fiction* – where Vince accidentally shoots his friend in the face, leaving bits of brain scattered throughout the back of the car, to be cleaned out in a later scene – Soderbergh shows a great deal of restraint, restricting what the audience can and cannot see. The camera lens is spray painted by one of Glenn's would-be compatriots, leaving just enough room in the frame for the viewer to see the motion of a shaken Zahn nervously shooting a pistol. This is followed by a series of jump-cuts of Glenn's arm as he repeatedly swings a hatchet. The audience still witnesses Glenn's horror in the situation, while the film suggests just enough violence for viewers to fill in the details themselves. Perhaps influenced by one of the few genres he himself has not tried, Soderbergh utilises the convention of the horror genre: the most truly horrifying is that which remains unseen.

The racial and class compositions in these films are also significant to the way
that these stories function. In the case of Karen, she has to overcome the prejudices
inherent in her being a Latina woman in law enforcement. In this vein, it is important that Buddy is black and Jack is white, although neither speaks of his position-
ality. What they have in common is their ability and desire to operate outside of the
parameters of their respective fields (law and crime) in order to fulfill their respective
needs. The relationship between Karen and Jack is dictated by the fact that each of
them stands as outsiders within their respective professions. For Karen, this means
that her status as a woman in the dangerous job of a county sheriff puts her at odds
in a male dominated profession, whereas for Jack, this means that he is often enough
an outcast, namely a gentleman among a cadre of criminals. Despite the fact that his
chosen profession is full of killers, Jack eschews the use of violence, to the point that
he has never used a gun in his career of bank robberies but instead has effectively

charmed his way through all of these enterprises. What Jack Foley and Danny Ocean share, besides the actor who portrays them, is the assertion that were it not for either outside circumstances (Jack's partner Buddy calling to confess on their penultimate job) and Danny's 'self-destructive phase' where he allowed himself to be caught, they would have continued their successful, charming careers. Thus, Soderbergh overlays a particular moral ambivalence and ambiguity (robbing from the rich, never from the poor, and never using violence to fulfill one's needs) over the Manichean ethics of the traditional Hollywood crime film.

Although Foley is presumably brought to justice at the end of *Out of Sight*, the film provides a unique subversion of Hollywood closure. Though Karen upholds the law and arrests Foley, going so far as to shoot him in the leg so he cannot escape in their showdown, she also arranges to give him a ride back to prison accompanied by an expert lock picker and escape artist (played by Samuel L. Jackson in a cameo). A testament to the paradoxical nature of Soderbergh's anti-crime practice, Foley ends up achieving freedom, money, and love through his criminal enterprise, while Karen exploits a loophole to fulfill her duty as a defender of the law. The traditional romantic coupling established, they drive off into the sunset, as is the Hollywood custom, except this time it is in an armoured police van and a literal chain barrier between crime and law sits between them.

Notes

1   John Pierson, *Spike, Mike, Slackers & Dykes: A Guided Tour Across a Decade of American Independent Cinema* (New York: Miramax Books/Hyperion, 1997), 218.

2   Emanuel Levy, *Cinema of Outsiders: The Rise of American Independent Film* (New York: New York University Press, 1999). The chapter entitled 'Resurrection of Noir' provides a comprehensive overview of crime films in the 1990s.

3   Waxman, *Rebels on the Backlot*.

4   James Mottram, *Sundance Kids*.

5   The films he has produced also typically involve crime, such as *Criminal* and *Welcome to Collinwood*.

6   Thomas Leitch, *Crime Films* (New York: Cambridge University Press, 2002), 1.

7   David Desser, 'Global Noir: Genre Film in the Age of Transnationalism,' in *Film Genre Reader III*, ed. Barry Keith Grant (Austin, TX: University of Texas Press, 2003), 518. Desser suggests that the noir resurgence begins with *Pulp Fiction*, stating '[with the success of *Pulp Fiction*, neo-noir extended itself later into the nineties, with *Pulp Fiction*, as such, becoming the standard of generic definition.'

8   See Michael Ryan and Douglas Kellner, *Camera Politica: The Politics and Ideology of Contemporary Hollywood Film* (Bloomington: Indiana University Press, 1988); Robin Wood, *Hollywood from Vietnam to Reagan – and Beyond* (2003).

9   Leitch, *Crime Films*, 46.

10   Ibid., 15.

11   Nicole Rafter, *Shots in the Mirror: Crime Films and Society* (New York: Oxford University Press, 2000), 3.

12 Monaco, *The New Wave*, 17.

13 Richard John Neupert, *A History of the French New Wave Cinema* (Madison, WI: University of Wisconsin Press, 2002), 68.

14 Leitch, *Crime Films*, 2.

15 Rafter, *Shots in the Mirror*, 13.

16 Letich, *Crime Films*, 15.

17 Peter Biskind, *Easy Riders, Raging Bulls: How the Sex-Drugs-and-Rock-'n'-Roll Generation Saved Hollywood* (New York: Simon & Schuster, 1998), 17.

18 Alexander Horwath, Noel King, and Thomas Elsaesser, *The Last Great American Picture Show: Traditions, Transitions and Triumphs in 1970s Cinema* (Amsterdam: Amsterdam University Press, 2003).

19 See Thomas Elsaesser, 'Notes on the Unmotivated Hero: Pathos of Failure in the 1970s,' in *The Last Great American Picture Show: Traditions, Transitions and Triumphs in 1970s Cinema*, eds. Alexander Horwath, Noel King, and Thomas Elsaesser, (Amsterdam: Amsterdam University Press, 2003), 279–292.

20 See Mia Mask, '1971 – Movies and the Exploitation of Excess,' in *American Cinema of the 1970s: Themes and Variations*, ed. Lester D. Friedman (Oxford: Berg, 2007), 63.

21 We are borrowing this phrase from Fred Botting and Scott Wilson, whose 'The Tarantinian Ethics' suggests a slightly more complicated view than a Manichean universe of good and evil. Fred Botting and Scott Wilson, *The Tarantinian Ethics* (London: Sage, 2001).

22 See Robin Wood, 'Ideology, Genre, Auteur' in *Film Genre Reader III*, ed. Barry Keith Grant, (Austin, TX: University of Texas Press, 2003), 60–74.

23 This is exactly what occurs in *Get Shorty*, where gangster Chili Palmer (John Travolta) finds it more rewarding to become a Hollywood producer than to collect the vig (interest on a loan) from his criminal counterparts. While Chili eventually does have to enforce the will of his gang, he simultaneously forms solid bonds between the out-of-work ex-scream queen Karen (Rene Russo) and the director Harry Zimm (Gene Hackman).

24 … and earns *Entertainment Weekly*'s award for Sexiest Movie.

25 Perhaps inspired by a memorable montage sequence in Mike Nichols' 1967 landmark film *The Graduate*, where the protagonist Benjamin (Dustin Hoffman) moves between past, present, and future within the course of two Simon & Garfunkel songs. As Soderbergh has long stated his reverence for the film, going so far as to provide the audio commentary on the DVD Anniversary edition, it is a safe bet that he is aware of Nichols' earlier achievement with this film. Likewise, the distinctive love scene in *Don't Look Now* (Nicolas Roeg, 1973) seems another likely influence given Soderbergh's cinephelia and specific love of 1970s' films.

26 In *Haywire*, this ethos is reflected in Ewan McGregor's pronouncement that the only value system is 'More money.' This value is juxtaposed against Michael Douglas's official governmental position, which stands counter to the fickle nature of the 'private sector' in this film, which is always inherently open to the highest bidder.

CHAPTER EIGHT

The Ethical Heist: Competing Modes of Capital in the Ocean's Trilogy

It's a throwback. Nobody gets killed. There's no bad language. It's just an old-fashioned heist movie with lots of stars.

Steven Soderbergh[1]

What is the robbing of a bank compared to the founding of one?

Bertolt Brecht[2]

Spanning a six-year period, *Ocean's Eleven*, *Ocean's Twelve*, and *Ocean's Thirteen* are Soderbergh's most outright popular and commercially successful films, and they are also some of his most well-received, particularly the first entry in the series. Though these are quite clearly mainstream movies intended for a broad, multiplex audience, they nevertheless retain the signature stylistics that we have thus far attributed to the director. *Ocean's Twelve* is even truer to Soderbergh form than the first film, comprised of reflexive storytelling and technique, which may account for some of its critical backlash. The third film then returns the characters to the space and place that made them so appealing in the first place; the Rat Pack reborn, the gang takes on the indifferent forces of excessive capitalism and unethical business practices. The national and class tensions in each of these films is overt, and through the means of the heist, Soderbergh presents two competing modes of capital: the all-American underdogs versus the bullies of global capitalism, with the little guys triumphing in the face of overwhelming odds.

It is worth documenting just how enormously successful these movies were in the global marketplace, and the degree to which they were an international phenomenon. Soderbergh's first number one box-office opening, *Ocean's Eleven* earned a significant $183 million domestically, but with its highly marketable A-list cast and classical Hollywood panache, earned another $267 million in foreign markets, making it the fifth highest worldwide earner in 2001. *Ocean's Twelve* also opened at number one at the box office earning $125 million domestically, and another $237 million internationally. Finally, *Ocean's Thirteen* completed the hat trick, with another number one box-office opening and another $117 million domestically, $194 million internationally. A testament to the new economics of Hollywood mathematics and its increasing reliance on foreign box office to recoup studio investment, these foreign markets account for more than sixty percent of the total worldwide gross of the trilogy, a mammoth $1.1 billion. 'Ancillary' markets such as DVD, pay-television, and broadcast television[3] tend to bring in as much as the theatrical gross, or more, so it's safe to say the actual gross of the *Ocean's* trilogy is in the $2 billion range. Soderbergh had come a long way from the scant $10,000 that *Schizopolis* grossed.[4]

As caper films, the *Ocean's* trilogy presents a utopian allegory of America at the turn of the new century, in which American values need to be renegotiated in the face of globalised and multinational business practices. In effect, the Ocean's gang repopulates Las Vegas with a pan-American cadre of likable personalities, and by emulating the Rat Pack, supplants the contemporary reality by replacing it with a utopian fantasy. As in much of Hollywood cinema, these tensions within the film evoke wish-fulfillment on the part of the spectator, as well as expressing a somewhat subversive message, wherein the protagonists always end up 'getting away with it,' winning love and money at the end of the film.

This chapter will examine the evolving stylistic, thematic, and narrative concerns that pepper the trilogy as Soderbergh revisits it throughout the decade, with each subsequent effort seeking to complicate, rather than solve, the ongoing issues of capital. Using *Ocean's Eleven* as our main example, we will analyse the film with an eye to what we see as its allegory of capital, laying the foundation for our work on the other films in the trilogy. This involves a thorough examination of the heist genre, taking into account the qualities that the first installment adheres to and resists. For *Ocean's Twelve,* we will revisit its reflexive traits, and its deployment of the international star system, in addition to suggesting that these are exactly the reasons for its success in Europe and its critical (but not commercial) failure in the US. Finally, we will suggest that *Ocean's Thirteen* rounds out the trilogy with its most explicit message of philanthropy, corporate responsibility, and the redistribution of wealth. These films should not be dismissed as trivial, Hollywood blockbuster fare; following Jameson, we will assert that the more popular and successful these films are – in other words, mass – the more political and subversive they can be.

Ocean's Eleven: An Allegory of Capital

In the first moments of *Ocean's Eleven*, dishevelled protagonist Danny Ocean is released from prison after doing four years of hard time. He stands as a man out of sorts: an unshaven ex-con in a tuxedo, hoping to reassert his male utility in the face of overwhelming odds. This image echoes Ocean's earlier conversation with his parole board, when he announces that he allowed himself to be caught after his wife left him, part of his admitted 'self-destructive phase.' The juxtaposition of Ocean in his tuxedo, set against the backdrop of the prison, presents him as a man 'out of time' as well, an anachronistic, nostalgic version of 'manliness' set against the stark representation of a present-day prison.

In this remake of the Rat Pack classic *Ocean's Eleven* (Lewis Milestone, 1960), Soderbergh consciously exploits the cultural cachet of the earlier picture, but with several profound modifications. Here, as in the Frank Sinatra film, an amiable band of outlaws performs the ultimate act of male solidarity and utility – a heist – achieving something far greater than they could have accomplished individually. The heist expresses the desire for two complementary value systems. The first of these is money, as seen in *Ocean's Eleven* in which the gang will attempt to rob $165 million to divide evenly among themselves. The second value is directly related to the heist genre's ongoing appeal, embodying the way that men, each possessing unique and highly-specialised sets of skills, are supposed to use them within the contemporary setting. These depictions of male solidarity, camaraderie, and friendship allow the best of both worlds, the reward of direct monetary compensation for their efforts, and fulfillment of the more important values of love and solidarity. Thus, the film offers a typical Hollywood reward of love and money for those who deserve it. In this vein, *Ocean's Eleven* not only foregrounds these value systems that the heist group embodies, but also the competing modes of capital that jockey for position throughout the film. The movie is a comedy of remarriage, which has its own connotations in terms of genre and the depiction of class, reuniting Clooney and Roberts at the end of the film and overlaying yet another value system upon an already rich tapestry of values.

Another tension within Soderbergh's remake is the film's depiction of real-life history (circa 2001) set against a present-tense, albeit fictional, 'reality.' After his release, Ocean reads a newspaper headline: 'Las Vegas Landmark to Be Razed: Former Casino Owner Denounces Plan,' which is accompanied by photographs of Reuben Tishkoff (Elliot Gould) and Terry Benedict (Andy Garcia). According to the newspaper, 'Terry Benedict, the new owner of the Xanadu casino announced his plan to demolish the resort and replace it with "something the whole world will treasure."' Danny's viewing of the article is significant, as it points to his greater involvement in the problem, as well as his business in producing a solution to it. This conflict could not be clearer. Gould's Reuben Tishkoff, the nostalgic embodiment of American capital that Las Vegas used to stand for, runs counter to Garcia's suave, vaguely-European Terry Benedict, who embodies the new global monetary system that is in the process of transforming the site of Vegas from 'America's Playground' and 'Sin City' to a destination for global and familial tourism. *Ocean's Eleven* highlights several issues regarding history, memory, and globalisation, overwriting contrasting value systems on the palimpsest of Las Vegas.

First, it utilises the cultural cachet of an earlier historical moment (the Rat Pack and the original film) to nostalgically evoke post-World War II American affluence within the contemporary global setting of present-day Vegas. Second, the heist is a utopian effort to provide an alternative to capital, both local and global, depicting a parallel system that is populated by 'real' people and places. In this world, it is still possible to realign the system by rewriting the rules, 'taking the house' through the ultimate act of collective male solidarity. In doing so, the film imagines how collective efforts realign contemporary cultural values by imposing a different set of moral and monetary rewards. Third, as the most classic of Hollywood tropes, true love is the overarching goal, and true to the American dream, the reward for embodying these American values includes the love of an unattainable woman, in addition to riches.

As a work of mass culture in the early twenty-first century, *Ocean's Eleven* stands as an allegory for the present-day setting that it emerges from. This is to say that it mediates this history, for the viewer, within the film itself. The setting here is crucial, not only because Vegas is the staging ground for early postmodern theory but also because it serves as the ongoing site of hyper-accelerated transition. The continued destruction and reconstruction of its landmarks allows us to view, in real time, the global flow of money in and out of the Strip.[5] It is this historical actuality – the replacement of older structures with newer ones – that can be seen as the transitional space of economic modes as they transform from modern to postmodern capital.

The meaning of the heist film can be traced through its various, historically-motivated reappearances that are symptomatic of overall socio-economic trends. *Ocean's Eleven* is emblematic of the transformation of economic modes (the transitional moment of capital) which simultaneously embodies and criticises the cultural logic of Hollywood. To wit, Soderbergh employs both allegorical and utopian strategies in order to reveal the film's alternate value system in play. Opposing arguments posed by Thomas Schatz[6] or Justin Wyatt[7] that the New Hollywood's 'high concept' fare ushered in a new era of apolitical cinema, Fredric Jameson's reading of *Jaws* highlights the inherent tensions between high and low culture and argues that mass culture can be just as semiotically and politically rich as other works.[8] By taking *Jaws,* the film that ultimately ushered in the 'apolitical New Hollywood,' Jameson argues for the usefulness of a new mode of analysis, one which recognises the utopian potential within a work of mass culture. Jameson suggests that it is not the shark itself that needs to be questioned, but rather the formation (and class composition) of the group of people who band together to defeat it. Following this logic, we should put aside our impulse to 'interpret' the shark as an outright symbol and instead accept its figuration as 'polysemous.'[9] *Jaws* not only serves as a fitting example of how ideology is folded back into texts, but it also shows the way that social and historical issues can be figured within movies in order to 'be the object of the successful manipulation and containment.'[10] Thus, we can use this method to read the heist film as a utopian imagining of a competing value system.

Ocean's Eleven operates in this way, assembling a set of heroes who rally against the 'mythical' conjuration of a 'monster.'[11] Terry Benedict, then, need not be interpreted as the outright symbol of 'capital,' but instead the 'monster' that the protagonists of the film will rally against. Danny's goal is not only to repatriate his male utility but also to find a place for himself in the new system of capital, which can be achieved only by opposing Benedict. This opposition links him to Reuben and both characters must negotiate their 'past-ness' in the present day. Danny supplements the credo, 'the house always wins,' with his optimistic assertion that betting big will still let you take the house. Danny has spent his time in prison scheming to steal from the most impervious vaults in Las Vegas and has calculated the spoils of the job as 'eight figures, divided equally.' Rusty, Danny's right-hand man, claims a heist this complex will require ten or eleven specialists in their field: 'at least a dozen guys doing a combination of cons.' Utilising the (fabricated) insider language of the con man, Rusty says they will need 'a Boesky, a Jim Brown, two Jethros, a Leon Spinks, a Miss Daisy and the biggest Ella Fitzgerald ever.' The formation of a diverse group relates to the central issue in almost all crime films, as men get to use their unique skills (denoted by Rusty's categories) in a 'proper' setting. In many ways, the logic and assembly of the group precedes the later structure of the super-hero film, where each of the super-powered individuals team up in order to oppose some larger global cataclysm, or super-villain's evil plot.

Before Danny assembles his rag-tag crew, each member has been wasting his talents in various locales across the country: Rusty has been teaching (rather unsuccessfully) Hollywood teen stars the ins and outs of poker, Reuben has been ousted from his casino and is doomed to witness its destruction at the hands of his rival Terry Benedict, Frank (Bernie Mac) has been dealing blackjack at a casino in Atlantic City, the Malloy twins (Scott Caan and Casey Affleck) have been entertaining themselves by annoying each other in Utah, electronics expert Livingston Dell (Eddie Jemison) has been working with an FBI drug squad, Yen (Shaobo Qin) has been employed as a Chinese acrobat, Saul (Carl Reiner) is retired in Florida and losing at the dog track, Linus (Matt Damon) has been trying to establish himself as a pickpocket in Chicago, and explosives specialist Basher (Don Cheadle) has assembled an inept gang of bank robbers and is about to get himself caught before Rusty finds him. Basher's reaction to Rusty's offer – 'It'll be nice working with proper villains again' – testifies to the bind in which all these characters have found themselves. Their impressive skills and talents are being squandered because they lack the opportunity to express them in the contemporary cultural context.

The pan-American composition of the group is also important, recalling a generic precursor, the World War II combat film.[12] The diverse constitution of the group came to stand as a rallying point for the construction of the mythical American character within the context of the nation-building project and also showed the many teams, all of whom opposed Hitler and Nazism. This diversity finds its expression in the *Ocean's Eleven* ensemble, who represent the multi-faceted geographic, regional, and racial constituencies in America. In this vein, it is worth noting that Danny hails from New York, Frank is from New Jersey, Rusty resides in LA, the Malloys are Mormons from Utah, Saul is retired in Florida, Livingston is in California, Linus is in Chicago, and Reuben, who is Jewish, lives in Las Vegas. The inclusion of Basher (a black Englishman) and Yen (a Chinese import) is also significant, as they expand the parameters of the group's resistance to globalisation by themselves representing a globalised alternative to the contemporary mode of capital.

If what is at stake for Danny is the repatriation of his male utility (a common theme in the less violent examples of the heist genre), revisiting the sub-genre's history is essential, as the heist genre contains the traits and iconography that *Ocean's Eleven* inherits and subverts. For Jameson, the historical transformation of the criminal protagonist (from reprehensible to sympathetic) is a cipher for a larger perception of masculinity. *The Godfather* 'is a permutation of a generic convention' through which 'one could write a history of the changing social and ideological functions of this convention, showing how analogous motifs are called upon in distinct historical situations to emit strategically distinct, yet symbolically intelligible messages.'[13] While Edward G. Robinson's *Little Caesar* (Mervyn LeRoy, 1931) and James Cagney's Tom Powers in *The Public Enemy* (William A. Wellman, 1931) in the 1930s were 'psychopaths,' in the postwar Hollywood setting, the criminal protagonists 'have unexpectedly become invested with tragic pathos' that expressed 'the confusion of veterans returning from World War II.'[14] Considering this transformation of the cinematic criminal, we are prompted to ask whether audiences were either allied or opposed to these conceptions, recalling the earlier suggestion that the audience of a crime film suspends their disbelief as well as their moral judgement.[15] Today, cinematic criminals (and Ocean's gang in particular) are seen as heroic, sympathetic, and ultimately justified in their actions. Thus, Danny Ocean is our surrogate, playing out our thoughts, wishes, and anxieties regarding American identity, capitalism, friendship, and even love.

In the original *Ocean's Eleven* film, the merry band of criminals comprise the remnants of an ex-World War II platoon that had operated as a crack commando unit under the charge of Frank Sinatra's Danny Ocean. The restless ex-GIs find themselves unsuited to the new conditions of postwar society, and must operate outside this framework in order to find personal fulfillment. The heist connects them directly to these new historical circumstances and class relations, with the heist group attempting to carve out a small niche for themselves within the new world system. The depiction of class is central to this discussion. The heist film has always served as a site for this debate, dating from the earliest example of the sub-genre, *Asphalt Jungle* (John Huston, 1950). In this film, former soldier Dix (Sterling Hayden) is unable to adapt to the new conditions of postwar society and his gambling and drunkenness are both symptoms of this listlessness. His contemporaries are the other lost souls who reside in the purgatory of the criminal underworld. They are not perceived as evil, but simply seek the 'one big score' that will allow them to utilise their skills and redeem their personal pride. The neutral morality of this depiction is a key feature of this work, as the gang attempts to overcome their current circumstances through teamwork, planning, and a non-violent crime. This emphasis on collective action corresponds neatly with the postwar eruption of the heist film, in which individuals align with others in order to accomplish something bigger than themselves and attain greater rewards. Jameson accounts for these shifts in the genre, stating that 'this very distinctive narrative content…can at once be structurally differentiated from the older paradigms by its collective nature: in this, reflecting an evolution towards organizational themes and team narratives.'[16]

This logic presupposes that the heist genre reappears and disappears at various historical junctures and that each version expresses different values than the last. Recalling Schatz, a genre evolves in stages from Classical to Mannerist to Baroque.[17] To this we will add that these stages move in cycles and can often operate simultaneously in different spaces and places across the world.

Though the heist genre did not initially last long in the United States, peaking in the 1950s, it found greater life in Europe, where several key texts modified its conventions. In the heist's reconstitution in France – with *Rififi* (Jules Dassin, 1955) and *Bob le flambeur* – the genre continued to highlight the exploits of the noble, yet downtrodden protagonist. In *Rififi*, the protagonist is an ex-con who appears to have tuberculosis, and in *Bob le flambeur*, the thief is, among other things, a heroin-addicted gambler. The genre mutated further when transplanted to Italy, where the heist emphasised comic rather than tragic dimensions. Interestingly enough, in Europe the genre depicts the problems of class conflict and poverty in a more explicit form. *Big Deal on Madonna Street* (*I soliti ignoti,* Mario Monicelli, 1958) traces the exploits of a hopeful, yet down-and-out gang of everyday people. What *Madonna Street* alters is the group as 'professional' criminals. While not immediately inclined towards crime, they assemble in order to transcend their meagre social conditions and poverty, as exemplified by the motivation of photographer Tiberio (Marcello Mastroianni) to use his share of the money simply to bail his wife out of jail and reopen his camera store.

When the heist genre returned to the United States in the early 1960s, the original *Ocean's Eleven* was the baroque incarnation of the form and its repatriation via the silly antics of the Rat Pack looting Vegas sent the heist genre into limbo for another long stretch, this time ending in the early 1990s. The original film takes the essential conventions of the genre and combines both their comic and tragic elements into a playful, reflexive romp for actors to play themselves within a formal structure and to sing songs in the middle of what was once presumably a venue for serious social reflection. This consideration will be important later, as it becomes one of the key features of the film's *doppelgänger*, Soderbergh's own version of *Ocean's Eleven*.

Soderbergh's film inherits and exploits the cultural capital of the heist film within the specific parameters of its contemporary historical moment. The heist film is the embodiment of countercultural trends, and possibly contains the utopian gesture that positively reconstitutes postmodern male utility. Danny's quest to bet large against the house can be seen as a monumental gesture in the face of the shift from modern (and American) capital to its postmodern and globalised counterpart. This tension between modes is embodied through the opposing real-life spaces of Las Vegas, as seen in the location shooting at the Bellagio casino, the 'found' footage of the actual destruction of the 'Xanadu,' as well as the synthesis of these sites within the film.

If the contemporary subject is increasingly fragmented by the system of late capital (characterised by Francis Fukuyama's famous declaration that the end of the twentieth century was the epoch of 'The End of History') then what occurs at this 'End' is the 'blockage of the historical imagination' within postmodernism.[18] Not only is *Ocean's Eleven*'s status as a remake symptomatic of this phenomenon, but presumably, we have arrived in an era that remains trapped in a singular mode of representation, reflecting the overall dominance of the singular vision of the market. Hollywood is an expression of these tensions, as movies are the ultimate product of the system of capital that produces them. What is needed at this point is allegorical reading that can help us to negotiate the 'real' and 'fictional' elements of the film, reconstituting them as allegorical within an equally distributed 'imaginary space.' We could then attempt to re-read the historical and 'real-life' appearances of actors playing themselves along with the depiction of historical buildings in the film. Here, the diegetic renaming of El Rancho (which was imploded in 2000 – the year the film was shot) to the Xanadu (a hotel that was never built, but whose designs feature prominently in the Las Vegas imaginary) demonstrates the allegorical relationship that the film has to reality.[19] This feature, in addition to the other real-life personalities within the film (including young stars Topher Grace and Joshua Jackson), along with Las Vegas luminaries (Wayne Newton, Siegfried and Roy, and Evander Holyfield), complicates the reading of the film when viewed head-on. One solution may be to link the concepts of allegory to Utopia, terms that for Jameson are inseparable.

Solidarity and Love, Entertainment and Utopia

Historically, the protagonists of the heist film largely eschew the use of violence in favour of ingenuity and skill, redeeming themselves through their loyalty to the group and the utility of the job itself.[20] Jameson's method projects allegorical and utopian features onto the site of the criminal organisation. For Jameson, the crime family (or heist group) becomes the imaginary mediation of the collective longing onto a construction that exists outside the everyday parameters of society, or rather, the 'figure of collectivity' is a fulfillment of 'Utopian longing, if not a Utopian envy.'[21] We can further link the heist group to the most basic of utopian desires: employment. As demonstrated in *Big Deal on Madonna Street* and its recent American remake, produced by Soderbergh and Clooney, *Welcome to Collinwood*, men are the products of their depressed socio-economic conditions, and when 'criminals' are forced to cope with the real facts of their poverty, they take action to alleviate their hardships through the criminal act. This logic suggests that the desire of the criminal is not simply to elevate one's social standing but merely to enter society. The act of viewing the heist, with the incorporation of the viewer and participants in the planning stages, also allies these two groups and expresses a collective, shared desire to redistribute wealth into the hands of the protagonists.

The crime of the heist needs to be perceived as victimless, lest the protagonists lose out on the audience's sympathies. This element is different from the various other sub-genres of the crime film, as many crimes include the probability of people (besides the robbers) not only getting robbed, but also getting hurt or killed. Instead, the job itself (as demonstrated in *Rififi*) involves a great deal of planning (including a trial run) and requires specialists in order to pull off the bloodless crime.[22] The 'score' usually takes place in a highly-insured space, such as a bank, a jewellery store, or a casino. The object that is stolen is not as consequential as what it will do to change the lives of the heist team for the better. Thus, as opposed to a straight-on bank robbery in which people can be harmed, the heist proposes both its 'victimlessness' (targeting insured material) and the possibility of achieving some sort of upward mobility in the era of late capital. The heist also stands as wish-fulfillment on the part of the spectator, who witnesses this redistribution of wealth while idolising the entrepreneurial intent of the group, which is essentially to steal from the rich. This idea extends throughout the *Ocean's* trilogy, in which the gang's final heist literally turns out to be a charitable enterprise rather than an effort for personal gain.

Viewing the heist as a utopian gesture means distinguishing, as Jameson does, between 'the Utopian form and the Utopian wish.'[23] Sometimes this means that the utopian work functions in a negative capacity, pointing towards an 'imaginary enclave' that is parallel to the world it springs from. By incorporating its negative potential within a system of dialectics, or rather, by its negativity, it points towards a possible future that no one actually *wants* but that everyone *imagines* is possible.[24] *Ocean's Eleven*, then, situates fictional characters in a real-life space and demonstrates how they can better themselves through the utopian gesture of the heist. The film's real footage of the actual implosion of the El Rancho casino complex – which follows the destruction of the Sands, the Dunes, the Hacienda, the Aladdin, the Landmark, and the subsequent implosion of the Desert Inn – is emblematic of the desire to intercede in the continuous destruction of the 'American' version of Vegas as represented through the nostalgic (and somewhat anachronistic) presence of Ocean's gang.

The opposite (or negative) key to reading this issue lies in the characterisation of Terry Benedict. The figurability of *über*-capitalist Benedict is an important part of this discussion as he sets up a binary opposition to his counterpart, Danny. Benedict is the reason for the destruction of the Xanadu, which the film depicts as part of the inevitable destruction of 'American' casinos in the face of a globalised future.[25] The viewer is thus presented with a face and a name on which to place their frustrations about the era. Anyone who stands counter to Benedict – with his destruction of landmarks, his accumulation of the canon of Western art, and his 'possession' of Danny's former wife Tess – will be worthy of our approval and our loyalty. Once again, we need to remind ourselves that Benedict is not the outright 'symbol' of capital, as he would be in a strictly binary reading, but resembles Jameson's characterisation of the shark in *Jaws*. As with the shark, 'a multiplicity' of readings attributable to Benedict allows for polysemous interpretation.[26] The protagonists in *Ocean's Eleven*, as in *Jaws*, oppose the antagonistic force, reconstituting class awareness and solidarity by the act of opposition. This conflict takes place within the system of capital that the heist opposes, presenting a utopian gesture that imagines a happy ending in the face of what we know the more likely alternative would be – the nearly inevitable loss of a gambler's money.

Paradoxically, robbing three of Benedict's casinos is *itself* a capitalist enterprise and must be bankrolled and planned in advance in order that the new sub-system of capital can compete with the overarching one. However, the heist is orchestrated by equals who can trust each other, offering a model to compete with Benedict's greed and showing us an alternate reality where a handshake still has inherent value. The heist film also functions within the confines of the global capitalist moment, but utilises its own brand of business: the star system. The presence of stars within a work and their interactions (and acting styles) account for an allegorical system of figurability through which viewers can assess the features of the society in which they reside.[27] The film essentially presents the *personalities* of the Hollywood system against the globalised and de-personalised system of global capital. The heist narrative is mobilised once again to present an alternative system of capital within the larger framework of capital proper.

The work of the text is to present the alternative in an affable fashion, which manages to redeem the moment of its conception with a utopian discourse.

Danny Ocean's heist will redeem his wounded male pride by expressing his utility in the era that obviously was the cause of his original downfall. The means through which he accomplishes this redemption is by robbing the three biggest casinos in Las Vegas on the night of their largest profit. Even more significant is Danny's redemption in his wife's eyes, as Tess realises by the end of the film that the heist is a grand declaration of his love for her. Ocean knows that it cannot be done alone and that he needs to recruit a face-to-face group of experts, who are themselves as downtrodden as he is. The reappearance of class in this endeavour is significant here, as the gang's constitution from all walks of life (and indeed different countries) accounts for the utopian element in the reconstitution of the capitalist enterprise and prefigures the global transformation of an alternative system that consists of different classes coming together to pull off one job. The reward of 'eight figures, divided equally' for the job presents an alternative reading of the contemporary capitalist enterprise and stands counter to Benedict's portrayal of the single CEO with hired underlings. This formation corresponds to Jameson's reading of *Jaws*, in which the specialised unit (the cop, the whiz kid and the salty sailor) faces off against the threat to society which Jameson characterises as the allegorical rendition of 'bad leadership,' but is transformed here into Benedict, who embodies globalised capital.

The film exploits a parallel narrative. This is Danny's redemption by winning back Tess. Danny utilises the device of the heist in order to win back his love, which can occur only by rendering the very construct of his limitation (namely money) moot. After Danny supposedly blows up Benedict's money, he faces off against him. Their confrontation implies that there is a greater value system at work here, namely love. When Ocean gets Benedict to admit that he would rather have his money back than Tess (Danny – 'What if I told you I could get your money back? Would you give up Tess? What would you say?' Benedict – 'I would say yes') he reveals the value system implicit in the work, and Danny wins both love *and* money in the end. This rendering of money as 'value-neutral' (as exemplified by its explicit onscreen demolition) attempts to place an alternative system of principles within the work and demonstrates a substitute set of ethics within the overarching milieu of the late capitalist era: the privileging of class solidarity and the bonds of friendship that can engender collective redemption.

That Danny gets all the things he wants within the span of the narrative, without the dire consequences that often befall characters in heists, is testament to the utopian dimension of *Ocean's Eleven*. Here the entrepreneurial collective rises to defeat the real conditions within the capitalist system by rendering the value of money moot. These are the ideological dimensions that the film disguises through the structure of its narrative, mediated and reconciled in an allegorical manner and refigured in the positive transformation of the genre – the happy ending of the film. The final collection of the gang for one last gathering at the illustrious fountain of the Bellagio is a testament to the success of the endeavour ('taking the house') and to the fleeting nature of the enterprise. Set to the introspective sounds of Claude Debussy's *Claire de lune dans la*

suite Bergamasque,[28] the group walks slowly from their nearby headquarters where they have stashed their winnings to assemble in wordless satisfaction at their triumphant feat. This image is juxtaposed by Tess's realisation that Danny has staged it all for her benefit, and she runs towards the federal marshals that whisk him away, yelling, 'Wait! That's my husband!' Danny wins both the girl and executes the perfect crime, solidifying the bonds of friendship and matrimony with a single gesture. As the group disperses, the camera lingers on each of their expressions as they look to each other, smile, and leave wordlessly. Tellingly, the camera moves last to Reuben, the nostalgic remnant of Vegas's past who puffs, satisfied, on his cigar.

Ocean's Twelve, Thirteen and Beyond: Soderberghian Ethics Revisited

Ocean's Eleven presents a utopian vision of the world that is very much steeped in the historical moment from which it emerges. In the era of postmodernism and global capital, it is worthwhile to resuscitate the utopian imagination with the tools that our world has at its disposal. In Fukuyama's assessment of the end of history, where alternatives to capitalism have collapsed in the post-Soviet era, paradoxically it is only within an overarching system of capital that alternatives can be explored. The allegorical heist that *Ocean's Eleven* presents is a confrontation between two opposing forces of capital

– one that employs the cultural cachet of the star system set against another that provides figurability to the destructive forces of multinational corporate capitalism. The film attempts to mediate the predominant tone of the resistance to the forces of globalisation by demonstrating that it is indeed possible to imagine an alternate world that is as enjoyable as it is hopeful. This is the impulse that the heist film has always expressed; it is *always* okay to steal from the rich, as long as you are prepared to face the consequences of your actions, consequences that are postponed to the film's sequel. If the profits can be redistributed by the characters into charitable works, as they are in the third film, or into real charities by the actors, such as Clooney's 'Save Darfur' enterprise, then all the better.

Despite their emphasis on criminal activity, the films are actually about something deeper. The heists, in these cases, are only excuses to develop and deepen bonds of friendship and to depict how people can work together, speaking, paradoxically, to the trilogy's utopian impulse. In the first film this idea consists initially of only Danny Ocean and his one big, dual-focused heist. While initially trying to win back the love of his ex-wife, the story expands to include rounding up a bunch of professionals. Together, they experience the joys of using their unique sets of skills, working together and discovering that they operate better as a unit. In the second film, the gang faces off against a mastermind criminal, perhaps suggesting that yet again, as a collective they are better than the individual. And the collective continues to expand, to the point where it is no longer entirely clear who the group consists of, or even what the title refers to. Is Tess the new addition to the gang in *Ocean's Twelve*, or is it Isabel (Catherine Zeta-Jones)? In *Ocean's Thirteen*, is Terry Benedict the new member or is it Roman Nagel (Eddie Izzard)? The collective itself, embodied in an A-list ensemble cast, becomes the true star.

Returning to our continuing development of 'Soderberghian ethics,' we should also consider each of the film's ethical thrusts. In the first film, as discussed, the values depicted in the heist are camaraderie and loyalty, as well as love. By the second film, the group re-bands to pay back Benedict, with interest. As each of the gang has largely been idle and complacent, spending their money aimlessly and generally returning to the jams that they got themselves out of in the first film, the individuals are shown to be complete only within the collective function. The gang's competition with a single, rival master thief shows the superiority of the group over the individual, especially as the singular competition is a pampered aristocrat. Finally, in *Ocean's Thirteen*, the point of the collective effort is no longer to 'steal from the rich,' but to 'bankrupt the rich,' to undermine the financial operations of an unethical businessman who dared to mess with one of the original gang, Reuben Tishkoff. To this end, a significant transfer of capital does take place, but by this point it is unclear whether the members of the gang are even criminals anymore, or whether they are just a bunch of tech-savvy mischief-makers with a grudge to settle.

In addition to the initial ethical thrust of each film, there is something to be said about the constitution of the collective and what becomes of it. In the first film, the difficulty that the gang's membership experiences is threefold: financial, as they are all struggling to make ends meet; personal, as they are all doing something that they do not

The transformation of Benedict over the course of the films also has an ethical trajectory, as he moves initially from the object of opposition to a co-conspirator, to the unwitting vehicle for philanthropy, wrapping up the series with another A-list cameo: Oprah Winfrey.

want to be doing; and utilitarian, as they are all squandering their unique talents. The overall class constitution is also significant, as the gang is comprised of ordinary Americans in a struggle against the increasingly nameless, faceless forces of globalised capital, as represented by Terry Benedict. In the second film, this class composition and opposition is even more pronounced, as the average American workers of the Ocean's gang oppose François Toulour, a *bona fide* count who does not even need the money, but steals for sheer pleasure. In the final film, the gang is once again reassembled and the main opposition remains that of 'good' industrialist Reuben versus cutthroat corruption, this time embodied in the not-so-subtly named character Willy Bank, played by Al Pacino. The juxtaposition is made explicit in one of the film's early scenes, when Reuben goes into a coma after learning that Bank has conned him out of his share of their joint business venture; at the end of the film, Reuben is miraculously 'healed' through the ongoing ministrations of the gang as they read Basher's heartfelt letters and evocations of friendship.

As the trilogy's final villain, he is richer, greedier, and an even more nefarious force of global capital than Benedict or Toulour. Just as the film returns to Las Vegas, the overarching theme of American nostalgia versus global capital also returns. Danny's disgust with Bank is crystallised in his parting line: 'You shook Sinatra's hand, you should know better.' The implication here is that Bank does not live up to the code of

By this third film, capital is no longer an object to be possessed, a symbol to be coded as nostalgic coopera-tion or globalised indifference; rather, the value of capital is essentially negated as seen in this long tracking shot of the casino with numerical overlays indicating the increasing winnings of all the patrons, which result in losses for Bank (Al Pacino). The heist has been transformed into a charitable enterprise rather than an effort for personal gain.

honour embodied in the Rat Pack and Ol' Blue Eyes. The evocation of Frank Sinatra and the 'good old days' of Las Vegas suggests several possibilities within a larger philos-ophy of Soderberghian ethics. For one, Sinatra and Vegas suggest a high point in the American consciousness – a postwar heyday when it felt unabashedly good to be American after the liberation of Europe as well as the pretence of consensus culture. Second, Sinatra's persona, friendships, philanthropy, and political activities suggest a model of success that all Americans could aspire to, one that includes loyalty, patri-otism, and hard work. Finally, the presence of a 'code' that passes along generations suggests that there is a system of honour and ethics that needs to be adhered to even within the context of criminal activities.

The transformation of Benedict over the course of the films also has an ethical trajectory, as he moves initially from the object of opposition to a co-conspirator, whose double-cross is punished in a complimentary fashion to Bank. By this third film, capital is no longer an object to be possessed, a symbol to be coded as nostalgic cooperation or globalised indifference; rather, the value of capital is essentially negated. For Bank, his casino is drained of capital by the gang's 'heist' of rigged machines, illustrated in a long tracking shot of the casino with numerical overlays indicating the increasing winnings of all the patrons. For Benedict, after attempting to steal from the gang, his portion of the take is donated to charity, so that he (unwittingly) becomes the vehicle for philanthropy, wrapping up the series with another A-list cameo: Oprah Winfrey. The only star capable of rivalling Clooney and Pitt's megastar status, Oprah's presence adds that final dose of self-reflexivity and Hollywood panache to send off the series on a pleasurable note. 'Entertainment does not…present models of utopian worlds, as in the classical utopias of Sir Thomas More, William Morris, *et al.*,' claims Richard Dyer. 'Rather the utopianism is contained in the feelings it embodies. It presents, head on as it were, what utopia would feel like [i.e., pleasure] rather than how it would be organized.'[29] The *Ocean's* trilogy can certainly lay claim to an embodiment of this type of utopian feeling. It is a testament to Soderbergh's anti-crime impulse and ethical imperative that he accomplishes such a feeling of utopian pleasure, all the while developing a sophisticated treatise against the abstracting indifference of global capitalism.

Notes

1   Quoted in 'Movie Preview,' *Entertainment Weekly*, October 22, 2001.
2   Bertolt Brecht, 'The Threepenny Opera,' *Bertolt Brecht Poems; Bertolt Brecht Collected Plays*, eds. Erich Fried, Ralph Manheim, and John Willett (London: Eyre Methuen, 1976), 76.
3   And it seems as though an instalment of the *Ocean's* trilogy is playing on some channel at any given time on American cable TV, solidifying it as a constant presence in popular culture beyond its initial release.
4   All figures courtesy of boxofficemojo.com
5   Robert Venturi, Denise Scott Brown, and Steven Izenour, *Learning From Las Vegas: The Forgotten Symbolism of Architectural Form* (Boston: The MIT Press, 1977).
6   Thomas Schatz, 'The New Hollywood,' in *Film Theory Goes to the Movies*, eds. Jim Collins *et al.* (New York: Routledge, 1993).
7   Justin Wyatt, *High Concept: Movies and Marketing in Hollywood* (Austin, TX: University of Texas Press, 1994).
8   Fredric Jameson, *Signatures of the Visible*. (New York: Routledge, 1990), 9–54.
9   Ibid., 26.
10 Ibid., 27.
11 Ibid.
12 For examples of the international composition of 'last stand' war films, see *Sahara* (Zoltan Korda, 1943), *Bataan* (Tay Garnett, 1943), *Bridge On the River Kwai* (David Lean, 1957), and *The Guns of Navarone* (J. Lee Thompson, 1961) .
13 Jameson, *Signatures*, 30.
14 Ibid., 30–31.
15 Leitch, *Crime Films*, 15.
16 Jameson, *Signatures*, 31.
17 Thomas Schatz, *Hollywood Genres: Formulas, Filmmaking, and the Studio System* (Philadelphia, PA: Temple University Press, 1981).

18 Fredric Jameson, "'End of Art' or 'End of History,'" in *The Cultural Turn: Selected Writings on the Postmodern, 1983–1998*, ed. Fredric Jameson (London: Verso, 1998), 73–92.

19 Another interesting intersection here is that the hotel was destroyed in order to make way for magnate Steve Wynn's (the real-life owner of the Bellagio, and possibly the model for Terry Benedict) new multinational mega-casino.

20 The notable exception is Stanley Kubrick's 1955 heist film, *The Killing*.

21 Jameson, *Signatures*, 32.

22 It should also be noted that the main conflict in the recent remake of *The Italian Job* (F. Gary Gray, 2003) is precisely between violent (embodied by bad guy Edward Norton's penchant for using guns) and non-violent (embodied by Mark Wahlberg's innovative planning) forms of the heist.

23 Fredric Jameson, *Archaeologies of the Future: The Desire Called Utopia and Other Science Fictions* (New York: Verso, 2005), 1.

24 Ibid., 15.

25 It is also interesting to note that the Wynn-owned Bellagio, where most of the film's interiors were shot, stands on the soil of The Sands, where Sinatra and his Rat Pack famously romped between takes of the original film.

26 Jameson, *Signatures*, 26–27.

27 Jameson, *Signatures*, 53–54.

28 The poem the movement is based on, 'Clair de Lune' by Paul Verlaine, concludes with a line about tall 'svelte' fountains amid white marble.

29 Richard Dyer, 'Entertainment and Utopia,' in *Genre: The Musical: A Reader*, ed. Rick Altman, (London: Routledge and Kegan Paul, 1981), 177.

CHAPTER NINE

Trafficking Social Change: The Global Social Problem Film in the 2000s

The idea was to address a social issue but sort of lay on the trappings of a thriller.

Steven Soderbergh[1]

As international relations scholar Justin Rosenberg succinctly states: '"Globalization" was the *Zeitgeist* of the 1990s.'[2] A critic of the method in which the implications of globalisation have been theorised and aggrandised, Rosenberg draws attention to the way globalisation was more a 'felt' phenomenon than the rapid acceleration of globalised flows that the theory's advocates would have us believe; it was the 'spirit of the times' to believe the world was in a state of increasing interconnection and integration. While debate continues over the conceptualisation and extent of globalisation and globalisation theory, it still seems undeniable that we live in a much more 'globalised' – however you wish to define the term – world than we did fifty, twenty, even ten years ago. In typical Hollywood style, it took some time for mainstream cinema to embody characteristics of this sweeping geopolitical, socio-economic shift and pick up on the *zeitgeist*, but its effects have now most certainly arrived. Hollywood has, of course, always been a global institution. But like globalisation itself, the transformation is not so much a matter of innovation, but degree. The changes taking place – both globally and cinematically – are not necessarily new, but what is new is the rapid rate at which they are occurring. From worldwide release patterns and digital technology[3] to rampant piracy and the 'New International Division of Cultural Labour,'[4] the effects of globalisation on Hollywood are ever-increasing. One such development – simultaneously an embodiment as well as an artistic response to transnational flows, and the problems that accompany them – is the re-emergence of the social problem film genre in the 21st century. Mostly absent since the early days of Hollywood, the social problem film has returned amidst a decidedly global context.

The decidedly global locations of Soderbergh's later films are indicated by the US/Mexico border in *Traffic*, the map of the global pandemic in *Contagion*, and the increasingly timely depictions of the drone attacks in *Syriana*.

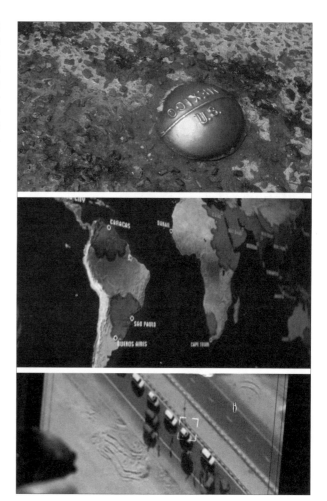

Steven Soderbergh can be seen as a key figure in this re-emergence, with his one-two punch of highly successful social problem films in the year 2000 – *Erin Brockovich* and *Traffic* – paving the way for a cycle of politically and socially conscious films to be released throughout the following decade. *Erin Brockovich* sets the stage for the director's anti-corporate politics to follow, as the film documents a successful class-action suit against the energy corporation Pacific Gas and Electric Company (PG&E) for their cancer-causing environmental pollution. At Section Eight, Soderbergh and Clooney also helped produce many other socially conscious films, such as the ambitious *Syriana* in 2005, with *Traffic* writer Stephen Gaghan writing and directing, and *Michael Clayton* in 2007, Tony Gilroy's story of legal impropriety on the part of an agricultural conglomerate knowingly selling a carcinogenic product, both films starring George Clooney. Section Eight also released Clooney's *Good Night, and Good Luck* in 2005, a morality play about media responsibility and the politics of fear as seen through the conflict between television journalist Edward R. Murrow and Senator Joseph McCarthy. *Ides of March* (2011), another film written and directed by Clooney, continues the filmmaker's preoccupation with American politics, this time casting himself as the corrupt, hypocritical presidential nominee in an even more corrupt system.

After completion of his own 'historical global social problem film' in the form of *The Good German* in 2006, which probed American complicity in Nazi war crimes following the end of World War II, Soderbergh would again return to the issue of global corporate malfeasance with *The Informant!* in 2009, this time matching the institutional insanity of global corporate corruption with a comic absurdity. In 2011, *Contagion* re-utilised the successful formula of *Traffic*, interweaving multiple plot lines and celebrities, this time to tackle the issue of public health in the era of globalisation. In the chapter that follows, we will use four case studies to outline and explore the global social problem (GSP) film:[5] the originator, *Traffic*, with its three intersecting plot lines exploring the illegal Mexican-American drug trade from the perspective of user, enforcer, politician, and trafficker; *Syriana*, a geopolitical thriller which explores the political, military, economic, legal, and social aspects of the global petroleum industry; *The Informant!*, a biographical comic thriller about the whistleblower who exposed the global Lysine price-fixing conspiracy during the mid-1990s; and *Contagion*, a disaster film that follows a pandemic as it circles around the globe, along with the ensuing social strife.

Non-Soderbergh related examples of the GSP include *Fast Food Nation* (Richard Linklater, 2006), the fictional interpretation of Eric Schlosser's 2002 exposé of the same name, detailing the economic, environmental, and social consequences of the fast food industry, weaving stories from across the United States and Mexico. *Babel* (Alejandro González Iñárritu, 2006) is another: this multi-language, globe-spanning mediation on (mis)communication follows a chain of events linking a couple of American tourists, a Japanese father and daughter, two Morrocan boys, and a Mexican nanny on a cross-border trip with two American children. *Munich* (Steven Spielberg, 2005) is another historical GSP film, detailing the Israeli government's retaliation for the massacre of Israeli athletes by terrorists during the 1972 Summer Olympics. Other notable GSPs include *The Constant Gardener* (Fernando Meirelles, 2005), which takes on the global pharmaceutical industry; *Blood Diamond* (Edward Zwick, 2006), concerning the war-profiteering of diamond sales, and *Lord of War* (Andrew Niccol, 2005), which documents global arms distribution.

As a genre cycle, the GSP is a result of postmodern genre hybridity, an integral characteristic of New Hollywood. As seminal genre theorist Steve Neale notes, 'New Hollywood can be distinguished from the old by the hybridity of its genres and films… this hybridity is governed by the multi-media synergies characteristic of the New Hollywood, by the mixing and recycling of new and old and low art and high art media products in the modern (or postmodern) world.'[6] And as he says of the social problem film directly, it is 'essentially a critical invention.'[7] Every film is to some degree dealing with socio-cultural 'problems,' and so any clear-cut structural grouping of the GSP film will itself be a problem. By no means an authoritative genre classification (though none is), our designation of the GSP will be those films whose hybridity is comprised of three main ingredients: the legacy of the original social problem film of early Hollywood cinema, including the use of melodramatic tone, with a focus on wider, global institutional problems; the distinct influence of documentary and docudrama, in an effort towards realism; and the distinct utilisation of a multi-linear, rhizomatic web-of-life plot line. There is usually a dash of thriller, a smidgen of crime, a pinch of sardonic wit, and the whole bastardised recipe occurs in a global melting pot.

The Evolution and Globalisation of the Social Problem Film

In one of the first systematic analyses of the social problem film, Peter Roffman and Jim Purdy explicitly define the genre by its didacticism: 'the central dramatic conflict revolves around the interaction of the individual with social institutions (such as government, business, political movements, etc.)… it deals with social themes very much on the surface of the dramatic action.'[8] Similarly, another analysis of the social problem film finds it 'distinguished by the way its subject was usually given as much weight as its stars or story: the films used individual human dramas to present a morality tale with wider social repercussions.'[9] *I Am a Fugitive from a Chain Gang* (Mervyn LeRoy, 1932), *The Grapes of Wrath* (John Ford, 1940), and *The Lost Weekend* (Billy Wilder, 1946) are three of the most notable, while Frank Capra carved out his own social problem niche, often incorporating elements of the screwball comedy, with *Mr. Deeds Goes to Town* (1936), *Mr. Smith Goes to Washington* (1939), and *Meet John Doe* (1941). Roffman and Purdy place the social problem film's rise and peak during the 1930s and 1940s, though Kay Sloan locates its origins in the silent era with what she terms, in the title of her book, *The Loud Silents* (1988), films in which reformist groups portrayed alcoholism, labour relations, and other social issues.[10]

Another short cycle of the social problem film can be located during the tumultuous times of the late 1960s and 1970s: the civil rights movement, the Vietnam War, and Watergate providing ample social strife. The controversial mixed race couple in *Guess Who's Coming to Dinner* (Stanley Kramer, 1967), the corrupt police force in *Serpico* (Sidney Lumet, 1974), the investigation into the Watergate scandal in *All the President's Men* (Alan J. Pakula, 1976), and the labour union organising in *Norma Rae* (Martin Ritt, 1979) are some of the most prominent examples. The 1980s are typically marked by the rise of apolitical blockbusters, but independent auteurs kept the spirit of the social problem film alive with works such as Mike Nichols' *Silkwood* (1983), John Sayles' *Matewan* (1987) and Spike Lee's *Do the Right Thing* (1989).

If the original social problem film was concerned with an individual in conflict with a social institution, the global social problem film multiplies both dimensions. Rather than a single individual, we get a multitude of interconnected individuals facing an array of problems; instead of a solitary institution, we get a network of immobilising social institutions. Both *Traffic* and *Syriana* follow a series of individuals in their interactions with the intertwined systems of law, military, economics, government, and media. *Contagion* expands its reach to the spread of disinformation now capable with new media – a contagion of another kind. Though *The Informant!* does follow a single figure, it also weaves law enforcement, government agents, lawyers, and international businessmen into a dense web of characters and institutions in order to tell the true story of a global conspiracy to fix prices, all the while illuminating the pathological nature of the corporate structure.

In *Traffic*, the multitude of problems stems from the flow of narcotics, and its symptoms of addiction, crime, and political corruption. *Syriana* tracks another addictive substance, oil, as the access to and control of it requires legal impropriety, illegal arms trafficking, corporate monopolisation, clandestine assassination, and the radicalisation of young Islamists. Ostensibly, the 'problem' in *Contagion* is the virus, but the conclusion of the film reveals that it was environmental destruction by a mining corporation that is the root cause of the disease travelling from a bat to a pig to a human. Furthermore, it is the all-too-human response to the pandemic – fear, distrust, violence, rioting – that is the real target of Soderbergh's GSP parable for a hyperconnected world.

Roffman and Purdy locate two key reasons for the emergence of the social problem film in the 1930s. The first was the strong sense of social consciousness that grew out of the Depression, as well as the rise of authoritarianism/fascism in Europe. As demonstrated by the success of the novels of John Steinbeck and the songs of Woody Guthrie, audiences were hungry for social and political commentary during such turbulent times. The second factor was the 'golden era' of the Hollywood studio system, when Hollywood rose to central prominence in the popular culture landscape. However, having earned a reputation for being 'morally questionable,' Hollywood established the Production Code, a basic set of conventions and a consistent ideological framework. Rather than face government interference, potentially losing control over its product, Hollywood took it upon itself to 'self-censor' and promote 'traditional values' in order to placate its detractors. Thus, the social problem film was able to capitalise on both the audience's desire for social consciousness and the industry's need to clean up its image.

Seventy years later, the GSP is in a similar situation, albeit a vastly different social and political climate. Though *Traffic* predates it, the terrorist attacks on the World Trade Center of 9/11 mark a certain entrance – whether desired or not – onto the global stage for America. As Slavoj Žižek remarked, 'On September 11, the United States of America were given the opportunity to realize what kind of a world it was part of.'[11] While Žižek correctly identifies America's largely ideologically-reaffirming response, we might also witness a more globally-oriented American social consciousness arising out of the ashes of Ground Zero. The reactionary Bush presidency and its aggressive foreign policy only fuelled this fire. Though certainly not limited to the events of 9/11 and its aftermath, this emerging global consciousness – a concern for the global ramifications of our actions and decisions – parallels the one that gave birth to the original social problem film.

From a production standpoint, the GSP is also in a similar situation in that it benefits from the current state of the Hollywood system, as well as appeals to a certain niche audience. Rather than a studio formula, the GSP is a product of the middle tier of filmmaking that developed in the 1990s, as outlined in chapter two. Negotiating the fine line between art and commerce, the major independents provide the opportunity for big-budget, heavily-marketed films that focus on artistic merit and message in order to win valuable film festival and awards season prestige. *Traffic* was developed with Universal's USA Films (now Focus Features), and won multiple Academy Awards and critics' awards; *Syriana* and *The Informant!* were developed by Soderbergh and Clooney's Section Eight, with financing from Warner Bros, and also earned multiple award nominations and wins, particularly the acting performances of George Clooney and Matt Damon. *Contagion* was set up through Participant Media (more on this company below), as well as Imagenation Abu Dhabi, lending some international funding alongside Warner Bros, and starred four Academy Awards winners and three nominees. Like its predecessor's emergence, the GSP benefited from a favourable industrial context and fulfilled its audience's desire for social consciousness following a major crisis.

Considering this political and industrial impetus, we can add some more groups of films from the 2000s that overlap with the qualities of the GSP film. Though they might not always exhibit a distinctly global scope, nor orient themselves primarily around a social problem, they do involve a wider, often international political realm, and they tend to insinuate larger social ramifications than just the interpersonal conflict typical of a Hollywood film. The re-emergence of the conspiracy film certainly took on a global scale, in films such as *Spy Game* (Tony Scott, 2001), *The Manchurian Candidate* (Jonathan Demme, 2004), *The Interpreter* (Sydney Pollack, 2005), and *State of Play* (Kevin Macdonald, 2009). Like *The Good German*, there were also other 'historical global social problem films' that revisited moments of conflict in history from a global perspective, such as *Ararat* (Atom Egoyan, 2002), *Hotel Rwanda* (Terry George, 2004), and *The Last King of Scotland* (Kevin Macdonald, 2006).

The 'War on Terror' also spawned some counter-terrorism thrillers with a GSP dimension, engaging with both the causes of terrorism and the efforts to contain it, such as *The Kingdom* (Peter Berg, 2007), *Body of Lies* (Ridley Scott, 2008) and *Zero Dark Thirty* (Kathryn Bigelow, 2012). And war being the ultimate 'global social problem,' a new era of armed conflict – in Iraq, Afghanistan, and elsewhere – spawned a new cycle of war films, which often attempted to pull various geopolitical interconnections together. By no means an exhaustive list, this cycle of global war films include *Jarhead* (Sam Mendes, 2005), *Lions for Lambs* (Robert Redford, 2007), *In the Valley of Elah* (Paul Haggis, 2007), *Rendition* (Gavin Hood, 2007), *Redacted* (Brian De Palma, 2007), *Stop-Loss* (Kimberly Peirce, 2008), and *The Hurt Locker* (Kathryn Bigelow, 2008). Genres continue to cross-pollinate and hybridise, and the act of genre classification becomes even more difficult; the global social problem film is another layer to be added to this increasingly diffuse mix.

Keeping it Real: The Documentary/Docudrama Impulse

Documentary filmmaking – and its fictionalised offshoot, docudrama – is the second key influence for the GSP film. As the primary focus of the GSP is to shed light on a real-world problem, the effort to achieve a sense of realism is vital. One of the key strategies that the GSP uses to achieve this realism is a reliance on non-fiction resources in the pre-production process. Although based on the British television miniseries *Traffik* (Alastair Reid, 1989), Stephen Gaghan made significant changes to his adap-

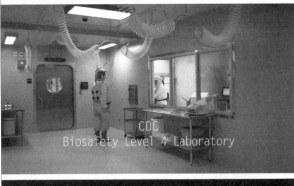

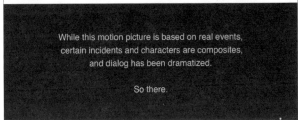

Elements of the docudrama include the intersections of real-life people and settings in fictionalized contexts, such as Michael Douglas' discussions of drug policy with actual Washington politicians in *Traffic* (here we see Senate Majority Leader Harry Reid), on-location shooting at the Center for Disease Control in *Contagion*, and the declaration that *The Informant!* is based on true events, but with a twist.

tation after a year's worth of obsessive research, interviews with key political figures in Washington, and investigative trips to San Diego and Tijuana. Most notably, the drug cartels were shifted from Columbia to Mexico and the drug was changed from heroin to cocaine, corresponding with the real-life relocation of drug production that occurred in the decades separating the television series and the film. Another element of realism is Gaghan's own drug addiction, which started in high school (the basis for Caroline, the prep-school drug abuser), continued throughout pre-production of the film, and became a promotional narrative during the publicity run-up to the film's release.[12]

Syriana's premise also comes from non-fictional origins; the term Syriana is a metaphor for foreign intervention in the Middle East, used by Washington think-tanks to describe a hypothetical reshaping of the region to ensure continued access to oil. The screenplay is loosely adapted[13] from former CIA case officer Robert Baer's memoirs, *See No Evil: The True Story of a Ground Soldier in the CIA's War Against Terrorism* (2003). Robert Baer became the basis for George Clooney's character, Bob Barnes, who similarly undertakes various clandestine Middle Eastern operations, including a failed assassination plot. Because of this fictionalising of non-fiction memoirs, the film carries this unique statement in the credits: 'While inspired by a non-fiction work, this motion picture and all of the characters and events portrayed in it (except for incidental archival footage), are fictional.' The fine line between 'real' and 'reel' is certainly blurred. *The Informant!* takes even more liberties with its source material: the non-fiction book *The Informant* (2001), by journalist Kurt Eichenwald. Heavily fictionalising and satirising the original true story, *The Informant!* also contains a unique statement in its opening credits: 'While this motion picture is based on real events, certain incidents and characters are composites, and dialog has been dramatized. So there.' This cheeky epilogue sets the stage for the absurdity to come, while also defusing any criticisms the film may face based on fictional distortion.

Contagion is the only GSP film of the four that is an original screenplay, yet it also employed a unique strategy in achieving a sense of realism: enlisting Dr. W. Ian Lipkin, Professor of Epidemiology and Director of the Center for Infection and Immunity at Columbia University, as the film's chief science advisor. In what was far more than a token consulting position, Dr. Lipkin was actively involved in the film during the script-writing phase and on set, assuring realistic depictions of the CDC (Centers for Disease Control and Prevention) and WHO (World Health Organization) operations, and working with the actors and set designers to depict proper laboratory technique. Dr. Lipkin and his team also designed the film's main star: the imaginary virus that drives the narrative. Based on the real-life Nipah virus, which caused a pandemic in Malaysia in the late 1990s, also originating from the transfer from bats to pigs to humans, the MEV-1 virus of the film was built as a 3-D model and then Dr. Lipkin and his team developed how it would evolve and how public health, medical communities, and governments would respond. 'Is this fiction?', Dr. Lipkin asks rhetorically in a *New York Times* op-ed published the weekend the film was released, 'Yes. Is it real? Absolutely.'[14]

As much as these films strive for realism, they are bound to the fictionalising process necessary to make them palatable as multiplex fare. The techniques of docudrama, then, are an essential influence on the GSP, and are the most explicit example of the grey area that exists between fact and fiction in these films. Docudramas typically involve recreations or dramatisations of documented events, and may involve real footage of the events themselves. *Syriana* and *The Informant!* are obvious examples of docudrama, having heavily dramatised their non-fictional source material, but *Traffic* contains a unique scene of docudrama as well. When Michael Douglas's drug czar character goes to Washington, D.C., he is seen at a party talking with actual, real politicians, both Democrat and Republican, such as US Senators Harry Reid, Barbara Boxer, Orrin Hatch, Charles Grassley, and Don Nickles, and Governor Bill Weld, as well as lobbyists and journalists. Entirely improvised, the sequence contains frank discussions about the drug war, and its public perception, edited together as a quick montage. This is a very Soderberghian scene; it simultaneously pulls in the viewer with its raw, 'uncut' realism, but distances with its artifice and fictional juxtaposition.

The aim of a docudrama is to concentrate on the facts and avoid editorialising or opinionated bias; in practice, of course, this rarely occurs. *Syriana* was subject to considerable criticism for its political bias. As is often the case in such a polarised public sphere, this 'liberal' cultural text that ventures criticism towards American governmental policy was met with accusations against those 'typical Hollywood liberals' and their 'anti-American' values. An op-ed in the *Washington Post*, entitled 'Oscars for Osama,' claimed that 'Osama bin Laden could not have scripted this film with more conviction.'[15] We will leave the validity of that statement to the reader's discretion.

Seth Feldman's analysis of the genre, 'Footnote to Fact: The Docudrama,' focuses on the function of such films.[16] His analysis of the three most popular incarnations of the docudrama – *Roots* (Marvin J. Chomsky and others, 1977), *Holocaust* (Chomsky, 1978), and *The Day After* (Nicholas Meyer, 1984) – finds them 'firmly grounded in events that had already achieved a central place in the public imagination. What all three programs then spoke to were the personal, psychological reasons for that centrality.'[17] The same could be said for *Traffic*'s engagement with the 'War on Drugs', *Syriana*'s interconnection of the 'War on Terror' with 'Big Oil', *The Informant!*'s satirical dismembering of 'Big Agriculture' and corporate profiteering, and *Contagion*'s frank portrayal of a globalised pandemic: prevalent issues in the forefront of the social imaginary seen through the eyes of a range of (mostly) sympathetic characters. However, it should be noted that unlike *Roots* and *Holocaust*, which are set in the past, *Traffic*, *Syriana*, *The Informant!* and *Contagion* engage with contemporary, ongoing issues that demand attention and action.

Furthermore, Feldman's reading of the conservative, comforting nature of the docudrama is not applicable to the GSP. *Roots*, *Holocaust*, and *The Day After* attempted to provide 'explanations of an incomprehensible world to the disenfranchised,' but failed to offer 'a deeper understanding of historical forces; rather it is the durability of [the] familial order' that is celebrated.[18] Conversely, the GSP's greatest strength is its illumination of geopolitical socio-economic forces through narrative means. By threading multiple stories together into a larger fabric, yet retaining character-based action and the pleasures of melodrama and the thriller, viewers get a glimpse of the sheer complexity and scope of these global problems. And while the GSP is also concerned with the familial order – *Syriana* has two sets of fathers and sons, one of the three plot lines in *Traffic* is a drug czar and his addict daughter, the titular informant is distinctly a 'family man,' and one of the key plot lines in *Contagion* is a recent widower coping with the loss of his wife and son while protecting his remaining daughter from the pandemic – here the solidarity of the family is seen to be in decay in the face of such dire global problems and interconnected corruption.

As realism is of central concern to the GSP, the use of ostentatious cinematography is rare, but if used, serves a utilitarian function. *Traffic*, for example, uses distinctive colour palettes to clearly distinguish its three plot lines: the East Coast scenes are shot in bright daylight to produce icy blue, monochromatic tones; the Mexican scenes are overexposed and use 'tobacco' filters for grainy, bleached-out sepia tones; and the San Diego scenes use the risky technique of 'flashing' the negative for a halo effect to

The final montage of *Syriana* oscillates between the interrelated dimensions of the global petroleum industry, as seen in images of the Middle East refinery, the awards ceremony for 'oil man of the year,' and the terrorist attack perpetrated by the young, radicalised Wasim (Mazhar Munir).

compliment the vibrant hues. *Contagion* uses a similar visual scheme, assisting the viewer to keep track of the various different geographic locations by shooting them in different hues: Minnesota is cold blues, Atlanta is warm oranges for example. *The Informant!* also uses a distinct colour palette in the service of its subject matter: a drab, claustrophobic yellow hue is cast over much of the film, emphasising the degree to which corn is used in an astonishing amount of everyday products, not just food.

Another utilitarian stylistic convention of the genre is the use of graphic matches with sound bridges to draw connections between narrative strands. In the conclusion of *Syriana*, for instance, a shot of the videotaped burial requests of a young Pakistani terrorist, Wasim (Mazhar Munir), slowly fades into a graphically-matched shot of the energy analyst's (Matt Damon) sole surviving son, while Wasim's chilling dialogue bridges the edit: 'From the dust a new person will be created.' Wasim commits this terrorist act in retaliation for the foreign exploitation of oil companies, an example of what is referred to by foreign policy specialists as 'blowback'; the generic convention of the graphic match renders this problem bare.

As a final note on the documentary/docudrama impulse, we would be remiss not to mention the recent resurgence in documentary filmmaking of works that are also largely concerned with global connections and consequences, resulting in something of a sibling cycle to the GSP. This parallel strain of GSP documentaries should be seen as a significant cycle in its own right. The all-time highest grossing documentary film is *Fahrenheit 9/11* (Michael Moore, 2004), which lampoons the Bush administration and its corporate cronyism for exploiting the 9/11 attacks to flex an aggressive foreign policy with dire global consequences. *An Inconvenient Truth* (Davis Guggenheim, 2006) is a passionate and informative plea for clarity and action against worldwide climate change. Other popular examples of the global social problem documentary include *The Fog of War* (Errol Morris, 2003), outlining the global threat of the American military as seen through the eyes of Robert S. McNamara, architect of the Vietnam War; *The Corporation* (Mark Achbar, 2003), a psychological examination of the corporate organisational model that has dominated economic, political, and social forces around the world; *Darwin's Nightmare* (Hubert Sauper, 2004), which explores the global network created around the Lake Victoria perch, from European supermarkets to Russian arms dealers to exploited Tanzanians; and *Why We Fight* (Eugene Jarecki, 2005), an exploration of the quest for global domination by the American military-industrial complex. That the GSP documentary should rise to popularity and critical acclaim in the same five-year span that the GSP film did should warrant their consideration as significant cycles of film production.

Everything is Connected: Networked Narratives, Productions, and Problems

The final essential ingredient to the GSP is its innovation on the web-of-life plot line. Instead of the traditional two primary lines of action, the 1990s saw a surge of films weaving together a variety of plot lines involving a multitude of characters, as we explored in the editing section of chapter one. Again, this is not a matter of precedence, but degree. The last fifteen years produced a tremendous increase in multi-linear filmmaking; some prominent examples include *Slacker*, *Reservoir Dogs*, *Short Cuts* (Robert Altman, 1993), *Pulp Fiction*, *Magnolia* (P.T. Anderson, 1999), *Snatch* (Guy Ritchie, 2000), *Amores Perros* (Alejandro González Iñárritu, 2002), and *Crash* (Paul Haggis, 2004). In his exploration of networked narratives and transnationalism, David Desser dates the multi-linear narrative back as far as *Intolerance* (1916), D.W. Griffith's silent-era epic spanning 2,500 years, paralleling four different ages in world history.[19] For our purposes, we might see *Intolerance* as the birth of the GSP nearly a century before its popularisation, though it concentrates on the enduring problem of intolerance throughout the ages, rather than its global interconnections. Multiple story lines focused on a single locale are also not uncommon in the history of Hollywood, *Grand Hotel* (Edmund Goulding, 1932) and *Dinner at Eight* (George Cukor, 1933) being the earliest incarnations. The disaster film also relies on multiple characters united in adversity, and *Contagion* is certainly influenced by such films as *The Poseidon Adventure* (Ronald Neame, 1972) and *The Towering Inferno* (John Guillermin, 1974). Many horror films, to a lesser degree, rely on a similar structure, such as the web of unrelated new characters in each entry of the *Saw* franchise (2004–present).

A pioneer of the web-of-life plot line is Robert Altman, and as such, he is a tremendous influence on the GSP. *Nashville* (1975) is a landmark film, not just for the GSP, but for cinema as a whole. With *Nashville*, Altman weaves a cinematic web the likes of which had never been seen before in mainstream film: densely interconnected story lines, a massive ensemble cast, and a satirical mixing of presidential politics with the business of country/gospel music. His *Short Cuts*, 'an L.A. jazz rhapsody,'[20] is inspired by nine short stories by Raymond Carver and follows 22 principal characters. Altman's signature style – overlapping dialogue and a wandering, zooming camera to capture his web of improvising actors/characters played by improvising actors – complements this formal experimentation, as it did in *Nashville*.

Utilising the web-of-life plot line creates an expectation within the viewer for unforeseen relations and causal connections among the film's disparate characters. With the GSP, the web-of-life is woven on a much larger scale: a global web-of-life. Thus, the connections made are far more startling and unexpected. For example, in *Traffic*, a teenage drug abuser in a Cincinnati prep school affects her father's ability as the newly appointed drug czar to combat a corrupt Mexican General (Tomás Milián) who has just enlisted the help of a double-crossing cop (Benicio Del Toro) in his effort to continue supplying cocaine to a jailed San Diego-based drug kingpin (Alec Roberts) whose wife (Catherine Zeta-Jones) continues the family business while under the surveillance of a rogue African-American DEA agent (Don Cheadle) who has just lost his Puerto-Rican partner (Luis Guzmán) to a Mexican hitman (Clifton Collins Jr.). This is, of course, just one line of connection between the central characters, and various 'connect-the-characters' trajectories could be traced in *Syriana*, *The Informant!*, and *Contagion* as well. It is here, in the limitless possibility of interconnection, that the GSP presents its most innovative act. We would like to pick up where Desser, in his consideration of 'global noir' and its broader impact on cinema itself, leaves off:

> Multiple storylines, the simultaneity of events forever skewing chronology and linearity, and chance encounters are, after all, not only the very core of global noir, but the very stuff of the hypertext that is digital and cyber technologies. Is global noir, then, the future of cinema, and is the future here?[21]

A detour to the philosophy of Deleuze and Guattari is necessary in order to answer Desser's rhetorical question.

Deleuze and Guattari set out to enact, among other things, a transformation of 'the image of thought.' Rather than the grand pursuit of truth or reason, they define philosophy as the creation of concepts that define a particular range of thinking with which to grapple with a certain reality. One such valuable conception is the *rhizome*, a multiplicity which aims to move away from the traditional binary structure of Western thought. A figure borrowed from biology, the rhizome is a model in strict opposition to the conventional figure of the tree which operates on the principles of foundation and origin. The rhizome, on the contrary, is proliferating and serial; it operates on the principles of connection and heterogeneity. There can be no static points or hierarchical positions within a rhizome: 'any point of a rhizome can be connected to anything other, and must be.'[22] Neither mimetic nor organic, a rhizome is a mobile and bifurcating series of lines; it only ever attempts to *map*, never resolve.

How appropriate, then, that *Syriana* deals with a hypothetical 'remapping' of the Middle East. As 'the rhizome pertains to a map that must be produced, constructed,

Despite his American origins, Soderbergh can be thought of as a global filmmaker: his movies have spanned a dizzying array of countries, oftentimes within the same film, as seen in *Contagion*, *Syriana*, *Che*, *The Good German*, *Haywire*, and *Ocean's Twelve*.

a map that is always detachable, connectable, reversible, modifiable, and has multiple entryways and exits and its own lines of flight,' *Syriana* works to outline the map of law, military, politics, economics, and terrorism that is the global petroleum industry.[23] The terrorist act shows this rhizome's detachability; the globe-spanning locales show its connectability; the double and double-double crossings by CIA agents show its reversibility; anti-trust regulators show its modifiability. The young Pakistani victimised by a post-Fordist disposable workforce and led astray by radical Islam simultaneously provides an entry into and an exit from this rhizome.

A rhizome 'has neither beginning nor end, but always a middle (*milieu*) from which it grows and which it overspills.'[24] Perhaps this explains the common reception of *Syriana*'s plot as too complex to follow. As Roger Ebert states with precision: 'we're not really supposed to follow [the plot], we're supposed to be *surrounded* by it. Since none of the characters understand the whole picture, why should we?'[25] The film has thus utilised the structure of the rhizome in the structure of its plot to illuminate the rhizomatic quality of its subject matter. The viewer is *supposed* to get lost in the film's complex story and be even more bewildered by its fruition. Like every useful answer to a difficult question, the GSP reveals even more complex questions instead of offering a tidy resolution.

In order to present this rhizomatic subject matter, the GSP's form must be rhizomatic, and in order to formally be a rhizome, it must have a rhizomatic production process. 'To attain the multiple, one must have a method that effectively constructs it.'[26] Referring to it as his '$49 million Dogme film,' Soderbergh directed and shot *Traffic* with the spontaneity and freedom he enjoyed with his self-financed efforts.[27] Three months, ten cities, 110 locations, and 163 speaking parts: the shoot was a frantic affair. The cast and crew travelled light and quick, 'like the Grateful Dead,' according to Benicio Del Toro.[28] Unable to secure permission to shoot in the White House, Soderbergh and Douglas went on a tour and stole footage guerrilla style. This is true rhizomatic style: 'Speed turns the point into a line!'[29] *Syriana* was a similarly complex endeavour; shooting took place in over a dozen locations around the globe, including Geneva, Dubai (the first Hollywood production in the U.A.E.), Egypt, Tehran, London, Morocco, New York, Texas, Maryland, Baltimore, and Washington D.C. *The Informant!* was also filmed around the world, with location shooting in Illinois, California, Missouri, Paris, Switzerland, and Hawaii, and additional scenes set in Mexico City, Tokyo, and Hong Kong. Naturally, *Contagion* would require a globalised production, with shooting in Hong Kong, Macao, Chicago, Atlanta, San Francisco, Casablanca, London, and Geneva.

A further rhizomatic dimension to *Syriana*, *The Informant!*, and *Contagion* is the involvement of production company Participant Media (formerly Participant Productions) in the development and marketing process. Founded in 2004 by Jeffrey Skoll, the billionaire entrepreneur and first president of eBay, Participant Media produces socially relevant films and documentaries that aim to be 'compelling entertaining stories that also create awareness of the real issues that shape our lives.'[30] Adding an educative and activist dimension to its criteria of choosing which projects to finance, Participant Media typically produces films that are based on current events and topical subjects which lend themselves to the kind of social action campaigns that are enacted in tandem with associated non-profit organisations around a film's release. As an example, the social action campaign that was launched alongside *Contagion* included an informational hub with a range of material on pandemics – history, profiles, precautions – complete with videos, infographics, interactive quizzes, and a social networking experience meant to mimic the viral nature of a pandemic. Participant Media also partnered with HealthMap, an online information system that monitors and visualises the global state of infectious diseases.

In addition to *Syriana*, *The Informant!*, and *Contagion,* Participant Media has produced more than three dozen films since 2004, making it a key catalyst and financial driver of the GSP cycle of Hollywood filmmaking. A few of the GSP narratives are *Fast Food Nation*, *North Country* (Niki Caro, 2004), *Charlie Wilson's War* (Mike Nichols, 2007), and *Fair Game* (Doug Liman, 2010), while the GSP documentaries include *An Inconvenient Truth*, *Darfur Now* (Ted Braun, 2007), *Food Inc.* (Robert Kenner, 2008), *The Cove* (Louie Psihoyos, 2008), and *Countdown to Zero* (Lucy Walker,

2010). Of course, corporate encouragement to 'participate' is both successful branding and innovative 'lifestyle' and 'viral' marketing. It would be easy to take a cynical view of such a crass venture funded by a billionaire who has turned to Hollywood through the guise of philanthropy, but the fact remains that Participant Media has produced dozens of films with social and educational messages at their core, leveraging the power of social networks and the rhizome structure to produce something more than 'mere entertainment.'

The GSP then – in construction, structure, finance, and theme – is a true personification of the rhizome. To return to Desser's question: *yes*, hypertext is at the core of the future of cinema, *but* its truest contemporary incarnation is not the global noir and its flaccid intertextualisation, but the GSP and its rhizomatic embodiment. And *yes*, the future of cinema is here *if* filmmakers use the logic of Deleuze and Guattari's rhizome. According to Roffman and Purdy, 'the Hollywood social problem film represents a significant social and artistic achievement, marshalling the resources of film to provide a vivid commentary on the times.'[31] Through its propagation of a global social consciousness, its commitment to realism, and a utilisation of the rhizome structure, the GSP has reinvigorated the potential for far-reaching social and political commentary in mainstream Hollywood cinema. To rewrite Manuel Castells' famous proclamation about the network society: the logic *of* the rhizome is more powerful than the power *in* the rhizome.[32]

Though there are definite antecedents to the GSP film, both in form and in content, there is a distinct enough wave of films that occurs just after the turn of the century that warrants this demarcation of the GSP film. That these films explicitly engage with some of the largest cultural and sociopolitical shifts of the last quarter-century – globalisation and digital technology, and the increasing interconnectedness that each brings – means they deserve further scrutiny. As opposed to Hollywood's ever-increasing reliance on over-blown spectacle and reformatted properties, this wave of films engages with its world directly and provocatively, with a unique formal and stylistic approach. Steven Soderbergh's role in this significant wave of filmmaking should not go unnoticed. *Traffic* is patient zero in this pandemic, with *Syriana*, *The Informant!*, and *Contagion* spreading the 'global social problem virus' to new hosts. As with his innovative financial practices, his cinematographic and digital experimentation, his generic preoccupations, and his intertextual reworkings, where ever there are significant developments in Hollywood filmmaking to be seen in the last twenty-five years, Soderbergh is there.

Notes

1   Quoted in Richardson, 'Life Of Steven Soderbergh.'
2   Justin Rosenberg, 'Globalization Theory: A Post Mortem,' *International Politics* 42 (2005), 2.
3   Robert E. Davis, 'The Instantaneous Worldwide Release: Coming Soon to Everyone, Everywhere,' in *Transnational Cinema: The Film Reader*, ed. Elizabeth Ezra and Terry Rowden (New York: Routledge, 2006), 73–80.

4   Toby Miller, Nitin Govil, John McMurria, and Richard Maxwell, *Global Holly-wood 2* (London: BFI, 2005).

5   In a nod to Miller *et al.*'s convenient dropping of a letter in their acronym, NICL (New International Division of Cultural Labour), we have taken the liberty of dropping a letter in ours, GSP, to parallel such other globally used acronyms as GNP and GDP.

6   Steve Neale, *Genre and Hollywood* (New York and London: Routledge, 2000), 248.

7   Ibid., 105.

8   Peter Roffman and Jim Purdy, *The Hollywood Social Problem Film: Madness, Despair, and Politics from the Depression to the Fifties* (Bloomington, IN: Indiana University Press, 1981), viii.

9   Michael Brooke, 'Social Problem Films: British Cinema and Postwar Social Change,' *ScreenOnline*, accessed February 15, 2010, http://www.screenonline.org.uk/film/id/1074067/index.html.

10 Kay Sloan, *The Loud Silents: Origins of the Social Problem Film* (Chicago: University of Illinois Press, 1988).

11 Slavoj Žižek, *Welcome to the Desert of the Real: Five Essays on September 11* (London: Verso, 2002), 47.

12 Waxman, *Rebels on the Backlot*, 325.

13 To Gaghan's dismay, *Syriana* was deemed an Original Screenplay by the Academy of Motion Picture Arts and Sciences.

14 W. Ian Lipkin, 'The Real Threat of "Contagion,"' *New York Times*, September 11, 2011.

15 Charles Krauthammer, 'Oscars for Osama,' *The Washington Post*, March 3, 2006,   http://www.washingtonpost.com/wp-dyn/content/article/2006/03/02/AR2006030201209.html.

16 Seth Feldman, 'Footnote to Fact: The Docudrama,' in *Film Genre Reader*, ed. Barry Keith Grant (Austin, TX: University of Texas Press, 1986).

17 Ibid., 349.

18 Ibid.

19 David Desser, 'Global Noir,' 516–536.

20 Michael Wilmington, 'Short Cuts: City Symphony,' *The Criterion Collection*, November 15, 2004, http://www.criterion.com/current/posts/349-short-cuts-city-symphony.

21 Desser, 'Global Noir,' 534.

22 Gilles Deleuze and Felix Guattari, *A Thousand Plateaus: Capitalism and Schizophrenia Vol. 2*, trans. Brian Massumi (Minneapolis, MN: University of Minnesota Press, 1987), 7.

23 Ibid., 21.

24 Ibid.

25 Emphasis added. Roger Ebert, 'Review: Syriana,' *rogerebert.com*, December 9, 2005, http://rogerebert.suntimes.com/apps/pbcs.dll/article?AID=/20051208/REVIEWS/51130002/1023.

26 Deleuze and Guattari, *A Thousand Plateaus*, 22.

27 Quoted in Waxman, *Rebels*, 315.

28 Ibid., 317.

29 Deleuze and Guattari, *A Thousand Plateaus*, 24.

30 'Our Mission,' *Participant Media*, accessed January 15, 2011, http://www.partici-pantmedia.com/company/about_us.php.

31 Peter Roffman and Jim Purdy, *The Hollywood Social Problem Film*, vii.

32 The original statement is: 'The logic of the network is more powerful than the power in the network,' Manuel Castells, *The Rise of the Network Society. The Information Age: Economy, Society, and Culture* (Oxford: Blackwell, 2000), 500.

Conclusion

At the end of Soderbergh's book – *Getting Away With It: Or, The Further Adventures of the Luckiest Bastard You Ever Saw*, which is part diary, part interview with Richard Lester – he looks back at the career of his interview subject and provides a tidy yet generous summary. In Soderbergh's view, Lester made 'three Masterpieces,' 'four Classics,' 'six worthwhile *divertissments*', and 'three Really Fascinating Films That Get Better With Age.'[1] As opposed to the overwrought prescriptions of auteur theory, Soderbergh's criteria appear reasonable and humble, and it is worth holding the filmmaker to his own standards. In our estimation, we contend that Soderbergh has made three Master-pieces (*Out of Sight*, *The Limey*, and *Traffic*), four Classics (*sex, lies, and videotape*, *Erin Brockovich*, *The Informant!*, and *Contagion*), one Beloved Trilogy (*Ocean's Eleven, Twelve,* and *Thirteen*), four Formal-Philosophical Experiments That Get Better With Age (*Kafka*, *The Underneath*, *Schizopolis*, and *Solaris*), five Significant Historical Docu-ments (*King of the Hill*, *Gray's Anatomy*, *The Good German*, *Che*, and *And Everything Is Going Fine*), five digital *divertissments* (*Full Frontal*, *K-Street*, *Unscripted*, *Bubble*, *Haywire*), three Erotic Experiments (*The Girlfriend Experience*, *Magic Mike*, and *Behind the Candelabra*) and at least a dozen Really Great Films That Might Not Have Happened Or Turned Out As Well Without His Production Assistance (*Pleasantville* [Gary Ross, 1998], *Confessions of a Dangerous Mind*, *Insomnia*, *Far From Heaven*, *Good Night, and Good Luck*, *Syriana*, *A Scanner Darkly*, *Michael Clayton*, *I'm Not There* [Todd Haynes, 2007], *We Need to Talk About Kevin* [Lynne Ramsay, 2011], etc.). After cataloguing Lester's career, Soderbergh concludes his book by simply stating, 'I hope to do as well with my career.'[2] We would assure him that he has.

As for our own book, we would also hope to have done as well. In our nine chapters, we aim to have achieved some provocative thought experiments (Dialectical Signature, Guerrilla Auteur), useful genre classifications (New Crime Wave, Global Social Problem Film), necessary correctives (Sellebrity Auteur, *Ocean's* trilogy as Allegory of Capital), and intriguing theoretical enquiries (Schizophrenic Detective, Blend of History). We hope to have illuminated the inherently paradoxical nature of Soderbergh and his body of work, and that this messy deconstruction has led to some productive analysis of both the films and the wider cultural, social, and technological implications. As a director-focused study, we aim to have expanded the notion of cinematic authorship analysis in our attempts at looking at some outlying factors: contradiction, economics, celebrity, guerrilla tactics, imperfectness, and intertextuality. In constructing such an unwieldy network of ideas and analyses, we hope that the end product is more than the sum of its parts.

Eighty-thousand words later, do we think that we have 'solved a problem like Steven Soderbergh'? Not exactly. His career is too unstable, too fast, too varied, and too unpredictable to ever be contained by a single, albeit multifarious analysis. During the process of writing this book, he released *six* more films, a fascinating, mostly digital surge that probably warrants its own book in and of itself. How could we pretend to have pinned down a moving target? No, we do not claim to have figured out Steven Soderbergh, nor would we have thought it at all possible. In many ways, this book is not even about him; instead, it concerns American film history of the last two decades. Of course, Soderbergh provides the perfect entry point into such a history, him and his films having embodied most of its various incarnations.

It is a testament to Soderbergh's body of work that between the wide-ranging trajectory of our *The Cinema of Steven Soderbergh*, the 16 excellent individual essays in *The Philosophy of Steven Soderbergh* (2010), and the astute, bi-lateral analysis of Aaron Baker's *Steven Soderbergh* (2011), there is still much that remains unsaid about the prolific filmmaker. We regret not spending more time on the collaborative nature of Soderbergh's filmmaking practice, including screenwriters, actors, producers and other creative talent, but Mark Gallagher's intriguing *Another Steven Soderbergh Experiment: Authorship and Contemporary Hollywood* (2013) employs that very perspective. Though we abstractly covered his 'minor' cinema, we would have liked to have spent more time with his smaller-scale features, all of which contain intriguing ideas, whether aesthetic, philosophic, or thematic. The digital films, in particular, demand more attention; we suspect that the significance of his ground-breaking digital experiments will reveal itself more fully as the medium develops. We have written extensively on these outlying films, but decided against including them in consideration of sustaining an overall trajectory. We intend to post them as mini-essays on our website – cinemaofsteven-soderbergh.com – along with continuing analysis of Soderbergh's upcoming and final films. As he wraps up this stage of his career, foregoing cinema for new possibilities in different media, we will track his latest work with enduring interest, confident that he will continue to experiment, investigate, and challenge. Despite years of over-analysis and dissection of every frame, we keep coming back to Soderbergh for more. By no means is every film a masterpiece, but there is *always* an idea worth exploring. After nearly thirty films, ranging across forms and styles and genres and formats, provocation is the one reliable thing we have come to expect. One final designation then: Steven Soderbergh, Provoc-auteur.

Notes

1   Steven Soderbergh and Richard Lester, *Getting Away With It: Or, The Further Adventures of the Luckiest Bastard You Ever Saw*, 216. The full quote is: 'I obviously hope this book, if read or perused, will ignite an interest in the reader to experience or re-experience [Richard Lester's] work. After all, the man has made, in my opinion, three Masterpieces (*A Hard Day's Night, The Knack, Petulia*), four Classics (*The Three Musketeers, The Four Musketeers, Juggernaut, Robin and Marian*), six worthwhile *divertissements* (*It's Trad, Dad, Help!, A Funny Thing Happened on the Way to the Forum, Royal Flash, The Ritz, Superman 2 and 3*) and three Really Fascinating Films That Get Better With Age (*How I Won the War, The Bed Sitting Room, Cuba*). I hope to do as well with my career, and I will always be thankful for the time he gave me.'

2   Ibid.

FILMOGRAPHY

1. Films Directed by Soderbergh

* Note: All release dates refer to American theatrical release unless otherwise noted. Budgets are estimated, and come from various internet sources (thus unreliable). Box-office figures are total worldwide gross, courtesy of boxofficemojo.com. 'Metascore' comes from Metacritic.com, a website which 'distills the opinions of the most respected critics writing online and in print to a single number,' whereas RottenTomatoes.com agglomerates as many critics as possible, leading to a much broader survey. CinemaScore ratings result from opening-day audience surveys managed by a marketing firm. IMDb ratings are generated from online user ratings on the popular Internet Movie Database website.

2013 – *Behind the Candelabra*
Director: Steven Soderbergh
Producer: Jerry Weintraub
Writer: Richard LaGravenese
Starring: Michael Douglas, Matt Damon, Rob Lowe, Debbie Reynolds
Distributor: HBO Films

2013 – *Side Effects*
Director: Steven Soderbergh
Producers: Lorenzo di Bonaventura, Gregory Jacobs, Scott Z. Burns
Writer: Scott Z. Burns
Starring: Jude Law, Rooney Mara, Catherine Zeta-Jones, Channing Tatum
Music: Thomas Newman
Cinematography: Steven Soderbergh (as Peter Andrews)
Editor: Steven Soderbergh (as Mary Ann Bernard)
Studio: Endgame Entertainment
Distributor: Open Road Films
Release date: February 8, 2013

2012 – *Magic Mike*
Director: Steven Soderbergh
Producers: Reid Carolin, Gregory Jacobs, Channing Tatum, Nick Wechsler
Writer: Reid Carolin
Starring: Channing Tatum, Alex Pettyfer, Cody Horn, Matt Bomer, Olivia Munn, Joe Manganiello, Matthew McConaughey
Music Supervisor: Frankie Pine
Cinematography: Steven Soderbergh (as Peter Andrews)

Editor: Steven Soderbergh (as Mary Ann
  Bernard)
Studio: Nick Weschsler Productions
Distributor: Warner Bros.
Release date: June 29, 2012
Budget: $7 million
Gross revenue: $167 million
Reception: Metascore: 72. Rotten
  Tomatoes Score: 80. CinemaScore
  Rating: B. IMDb Rating: 6.1.

2012 – *Haywire*
Director: Steven Soderbergh
Producers: Gregory Jacobs, Ryan
  Kavanaugh
Writer: Lem Dobbs
Starring: Gina Carano, Antonio Banderas,
  Michael Douglas, Bill Paxton, Ewan
  McGregor, Channing Tatum
Music: David Holmes
Cinematography: Steven Soderbergh (as
  Peter Andrews)
Editor: Steven Soderbergh (as Mary Ann
  Bernard)
Studios: Relativity Media, Lakeshore
  Entertainment
Distributors: Lionsgate, Overture Films
Release date: January 20, 2012
Budget: $23 million
Gross revenue: $33 million
Reception: Metascore: 67. Rotten
  Tomatoes Score: 80. CinemaScore
  Rating: D+. IMDb Rating: 6.6.

2011 – *Contagion*
Director: Steven Soderbergh
Producers: Steven Soderbergh, Gregory
  Jacobs, Michael Shamberg, Stacey Sher,
  Arnon Milchan
Writer: Scott Z. Burns
Starring: Marion Cotillard, Matt Damon,
  Laurence Fishburne, Jude Law, Demetri
  Martin, Gwyneth Paltrow, Kate Winslet,
  Bryan Cranston, Jennifer Ehle
Cinematographer: Steven Soderbergh (as
  Peter Andrews)

Music: Cliff Martinez
Editor: Stephen Mirrione
Studios: Imagenation Abu Dhabi, Double
  Feature Films, Participant Media
Distributor: Warner Bros.
Release date: September 9, 2011
Budget: $60 million
Gross revenue: $135 million
Reception: Metascore: 70. Rotten
  Tomatoes Score: 84. CinemaScore
  Rating: B-minus. IMDb Rating: 6.9.

2010 – *The Last Time I Saw Michael Gregg*
Starring: Cate Blanchett, Steven
  Soderbergh, Wayne Blair, Zoe Carides,
  Essie Davis, Genevieve Hegney, Damon
  Herriman, Rhys Muldoon
Release date: Unreleased

2010 – *And Everything Is Going Fine*
Director: Steven Soderbergh
Producers: Kathie Russo, Amy Hobby,
  Joshua Blum
Starring: Spalding Gray
Music: Forrest Gray
Editor: Susan Littenberg
Release date: January 2010 (Slamdance)
Reception: Metascore: 76. Rotten
  Tomatoes Score: 89. IMDb Rating: 7.7.

2009 – *The Informant!*
Director: Steven Soderbergh
Producers: Gregory Jacobs, Jennifer Fox,
  Michael Jaffe, Howard Braunstein, Kurt
  Eichenwald
Writer: Scott Z. Burns
Based on: *The Informant* by Kurt
  Eichenwald
Starring: Matt Damon, Scott Bakula, Joel
  McHale, Melanie Lynskey, Tom Papa
Music: Marvin Hamlisch
Cinematography: Steven Soderbergh (as
  Peter Andrews)
Editor: Stephen Mirrione
Studios: Participant Media, Groundswell
  Productions, Section Eight

Distributor: Warner Bros.
Release date: September 18, 2009
Budget: $22 million
Gross revenue: $41.7 million
Reception: Metascore: 66. Rotten
  Tomatoes Score: 78. CinemaScore
  Rating: C-minus. IMDb Rating: 6.6.

2009 – *The Girlfriend Experience*
Director: Steven Soderbergh
Producers: Mark Cuban, Gregory Jacobs,
  Todd Wagner
Writers: Brian Koppelman, David Levien
Starring: Sasha Grey, Chris Santos, Glenn
  Kenny, Peter Zizzo
Distributor: Magnolia Pictures
Release dates: January 20, 2009
  (Sundance), May 22, 2009 (US)
Budget: $1.3 million
Gross revenue: $1 million
Reception: Metascore: 66. Rotten
  Tomatoes Score: 64. IMDb Rating: 5.7.

2008 – *Che*
Director: Steven Soderbergh
Producers: Laura Bickford, Benicio Del
  Toro
Writers: Peter Buchman, Benjamin A. van
  der Veen
Starring: Benicio Del Toro, Franka
  Potente, Catalina Sandino Moreno
Music: Alberto Iglesias
Cinematography: Steven Soderbergh (as
  Peter Andrews)
Editor: Pablo Zumárraga
Studios: Telecinco Cinema, Wild Bunch
Distributors: IFC Films (USA), Optimum
  Releasing (UK)
Release dates: May 21, 2008 (Cannes),
  December 12, 2008 (US)
Budget: $58 million
Gross revenue: $41 million
Reception: Metascore: 64. Rotten
  Tomatoes Score: 67 (Part One), 80 (Part
  Two). IMDb Rating: 7.3 (Part One), 6.9
  (Part Two).

2007 – *Ocean's Thirteen*
Director: Steven Soderbergh
Producer: Jerry Weintraub
Writers: Brian Koppelman, David Levien
Starring: George Clooney, Brad Pitt, Matt
  Damon, Andy García, Don Cheadle,
  Bernie Mac, Ellen Barkin, Al Pacino,
  Casey Affleck, Scott Caan, Eddie Izzard,
  Eddie Jemison, Shaobo Qin, Carl
  Reiner, Elliott Gould
Music: David Holmes
Cinematography: Steven Soderbergh (as
  Peter Andrews)
Editor: Stephen Mirrione
Studio: Village Roadshow Pictures
Distributor: Warner Bros.
Release date: June 8, 2007
Budget: $85 million
Gross revenue: $311 million
Reception: Metascore: 62. Rotten
  Tomatoes Score: 70. CinemaScore
  Rating: B+. IMDb Rating: 6.9.

2006 – *The Good German*
Director: Steven Soderbergh
Producers: Ben Cosgrove, Gregory Jacobs
Writer: Paul Attanasio
Based on: *The Good German* (novel) by
  Joseph Kanon
Starring: George Clooney, Cate Blanchett,
  Tobey Maguire
Music: Thomas Newman
Cinematography: Steven Soderbergh (as
  Peter Andrews)
Editor: Steven Soderbergh (as Mary Ann
  Bernard)
Studios: Virtual Studios, Section Eight
Distributor: Warner Bros.
Release date: December 8, 2006
Budget: $32 million
Gross revenue: $6 million
Reception: Metascore: 49. Rotten
  Tomatoes Score: 32. IMDb Rating: 6.1.

2005 – *Bubble*
Director: Steven Soderbergh
Producer: Gregory Jacobs

Writer: Coleman Hough
Starring: Debbie Doeberener, Dustin
James Ashley, Misty Dawn Wilkins
Music: Robert Pollard
Cinematography: Steven Soderbergh (as
Peter Andrews)
Editor: Steven Soderbergh (as Mary Ann
Bernard)
Distributor: Magnolia Pictures
Release date: January 27, 2006
Budget: $1.6 million
Gross revenue: $261,000
Reception: Metascore: 63. Rotten
Tomatoes Score: 72. IMDb Rating: 6.7.

2004 – *Ocean's Twelve*
Director: Steven Soderbergh
Producer: Jerry Weintraub
Writer: George Nolfi
Starring: George Clooney, Brad Pitt, Matt
Damon, Catherine Zeta-Jones, Andy
García, Don Cheadle, Bernie Mac, Julia
Roberts, Casey Affleck, Scott Caan,
Vincent Cassel, Eddie Jemison, Shaobo
Qin, Carl Reiner, Elliott Gould
Music: David Holmes
Cinematography: Steven Soderbergh (as
Peter Andrews)
Editor: Stephen Mirrione
Studio: Village Roadshow Pictures
Distributor: Warner Bros.
Release date: December 9, 2004
Budget: $110 million
Gross revenue: $362 million
Reception: Metascore: 58. Rotten
Tomatoes Score: 55. IMDb Rating: 6.1.

2004 – *Eros* (segment "Equilibrium")
Director: Steven Soderbergh
Producer: Gregory Jacobs
Writer: Steven Soderbergh
Starring: Robert Downey Jr., Alan Arkin,
Cinematography: Steven Soderbergh (as
Peter Andrews)
Editor: Steven Soderbergh (as Mary Ann
Bernard)

Distributor: Warner Independent Pictures
Release date: September 10, 2004
Gross revenue: $1.5 million
Reception: Metascore: 51. Rotten
Tomatoes Score: 35. IMDb Rating: 5.9.

2003 – *K Street*
Director: Steven Soderbergh
Producers: Steven Soderbergh, George
Clooney
Writer: Henry Bean
Starring: James Carville, Mary
McCormack, John Slattery, Roger
Guenveur Smith, Mary Matalin
Cinematography: Steven Soderbergh
Editor: Steven Soderbergh
Distributor: HBO
Release date: September 14, 2003
Reception: IMDb Rating: 5.9.

2002 – *Solaris*
Director: Steven Soderbergh
Producers: James Cameron, Jon Landau,
Rae Sanchini
Writer: Steven Soderbergh
Based on: *Solaris* by Stanisław Lem
Starring: George Clooney, Natascha
McElhone, Viola Davis, Jeremy Davies,
Ulrich Tukur
Music: Cliff Martinez
Cinematography: Steven Soderbergh (as
Peter Andrews)
Editor: Steven Soderbergh (as Mary Ann
Bernard)
Studio: Lightstorm Entertainment
Distributor: 20th Century Fox
Release date: November 29, 2002
Budget: $47 million
Gross revenue: $30 million
Reception: Metascore: 65. Rotten
Tomatoes Score: 65. CinemaScore
Rating: F. IMDb Rating: 6.2.

2002 – *Full Frontal*
Director: Steven Soderbergh
Producers: Gregory Jacobs, Scott Kramer

Writer: Coleman Hough
Starring: David Duchovny, Nicky Katt, Catherine Keener, Mary McCormack, David Hyde Pierce, Julia Roberts
Music: Jacques Davidovici
Cinematography: Steven Soderbergh (as Peter Andrews)
Editor: Sarah Flack
Distributor: Miramax
Budget: $2 million
Gross revenue: $3.4 million
Reception: Metascore: 45. Rotten Tomatoes Score: 38. IMDb Rating: 4.8.

2001 – *Ocean's Eleven*
Director: Steven Soderbergh
Producer: Jerry Weintraub
Writers: George C. Johnson, Jack G. Russell, Harry Brown, Charles Lederer, Scott Corwon, Ted Griffin
Starring: George Clooney, Brad Pitt, Matt Damon, Andy García, Julia Roberts, Bernie Mac, Don Cheadle, Casey Affleck, Scott Caan, Elliott Gould, Eddie Jemison, Shaobo Qin, Carl Reiner
Music: David Holmes
Cinematography: Steven Soderbergh (as Peter Andrews)
Editor: Stephen Mirrione
Studios: Village Roadshow Pictures, JW Productions
Distributor: Warner Bros.
Release date: December 7, 2001
Budget: $85 million
Gross revenue: $451 million
Reception: Metascore: 74. Rotten Tomatoes Score: 82. IMDb Rating: 7.7.

2000 – *Traffic*
Director: Steven Soderbergh
Producers: Laura Bickford, Edward Zwick, Marshall Herskovitz
Writer: Stephen Gaghan
Based on: *Traffik* by Simon Moore
Starring: Michael Douglas, Don Cheadle, Benicio Del Toro, Luis Guzmán, Dennis

Quaid, Catherine Zeta-Jones, D.W. Moffett, Jacob Vargas, Miguel Ferrer, Erika Christensen, Steven Bauer, Clifton Collins, Jr., Topher Grace, Salma Hayek
Music: Cliff Martinez
Cinematography: Steven Soderbergh (as Peter Andrews)
Editor: Stephen Mirrione
Studio: Bedford Falls Productions, Compulsion Inc., Initial Entertainment Group (IEG), Splendid Medien AG, USA Films
Distributor: USA Films
Release date: December 27, 2000
Budget: $46 million
Gross revenue: $207 million
Reception: Metascore: 86. Rotten Tomatoes Score: 91. IMDb Rating: 7.7.

2000 – *Erin Brockovich*
Director: Steven Soderbergh
Producers: Danny DeVito, Stacey Sher, Michael Shamberg, Gail Lyon, John Hardy
Writer: Susannah Grant
Starring: Julia Roberts, Albert Finney, Aaron Eckhart
Music: Thomas Newman
Cinematography: Ed Lachman
Editor: Anne V. Coates
Studio: Jersey Films
Distributors: Universal Studios, Columbia Pictures
Release date: March 17, 2000
Budget: $51 million
Gross revenue: $256 million
Reception: Metascore: 73. Rotten Tomatoes Score: 83. IMDb Rating: 7.2.

1999 – *The Limey*
Director: Steven Soderbergh
Producers: John Hardy, Scott Kramer
Writer: Lem Dobbs
Starring: Terence Stamp, Lesley Ann Warren, Luis Guzmán, Peter Fonda, Joe Dallesandro, Barry Newman

Music: Cliff Martinez
Cinematography: Edward Lachman
Editor: Sarah Flack
Distributor: Artisan Entertainment
Release date: October 8, 1999
Budget: $10 million
Gross revenue: $3.2 million
Reception: Metascore: 73. Rotten
    Tomatoes Score: 92. IMDb Rating: 7.1.

1998 – *Out of Sight*
Director: Steven Soderbergh
Producers: Danny DeVito, Barry Sonnenfeld
Writer: Scott Frank
Based on: *Out of Sight* by Elmore Leonard
Starring: George Clooney, Jennifer Lopez,
    Ving Rhames, Don Cheadle, Steve
    Zahn, Albert Brooks, Dennis Farina,
    Luis Guzman, Nancy Allen, Isaiah
    Washington, Michael Keaton
Music: David Holmes
Cinematography: Elliot Davis
Editor: Anne V. Coates
Distributor: Universal Pictures
Release date: June 26, 1998
Budget: $48 million
Gross revenue: $78 million
Reception: Metascore: 85. Rotten
    Tomatoes Score: 93. IMDb Rating: 7.1.

1996 – *Schizopolis*
Director: Steven Soderbergh
Producers: John Hardy, Lawrence Ré
Writer: Steven Soderbergh
Starring: Steven Soderbergh, David Jensen,
    Mike Malone
Music: Cliff Martinez, Steven Soderbergh
Cinematography: Steven Soderbergh
Editors: Steven Soderbergh, Sarah Flack
Distributor: Miramax Films
Release dates: September 13, 1996
    (premiere at TIFF), April 9, 1997
Budget: $250,000
Gross revenue: $10,580
Reception: Metascore: 44. Rotten
    Tomatoes Score: 59. IMDb Rating: 7.0.

1996 – *Gray's Anatomy*
Director: Steven Soderbergh
Producer: John Hardy
Writers: Spalding Gray, Renee Shafransky
Starring: Spalding Gray
Music: Cliff Martinez
Cinematography: Elliot Davis
Editor: Susan Littenberg
Release date: 1996
Budget: $350,000
Gross revenue: $29,090
Reception: Rotten Tomatoes Score: 53.
    IMDb Rating: 6.9.

1995 – *The Underneath*
Director: Steven Soderbergh
Producer: John Hardy
Writer: Steven Soderbergh
Based on: *Criss Cross* by Don Tracy
Starring: Peter Gallagher, Alison Elliott
Music: Cliff Martinez
Cinematography: Elliot Davis
Editor: Stan Salfas
Release date: 28 April 1995
Gross Revenue: $536, 023
Reception: Rotten Tomatoes Score: 57.
    IMDb Rating: 6.2.

1993 – *King of the Hill*
Director: Steven Soderbergh
Producers: Albert Berger, John Hardy,
    Barbara Maltby, Ron Yerxa
Writer: Steven Soderbergh
Based on: *King of the Hill* by A. E.
    Hotchner
Starring: Jesse Bradford, Jeroen Krabbé,
    Spalding Gray, Adrien Brody, Elizabeth
    McGovern, Joe Chrest
Music: Cliff Martinez, Michael Glenn
    Williams
Cinematography: Elliot Davis
Editor: Steven Soderbergh
Distributor: Universal Pictures
Release date: August 20, 1993
Gross revenue: $1.2 million
Reception: Rotten Tomatoes Score: 96.
    IMDb Rating: 7.4.

1991 – *Kafka*
Director: Steven Soderbergh
Producers: Harry Benn, Stuart Cornfeld
Writer: Lem Dobbs
Starring: Jeremy Irons, Theresa Russell, Ian Holm, Joel Grey
Music: Cliff Martinez
Cinematography: Walt Lloyd
Editor: Steven Soderbergh
Distributor: Miramax Films
Release date: November 15, 1991
Budget: $11 million
Gross Revenue: $1.05 million
Reception: Rotten Tomatoes Score: 57. IMDb Rating: 6.9.

1989 – *sex, lies, and videotape*
Director: Steven Soderbergh
Producers: John Hardy, Robert Newmyer
Writer: Steven Soderbergh
Starring: James Spader, Andie MacDowell, Peter Gallagher, Laura San Giacomo
Music: Cliff Martinez
Cinematography: Walt Lloyd
Editor: Steven Soderbergh
Distributor: Miramax Films
Release date: August 18, 1989
Budget: $1.2 million
Gross revenue: $24.7 million
Reception: Metascore: 86. Rotten Tomatoes Score: 98. IMDb Rating: 7.1.

2. Films Produced by Soderbergh

1994: *Suture*
1996: *The Daytrippers*
1998: *Pleasantville*
2001: *Tribute* (Documentary)
2001: *Who Is Bernard Tapie?* (Documentary)
2002: *Far From Heaven*
2002: *Confessions of a Dangerous Mind*
2002: *Insomnia*
2002: *Welcome to Collinwood*
2002: *Naqoyqatsi* (Documentary)
2003: *K Street* (TV Series)
2004: *Keane*
2004: *Criminal*
2004: *Able Edwards* (Documentary)
2005: *Symbiopsychotaxiplasm: Take 2 ½* (Documentary)

2005: *Syriana*
2005: *Good Night, and Good Luck*
2005: *The Jacket*
2005: *Rumor Has It…*
2005: *Unscripted* (TV Series)
2006: *Pu-239*
2006: *A Scanner Darkly*
2007: *I'm Not There*
2007: *Michael Clayton*
2007: *Wind Chill*
2008: *Roman Polanski: Wanted and Desired* (Documentary)
2008: *Tishomingo Blues* [in limbo]
2009: *Playground* (documentary)
2009: *Solitary Man*
2010: *Rebecca H. (Return to the Dogs)*
2011: *His Way* (TV Documentary)
2011: *We Need to Talk About Kevin*
2011: *Contagion*
2012: *Roman Polanski: Odd Man Out*

3. Films Written by Soderbergh

1989 – *sex, lies, and videotape* (written by)
1993 – *King of the Hill* (screenplay)
1995 – *Underneath* (screenplay/as Sam Lowry)
1996 – *Schizopolis* (written by – uncredited)
1997 – *Nightwatch* (screenplay)
2002 – *Solaris* (screenplay)
2004 – *Criminal* (screenplay/as Sam Lowry)
2004 – *Eros* (written by/segment 'Equilibrium')

4. Films Photographed by Soderbergh

1996 – *Schizopolis* (uncredited)
2000 – *Traffic* (as Peter Andrews)
2001 – *Ocean's Eleven* (as Peter Andrews)
2002 – *Full Frontal* (as Peter Andrews)
2002 – *Solaris* (as Peter Andrews)
2003 – *K Street*
2004 – *Eros* (segment 'Equilibrium'/as Peter Andrews)
2004 – *Ocean's Twelve* (as Peter Andrews)
2005 – *Bubble* (as Peter Andrews)
2006 – *The Good German* (as Peter Andrews)
2007 – *Ocean's Thirteen* (as Peter Andrews)
2008 – *Che* (as Peter Andrews)

2009 – *The Girlfriend Experience* (as Peter Andrews)
2009 – *The Informant!* (as Peter Andrews)
2011 – *Contagion* (as Peter Andrews)
2012 – *Haywire* (as Peter Andrews)
2012 – *Magic Mike* (as Peter Andrews)

5. Films Edited by Soderbergh

1985 – *Yes: 9012 Live* (video documentary)
1989 – *sex, lies, and videotape*
1991 – *Kafka*
1993 – *King of the Hill*
2002 – *Solaris* (as Mary Ann Bernard)
2003 – *K Street*
2004 – *Eros* (segment 'Equilibrium'/as Mary Ann Bernard)
2005 – *Bubble* (as Mary Ann Bernard)
2006 – *The Good German* (as Mary Ann Bernard)
2009 – *The Girlfriend Experience*
2012 – *Haywire* (as Mary Ann Bernard)
2012 – *Magic Mike* (as Mary Ann Bernard)

6. Films Assisted by Soderbergh

1998 – *Pleasantville* (Gary Ross) – Second Unit Director (uncredited)
2012 – *Hunger Games* (Gary Ross) – Second Unit Director

7. Films Produced by Section Eight

2001 – *Ocean's Eleven*
2002 – *Insomnia*
2002 – *Welcome to Collinwood*
2002 – *Confessions of a Dangerous Mind*
2002 – *Full Frontal*
2002 – *Far From Heaven*
2003 – *K Street*
2004 – *Criminal*
2004 – *Keane*
2004 – *Ocean's Twelve*
2005 – *Unscripted*
2005 – *The Jacket*
2005 – *Good Night, and Good Luck*
2005 – *Bubble*
2005 – *The Big Empty*
2005 – *Syriana*
2005 – *Rumour Has It… (co-production)*
2006 – *A Scanner Darkly*

2006 – *Pu-239*
2006 – *The Good German*
2007 – *Wind Chill*
2007 – *Ocean's Thirteen*
2007 – *Michael Clayton*
2008 – *Che: Part One* (*uncredited*)
2009 – *The Informant!*

8. Audio Commentaries by Soderbergh

Own films
1989 – *sex, lies, and videotape*, with filmmaker Neil LaBute
1996 – *Schizopolis*
1998 – *Out of Sight*, with screenwriter Scott Frank
1999 – *The Limey*, with screenwriter Lem Dobbs
2000 – *Traffic*, with screenwriter Stephen Gaghan
2001 – *Ocean's Eleven*, with screenwriter Ted Griffin
2002 – *Full Frontal*, with screenwriter Coleman Hough
2002 – *Solaris*, with producer James Cameron
2004 – *Ocean's Twelve*, with screenwriter George Nolfi
2005 – *Bubble*, with filmmaker Mark Romanek
2007 – *Ocean's Thirteen*, with screenwriters Brian Koppelman and David Levien
2009 – *The Girlfriend Experience*, with actress Sasha Grey
2009 – *The Informant!*, with screenwriter Scott Z. Burns

Others' films
1949 – *The Third Man*, with screenwriter Tony Gilroy
1962 – *Billy Budd*, with actor Terence Stamp
1966 – *Who's Afraid of Virginia Woolf?*, with director Mike Nichols
1967 – *The Graduate*, with director Mike Nichols
1967 – *Point Blank*, with director John Boorman
1970 – *Catch-22*, with director Mike Nichols
1989 – *Apartment Zero*, with screenwriter/producer David Koepp
1994 – *Clean, Shaven*, with director Lodge Kerrigan
2000 – *The Yards*, with director James Gray
2003 – *Seabiscuit*, with director Gary Ross

BIBLIOGRAPHY

Adler, Stella. *The Technique of Acting*. Toronto: Bantam Books, 1988.

Adorno, Theodor W. *Negative Dialectics*. New York: Seabury Press, 1973.

Andrew, Dudley. "The Unauthorized Auteur Today." In *Film and Theory: An Anthology*, edited by Robert Stam and Toby Miller, 20–9. Malden, MA: Blackwell, 2000.

Andrew, Geoff. "Again, With 20% More Existential Grief: Steven Soderbergh and George Clooney at the NFT." *Guardian Unlimited*, February 13, 2003. http://film.guardian.co.uk/interview/interviewpages/0,,897475,00.html.

Barthes, Roland. "The Death of the Author." *Image, Music, Text*. Translated by Stephen Heath, 142–8. New York: Hill and Wang, 1977.

Benjamin, Walter. "Theses on the Philosophy of History." *Illuminations*. New York: Harcourt, Brace & World, 1968.

Bernard, Sheila Curran. *Documentary Storytelling: Making Stronger and More Dramatic Nonfiction Films*. Burlington: Elsevier, 2007.

Biskind, Peter. *Easy Riders, Raging Bulls: How the Sex-Drugs-and-Rock-'n'-Roll Generation Saved Hollywood*. New York: Simon & Schuster, 1998.

_____ *Down and Dirty Pictures: Miramax, Sundance, and the Rise of the Independent Film*. New York: Simon & Schuster, 2004.

Bloom, Harold. *The Anxiety of Influence: A Theory of Poetry*. New York: Oxford University Press, 1973.

Boorstin, Daniel J. *The Image: A Guide to Pseudo-Events in America*. New York: Harper and Row, 1961.

Bordwell, David. *Narration in the Fiction Film*. Madison: University of Wisconsin Press, 1985.

_____ *The Way Hollywood Tells It: Story and Style in Modern Movies*. Berkeley: University of California Press, 2006.

Botting, Fred, and Scott Wilson. *The Tarantinian Ethics*. London: Sage, 2001.

Boym, Svetlana. *The Future of Nostalgia*. New York: Basic Books, 2001.

Branigan, Edward. *Narrative Comprehension and Film*. London: Routledge, 1992.

Brecht, Bertolt. "The Threepenny Opera." In *Bertolt Brecht Poems; Bertolt Brecht Collected Plays,* edited by Erich Fried, Ralph Manheim, and John Willett. London: Eyre Methuen, 1976.

Brooke, Michael. "Social Problem Films: British Cinema and Postwar Social Change." *ScreenOnline.* Accessed February 15, 2010, http://www.screenonline.org.uk/film/id/1074067/index.html.

Brooks, Xan. "Revolution in the air as Benicio Del Toro Meets Hugo Chávez." *The Guardian*, last modified March 5, 2008, http://www.guardian.co.uk/film/2009/mar/05/benicio-del-toro-hugo-chavez.

Buckland, Warren. "A Close Encounter with Raiders of the Lost Ark." In *Contemporary Hollywood Cinema*, edited by Steve Neale and Murray Smith, 166–77. London: Routledge, 1998.

——— "The Role of the Auteur in the Age of the Blockbuster: Steven Spielberg and DreamWorks." In *Movie Blockbusters*, edited by Julian Stringer, 84–98. London: Routledge, 2003.

——— *Puzzle Films: Complex Storytelling in Contemporary Cinema.* Chichester, West Sussex, U.K.: Wiley-Blackwell, 2009.

Burgoyne, Robert. *The Hollywood Historical Film*. Malden, MA: Blackwell, 2008.

Burr, Ty. "*Solaris* Remake is a Space Odyssey into the Human Heart." *Boston Globe*, November 27, 2002, D1.

Cameron, Allan. *Modular Narratives in Contemporary Cinema*. Basingstoke: Palgrave Macmillan, 2008.

"Casablanca." *Variety*. December 2, 1942, http://www.variety.com/review/VE11174 87980.html?c=31.

Castells, Manuel. *The Rise of the Network Society. The Information Age: Economy, Society, and Culture*. Oxford: Blackwell, 2000.

Caughie, John. *Theories of Authorship*. New York: Routledge, 2001.

Cawelti, John G. "*Chinatown* and Generic Transformation in Recent American Films." In *Mystery, Violence, and Popular Culture*. Madison: University of Wisconsin Press/Popular Press, 2004.

Cook, David A. *Lost Illusions: American Cinema in the Shadow of Watergate and Vietnam, 1970–1979*. New York: C. Scribner, 2000.

Cook, Pam. "The Point of Self-Expression in Avant-Garde Film." In *Theories of Authorship: A Reader*, edited by John Caughie, 271–81. London: Routledge, 2000.

Corrigan, Timothy. "The Commerce of Auteurism: A Voice Without Authority." *New German Critique* 49 (1990): 43–59.

——— *A Cinema Without Walls: Movies and Culture after Vietnam*. New Brunswick, N.J.: Rutgers University Press, 1991.

——— "Auteurs and the New Hollywood." In *The New American Cinema*, edited by Jon Lewis, 38–63. Durham: Duke University Press, 1998.

Dancyger, Ken, and Jeff Rush. "Narrative and Anti-Narrative: The Case of the Two Stevens: The Work of Steven Spielberg and Steven Soderbergh." In *Alternative Scriptwriting*, 58–75. Burlington: Elsivier Press, 2006.

Davis, Robert E. "The Instantaneous Worldwide Release: Coming Soon to Everyone, Everywhere." In *Transnational Cinema: The Film Reader*, edited by Elizabeth Ezra and Terry Rowden, 73–80. New York: Routledge, 2006.

deWaard, Andrew. "Joints and Jams: Spike Lee as Sellebrity Auteur." In *Fight the Power!: The Spike Lee Reader*, edited by Janice D. Hamlet and Robin R. Means Coleman, 345–61. New York: Peter Lang, 2008.

_____ "Intertextuality, Broken Mirrors, and *The Good German*." In *The Philosophy of Steven Soderbergh*, edited by R. Barton Palmer and Steven Sanders, 107–19. Lexington, KY: University Press of Kentucky, 2011.

Deleuze, Gilles. *Cinema 2: The Time Image*. London: Continuum, 2005.

Deleuze, Gilles, and Félix Guattari. "Kafka: Towards a Minor Literature," In *Theory and History of Literature* 30, translated by Dana Polan. Minneapolis: University of Minnesota Press, 1986. Translation of *Kafka: Pour une littérature mineure*. Paris: Les Editions de Minuit.

_____ *A Thousand Plateaus: Capitalism and Schizophrenia Vol. 2*, translated by Brian Massumi. Minneapolis: University of Minnesota Press, 1987.

Desser, David. "Global Noir: Genre Film in the Age of Transnationalism." In *Film Genre Reader III*, edited by Barry Keith Grant, 516–36. Austin, TX: University of Texas Press, 2003.

Dillon, Steven. *The Solaris Effect: Art & Artifice in Contemporary American Film*. Austin, TX: University of Texas Press, 2006.

Dyer, Richard, and Paul McDonald. *Stars*. London: BFI, 1998.

Dyer, Richard. "Entertainment and Utopia." In *Genre: The Musical: A Reader*, edited by Rick Altman, 175–89. London: Routledge and Kegan Paul, 1981.

_____ *Heavenly Bodies: Film Stars and Society*. London: BFI Macmillan, 1986.

Ebert, Roger. "*Syriana* [review]." *Chicago Sun-Times*. December 9, 2005. http://rogerebert.suntimes.com/apps/pbcs.dll/article?AID=/20051208/REVIEWS/51130002/1023.

Eco, Umberto. "*Casablanca*: Cult Movies and Intertextual Collage." *Travels In Hyperreality*, 197–212. San Diego: Harcourt Brace Jovanovich, 1986.

Eisenstein, Sergei. "Through Theater to Cinema." In *Film Form: Essays in Film Theory*, edited by Sergei Eisenstein and Jay Leyda, 3–17. New York: Harcourt, Brace, 1949.

Elsaesser, Thomas. "Notes on the Unmotivated Hero: Pathos of Failure in the 1970s." In *The Last Great American Picture Show: Traditions, Transitions and Triumphs in 1970s Cinema*, edited by Alexander Horwath, Noel King, and Thomas Elsaesser, 279–92. Amsterdam: Amsterdam University Press, 2003.

Espinosa, Julio Garcia. "For an Imperfect Cinema." *Jump Cut* 20 (1979): 24–6, translated by Julianne Burton, http://www.ejumpcut.org/archive/onlinessays/JC20folder/ImperfectCinema.html.

Esslin, Martin. *Bertolt Brecht*. New York: Columbia University Press, 1969.

Feldman, Seth. "Footnote to Fact: The Docudrama." In *Film Genre Reader*, edited by Barry Keith Grant, 344–56. Austin, TX: University of Texas Press, 1986.

Flanagan, Martin. "'The Hulk, An Ang Lee Film': Notes on the Blockbuster Auteur." *New Review of Film and Television Studies* 2, no. 1 (2004): 19–35.

Foucault, Michel. "What is an Author?." In *Textual Strategies: Perspectives in Post-Structuralist Criticism*, edited by Josué V. Harari, 141–60. Ithaca: Cornell University Press, 1979.

Fukuyama, Francis. *The End of History and the Last Man*. New York: Free Press, 1992.

Gallagher, Mark. *Another Steven Soderbergh Experience: Authorship and Contemporary Hollywood*. Austin: University of Texas Press, 2013.

Gamson, Joshua. *Claims to Fame: Celebrity in Contemporary America*. Berkeley: University of California Press, 1994.

Gerstner, David A., and Janet Staiger. *Authorship and Film*. New York: Routledge, 2003.

Gilmore, Richard. "The Dark Sublimity of *Chinatown*." *The Philosophy of Neo-Noir*, edited by Mark T. Conard, 119–36. Lexington: University Press of Kentucky, 2006.

Goss, Brian. "Steven Soderbergh's *The Limey*: Implications for the Auteur Theory and Industry Structure." *Popular Communication* 2, no. 4 (2004): 231–55.

Grant, Barry Keith. *Auteurs and Authorship: A Film Anthology*. Oxford: Blackwell, 2007.

Groen, Rick. "Soderbergh's Arc of Triumph." *The Globe and Mail*, March 23, 2001, R1.

_____ "Your Time Is Up: Steven Soderbergh." *The Globe and Mail*, August 24, 2002, R8.

Hills, Matt. "*Star Wars* in Fandom, Film Theory and the Museum: The Cultural Status of the Cult Blockbuster." In *Movie Blockbusters*, edited by Julian Stringer, 178–89. London: Routledge, 2003.

Hirsch, Foster. *A Method to Their Madness: The History of the Actors Studio*. New York: W.W. Norton, 1984.

Hoberman, James. "Nostalgia Trip." *The Village Voice*, December 5, 2006. http://www.villagevoice.com/2006–12–05/film/nostalgia-trip/.

Holson, Laura M. "Trying to Combine Art and Box Office in Hollywood." *New York Times*, January 17, 2005, http://www.nytimes.com/2005/01/17/business/media/17clooney.html.

Hornaday, Ann. "Stamp of Approval." *Sunday Herald*, October 31, 1999, 4.

Horwath, Alexander, Noel King, and Thomas Elsaesser. *The Last Great American Picture Show: Traditions, Transitions and Triumphs in 1970s Cinema*. Amsterdam: Amsterdam University Press, 2003.

Howell, Peter. "*Che*: A Revolution is not a Slumber Party." *Toronto Star*, February 20, 2009, www.thestar.com/article/590412.

Hutcheon, Linda. "Irony, Nostalgia and the Postmodern." Last modified January 19, 1998, http://www.library.utoronto.ca/utel/criticism/hutchinp.html.

"Interview with Steven Soderberg About *The Good German*." *The Good German Website*. Last modified October, 2006. http://thegoodgerman.warnerbros.com.

"Is *Che* This Year's *Southland Tales*?" *New York Magazine*, May 22, 2008, http://nymag.com/daily/entertainment/2008/05/is_che_this_years_southland_ta.html

Jameson, Fredric. *The Political Unconscious: Narrative As a Socially Symbolic Act*. Ithaca, N.Y: Cornell University Press, 1981.

____ *Signatures of the Visible*. New York: Routledge, 1990.

____ *Postmodernism, or, The Cultural Logic of Late Capitalism*. Durham: Duke University Press, 1991.

____ "'End of Art' or 'End of History.'" *The Cultural Turn: Selected Writings on the Postmodern, 1983–1998*, 73–92. London: Verso, 1998.

____ *Archaeologies of the Future: The Desire Called Utopia and Other Science Fictions*. New York: Verso, 2005.

Jones, Scott Kelton. "Straight Man: Joking Around, or Not, with *Limey* Director Steven Soderbergh." In *Steven Soderbergh: Interviews*, edited by Anthony Kaufman. Jackson: University Press of Mississippi, 2002.

Kaufman, Anthony. *Steven Soderbergh: Interviews*. Jackson: University Press of Mississippi, 2002.

Kehr, Dave. "You Can Make 'Em Like They Used To." *The New York Times*, November 12, 2006. http://www.nytimes.com/2006/11/12/movies/12kehr.html?emc=eta1.

Kennedy, Colin. "O Lucky Man!" *Empire Magazine*, March 2003.

King, Geoff. *New Hollywood Cinema: An Introduction*. New York: Columbia University Press, 2002.

____ *American independent cinema*. London: I.B. Tauris, 2005.

____ *Indiewood U.S.A: Where Hollywood Meets Independent Cinema*. London: I.B. Taurus, 2009.

____ "Consciousness, Temporality, and the Crime-Revenge Genre in *The Limey*." In *The Philosophy of Steven Soderbergh*, edited by R. Barton Palmer and Steven Sanders, 91–106. Lexington, KY: University Press of Kentucky, 2011.

Klein, Naomi. *No Logo*. London: Flamingo, 2001.

Krauthammer, Charles. "Oscars for Osama." *The Washington Post*, March 3, 2006, http://www.washingtonpost.com/wp-dyn/content/article/2006/03/02/AR2006030201209.html.

Lacan, Jacques and Jacques-Alain Miller. *The Seminar. 11, The Four Fundamental Concepts of Psychoanalysis*. New York: Norton, 1998.

La Capra, Dominick. *History and Criticism*. Ithaca: Cornell University Press, 1985.

Landon, Brooks. *Science Fiction After 1900: From the Steam Man to the Stars*. New York: Twayne Publishers, 1997.

Leitch, Thomas. *Crime Films*. New York: Cambridge University Press, 2002.

Levy, Emanuel. *Cinema of Outsiders: The Rise of American Independent Film*. New York: New York University Press, 1999.

Lewis, Jon. "The Perfect Money Machine(s): George Lucas, Steven Spielberg and Auteurism in the New Hollywood." *Film International* 1, no. 1 (2003): 12–26.

Lim, Dennis. "Sight Seeing: Steven Soderbergh Loosens Up," in *Steven Soderbergh: Interviews*, edited by Anthony Kaufman, 108–9. Jackson: University Press of Mississippi, 2002.

Lipkin, W. Ian. "The Real Threat of 'Contagion,'" *New York Times*, September 11, 2011.

"Making Che." *Che*. Supplementary DVD Material. 2008.

Martin, Michael T. "Introductory Notes," *New Latin American Cinema*, edited by Michael T. Martin. Detroit: Wayne State University Press, 1997.

Mask, Mia. "1971 - Movies and the Exploitation of Excess." In *American Cinema of the 1970s: Themes and Variations*, edited by Lester D. Friedman, Oxford: Berg, 2007, 48–70.

Maslin, Janet. "Schizopolis," *New York Times*, April 9, 1997.

McCarthy, Todd. "*Ocean's Twelve* [review]." *Variety*, December 8, 2004.

———. "*Che* [review]." *Variety* May 21, 2008.

McDonagh, Maitland. "The Exploitation Generation, or: How Marginal Movies Came in from the Cold." In *The Last Great American Picture Show: Traditions, Transitions and Triumphs in 1970s Cinema*, edited by Alexander Horwath, Noel King, and Thomas Elsaesser, 107–30. Amsterdam: Amsterdam University Press, 2003.

Miller, Frank. "The Devil Makes Three." *Turner Classic Movies*. Accessed January 12, 2010, http://www.tcm.com/thismonth/article.jsp?cid=154952ArticleId=154931.

Miller, Toby, Nitin Govil, John McMurria, and Richard Maxwell. *Global Hollywood 2*. London: BFI, 2005.

Monaco, James. *The New Wave: Truffaut, Godard, Chabrol, Rohmer, Rivette*. New York: Oxford University Press, 1976.

Morton, Drew. "*Schizopolis* as Philosophical Autobiography." In *The Philosophy of Steven Soderbergh*, edited by R. Barton Palmer and Steven Sanders, 173–93. Lexington, KY: University Press of Kentucky, 2011.

Moses, Michael Valdez. "*Solaris,* Cinema, and Simulacra." In *The Philosophy of Steven Soderbergh*, edited by R. Barton Palmer and Steven Sanders, 281–303. Lexington, KY: University Press of Kentucky, 2011.

Mottram, James. *Sundance Kids: How the Mavericks Took Back Hollywood*. New York: Faber and Faber, 2006.

"Movie Preview." *Entertainment Weekly*, October 22, 2001.

Naficy, Hamid. *An Accented Cinema: Exilic and Diasporic Filmmaking*. Princeton: Princeton University Press, 2001.

Nair, Natasha. "George Clooney Bares His Bottom In *Solaris*." *CinemaOnline*, , 2003, http://cinemaonline.com.my/news/news.asp?search=georgec.

Neale, Steve. *Genre and Hollywood*. New York: Routledge, 2000.

Neupert, Richard John. *A History of the French New Wave Cinema*. Madison: University of Wisconsin Press, 2002.

Newman, Michael Z. *Indie: An American Film Culture*. New York: Columbia University Press, 2011.

Olsen, Mark. "Soderbergh Takes a Revolutionary Approach to *Che*." *LA Times*, October 31, 2008, http://theenvelope.latimes.com/news/la-et-che1–2008nov01,0,4392866.story.

"Our Mission." *Participant Media*. Accessed 15 January 2011. http://www.participantmedia.com/company/about_us.php.

Palmer, R. Barton. "Alain Resnais Meets Film Noir in *The Underneath* and *The Limey*" In *The Philosophy of Steven Soderbergh*, edited by R. Barton Palmer and Steven Sanders, 69–90. Lexington, KY: University Press of Kentucky, 2011.

Perren, Alisa. "sex, lies and marketing: Miramax and the Development of the Quality Indie Blockbuster." *Film Quarterly* 55, no. 2 (2001): 30–9.

Petersen, Anne Helen. "The Rise and Fall of the $100 Million Paycheck: Hollywood Stardom Since 1990." In *American Film in the Digital Age*, edited by Robert Sickels, 123–42. Santa Barbara, CA: Praeger, 2011.

Picart, Caroline Joan, and David A. Frank. *Frames of Evil: The Holocaust As Horror in American Film*. Carbondale: Southern Illinois University Press, 2006.

Pierson, John. *Spike, Mike, Slackers & Dykes: A Guided Tour Across a Decade of American Independent Cinema*. New York: Miramax Books/Hyperion, 1997.

Rafter, Nicole. *Shots in the Mirror: Crime Films and Society*. New York: Oxford University Press, 2000.

Ramírez-Berg, Charles. "A Taxonomy of Alternative Plots in Recent Films: Classifying the 'Tarantino Effect.'" *Film Criticism* 31, no. 1+2 (Fall 2006): 5–61.

Richardson, John H. "The Very Boring Life Of Steven Soderbergh." *Esquire*, August 2002, http://www.esquire.com/ESQ0802-AUG_SODERBERGH.

Ritzer, Ivo. "Philosophical Reflections on Steven Soderbergh's Kafka." In *The Philosophy of Steven Soderbergh*, edited by R. Barton Palmer and Steven Sanders, 145–58. Lexington, KY: University Press of Kentucky, 2011.

Roffman, Peter and Jim Purdy. *The Hollywood Social Problem Film: Madness, Despair, and Politics from the Depression to the Fifties*. Bloomington: Indiana University Press, 1981.

Rogers, Everett M.and F. Floyd Shoemaker, *Communication of Innovations; a Cross-cultural Approach*. New York: Free Press, 1971.

Rosenberg, Justin. "Globalization Theory: A Post Mortem." *International Politics* 42 (2005): 2–74.

Rosenstone, Robert A. *Visions of the Past: The Challenge of Film to Our Idea of History*. Cambridge, MA: Harvard University Press, 1995.

Russell, James. *The Historical Epic and Contemporary Hollywood: From Dances with Wolves to Gladiator*. New York: Continuum, 2007.

Ryan, Michael, and Douglas Kellner. *Camera Politica: The Politics and Ideology of Contemporary Hollywood Film*. Bloomington: Indiana University Press, 1988.

Sarris, Andrew, *The American Cinema; Directors and Directions, 1929–1968*. New York: Dutton, 1968.

_____ "Notes on the Auteur Theory in 1962", Grant, Barry K. *Auteurs and Authorship: A Film Reader*. Malden, MA: Blackwell Pub, 2008.

Schatz, Thomas. *Hollywood Genres: Formulas, Filmmaking, and the Studio System*, Philadelphia, PA: Temple University Press, 1981.

_____ "The New Hollywood." In *Film Theory Goes to the Movies*, edited by Jim Collins, Hilary Radner and Ava Preacher Collins, 18–37. New York: Routledge, 1993.

_____ "The Studio System in Conglomerate Hollywood." In *The Contemporary Hollywood Film Industry*, edited by Paul McDonald and Janet Wasko, 11–42. Malden, MA: Blackwell Publishing, 2008.

_____ "New Hollywood, New Millennium." In *Film Theory and Contemporary Hollywood Movies*, edited by Warren Buckland, 19–46. New York: Routledge, 2009.

Scott, Allen J. "Hollywood and the World: The Geography of Motion-picture Distribution and Marketing." *Review of International Political Economy* 11, no. 1 (2004): 33–61.

Sloan, Kay. *The Loud Silents: Origins of the Social Problem Film*. Chicago: University of Illinois Press, 1988.

Soderbergh, Steven. *Getting Away With It or: The Further Adventures of the Luckiest Bastard You Ever Saw*. London: Faber and Faber Limited. 1999.

_____ *Moneyball*. Revised Version of Script, June 22, 2009.

Solanas, Fernando, and Octavio Getino. "Towards a Third Cinema: Notes and Experiences for the Development of a Cinema of Liberation in the Third World." In *New Latin American Cinema, Vol. 1*, edited by Michael T. Martin, translated by Julianne Burton and Michael T. Martin, 33–58. Detroit: Wayne State University Press, 1997.

Stam, Robert. "The Author: Introduction." In *Film and Theory: An Anthology*, edited by Robert Stam and Toby Miller, 1–6. Malden, MA: Blackwell, 2000.

Stanislavsky, Konstantin. *An Actor Prepares*. New York: Theatre Arts Books, 1948.

_____ *Building a Character*. New York: Routledge/Theater Arts Books, 1989.

Sterritt, David. "Schizoanalyzing the Informant." In *The Philosophy of Steven Soderbergh*, edited by R. Barton Palmer and Steven Sanders, 213–30. Lexington, KY: University Press of Kentucky, 2011.

Stewart, Ryan. "Steven Soderbergh: The Girlfriend Experience," *Suicide Girls*, May 21, 2009. http://suicidegirls.com/interviews/Steven+Soderbergh:+The+Girlfriend+Experience/.

Strasberg, Lee, and Evangeline Morphos. *A Dream of Passion: The Development of the Method*. Boston: Little, Brown, 1987.

Tait, R. Colin. "Competing Modes of Capital in *Ocean's Eleven*." In *The Philosophy of Steven Soderbergh*, edited by R. Barton Palmer and Steven Sanders, 231–45. Lexington, KY: University Press of Kentucky, 2011.

_____ "Piercing Steven Soderbergh's *Bubble*." In *The Business of Entertainment*, edited by Robert Sickels, 179–94. Westport, CT: Praeger Publishers, 2009.

Thompson, Anne. "Cannes: Che Meets Mixed Reaction." *Variety*, May 21, 2008, http://weblogs.variety.com/thompsononhollywood/2008/05/.html.

Thompson, Patricia. "Crazy for You: Steven Soderbergh Cuts Loose With *Schizopolis*." In *Steven Soderbergh: Interviews*, edited by Anthony Kaufman, 88–97. Jackson: University of Mississippi Press: 2002.

Todorov, Tzvetan. *The Fantastic; A Structural Approach to a Literary Genre*. Cleveland: Press of Case Western Reserve University, 1973.

Turner, Graeme. *Understanding Celebrity*. London: Sage, 2004.

Venturi, Robert, Denise Scott Brown, and Steven Izenour. *Learning From Las Vegas: The Forgotten Symbolism of Architectural Form*. Boston: The MIT Press, 1977.

Vonnegut, Kurt. *Slaughterhouse-five; or, The Children's Crusade, A Duty-dance with Death*. New York: Delacorte Press, 1969.

Wayne, Mike. *Political Film: The Dialectics of Third Cinema*. London: Pluto Press, 2001.

Waxman, Sharon. *Rebels on the Backlot: Six Maverick Directors and How They Conquered the Hollywood Studio System*. New York: Harper Entertainment, 2005.

Wexman, Virginia Wright. *Film and Authorship*. New Brunswick, NJ: Rutgers University Press, 2003.

White, Patricia. "Lesbian Minor Cinema." *Screen* 49, no.4 (2008): 410–25.

Willeman, Paul. "The Third Cinema Question: Notes and Reflections." In *New Latin American Cinema*, edited by Michael T. Martin. Detroit: Wayne State University Press, 1997.

Wilmington, Michael. "*Short Cuts*: City Symphony." *The Criterion Collection*, November 15, 2004, http://www.criterion.com/current/posts/349-short-cuts-city-symphony.

Wollen, Peter. "Godard and Counter-Cinema: *V'ent d' Est*." In *Narrative, Apparatus, Ideology: A Film Theory Reader*, edited by Philip Rosen, 120–30. New York: Columbia University Press, 1986.

Wood, Robin. *Hollywood from Vietnam to Reagan – And Beyond*. 2nd Edition. New York: Columbia University Press, 2003.

____ "Ideology, Genre, Auteur." In *Film Genre Reader III*, edited by Barry Keith Grant, 60–74. Austin, TX: University of Texas Press, 2003.

Wyatt, Justin. *High Concept: Movies and Marketing in Hollywood*. Austin, TX: University of Texas Press, 1994.

Yau, Ka-Fai. "Cinema 3: Towards a 'Minor Hong Kong Cinema.'" *Cultural Studies* 15, no. 3+4 (2001): 543–63.

Žižek, Slavoj. *The Sublime Object of Ideology*. New York: Verso, 1989.

____ "The Thing that Thinks: The Kantian Background of the *Noir Subject*." In *Shades of Noir: A Reader*, edited by Joan Copjec, 199–226. London: Verso, 1993.

____ *Welcome to the Desert of the Real: Five Essays on September 11*. London: Verso, 2002.

INDEX